SUSE® Linux Enterprise Server Security

Novell & Jason Eckert

THOMSON

COURSE TECHNOLOGY™

Australia · Brazil · Canada · Mexico · Singapore · Spain · United Kingdom · United States

THOMSON
COURSE TECHNOLOGY

SUSE® Linux Enterprise Server Security
is published by Course Technology

Director of Learning Solutions
Sandy Clark

Acquisitions Editor
Nick Lombardi

Product Manager
Molly Belmont

Managing Editor
Tricia Coia

Content Project Managers
Philippa Lehar, Jill Braiewa

Manufacturing Coordinator
Justin Palmeiro

Marketing Manager
Guy Baskaran

Editorial Assistant
Claire Jeffers

Cover Design
Laura Rickenbach

Text Designer
Joel Sadagursky

Compositor
International Typesetting
and Composition

Copy Editor
Kathy Orrino

Proofreader
Wendy Benedetto

Indexer
Sharon Hilgenberg

Brief Contents

Table of Contents

Introduction

Since its conception in 1991, Linux has fast become a major enterprise operating system and has led to the widespread adoption of Open Source Software in the computer industry. One good example is the Novell switch to SUSE Linux as their main enterprise platform. Today, there are millions of Linux users, administrators, and developers worldwide, and this community continually grows as companies adopt Linux and Open Source technologies.

However, as Linux grows in today's global marketplace, so does the need for Linux security. In this book, we examine the practices and procedures used to secure a SUSE Linux Enterprise Server in a network environment using the latest technologies such as cryptography, VPNs, firewalls, and AppArmor.

To provide benchmarks for hiring, many vendors such as CompTIA, Novell, Red Hat, and the Linux Professional Institute (LPI) have released Linux certification exams geared toward different skill sets required for common Linux job functions. The Novell Certified Linux Engineer 10 (CLE) certification is practicum-based, and focuses on advanced administration of SUSE Linux systems. Using carefully constructed examples, questions, and practical exercises, the *SUSE Linux Enterprise Server: Security (Course 3075)* text introduces you to the security concepts tested on the CLE certification exam.

Intended Audience

This book is appropriate for anyone who has experience administering Linux systems and who wishes to learn how to secure SUSE Linux systems, as well as for those who have experience administering SUSE Linux network services and who are currently preparing for the Novell Certified Linux Engineer 10 (CLE) certification. Although the concepts introduced in this book do not assume prior SUSE Linux experience, a general knowledge of Linux network and system administration concepts is assumed. Many of the concepts and procedures introduced in this book are transferable to most other Linux distributions.

Section Descriptions

There are 11 sections in this book, as follows:

Section 1, "General Considerations and Definition of Terms," outlines the process used to analyze the security of an organization and create a security analysis. In addition, this section also introduces the various technologies and concepts that may be used to secure a SUSE Linux Enterprise Server. Each of these technologies and concepts are discussed in depth throughout the textbook.

In **Section 2**, "Host Security," we discuss the technologies and procedures used to secure the file systems, software, and operating system settings on a local SUSE Linux Enterprise Server. Following this, we introduce the procedures used to test and document system security configuration.

Section 3, "AppArmor," discusses how to set up and configure the Novell AppArmor modules to restrict application access on a SUSE Linux Enterprise Server and prevent unauthorized access to key system programs and files.

In **Section 4**, "Cryptography: Basics and Practical Application," we examine how asymmetric and symmetric encryption may be used to protect data. Following this, we learn how to configure a Certification Authority to create the certificates used for asymmetric encryption as well as how to use GPG to provide asymmetric encryption support to applications without the use of a Certification Authority.

Section 5, "Network Security," introduces the various services and protocols used to transfer information on networks as well as the technologies used to secure them. Focus will be placed on TCP wrappers and SSL.

In **Section 6**, "General Firewall Design," we introduce you to the various types and uses of firewalls on Linux networks including packet filters, ALGs and DMZs. The configuration of these firewalls will be discussed in the following sections.

Section 7, "Packet Filters," teaches you how to configure the iptables/NetFilter firewall to secure a SUSE Linux Enterprise Server in a variety of different roles. In addition, you will learn how to use iptables/NetFilter to configure routing security and NAT.

Section 8, "Application-Level Gateways," examines the detailed configuration and usage of proxy server software including Squid, Dante, and rinetd.

In **Section 9**, "Virtual Private Networks," we discuss how VPNs may be used to secure network traffic as well as the components that make up a typical VPN. Following this, you learn how to configure an IPSec VPN as well as use packet filters on an IPSec VPN connection.

In **Section 10**, "Intrusion Detection and Incident Response," we examine the procedures and technologies used to detect and deal with security breaches. In addition, you will learn how to examine log files using various tools as well as configure several different Intrusion Detection Systems.

Section 11, "LiveFire Exercise," allows you to configure many of the technologies discussed in previous sections as part of a real-world exercise. This exercise is good practice for the Novell CLE certification candidates.

Features and Approach

SUSE® *Linux Enterprise Server Security* differs from other networking books in its unique hands-on approach and its orientation to real-world situations and problem solving. To help you comprehend how Linux security concepts and techniques are applied in real-world organizations, this book incorporates the following features:

- **Section Objectives**—Each section begins with a detailed list of the concepts to be mastered. This list gives you a quick reference to the section's contents and is a useful study aid.

- **Exercises**—Activities are incorporated throughout the text, giving you practice in setting up, managing, and troubleshooting a network system. The Exercises give you a strong foundation for carrying out network administration tasks in the real world. Because of the book's progressive nature, completing the Exercises in each section is essential before moving on to the end-of-section materials and subsequent sections.

- **Section Summaries**—Each section's text is followed by a summary of the concepts introduced in that section. These summaries provide a helpful way to recap and revisit the ideas covered in each section.

- **Key Terms**—Important terms within the section are gathered together in the Key Terms list at the end of the section. This provides you with a method of checking your understanding of all the terms introduced.

- **Review Questions**—The end-of-section assessment begins with a set of Review Questions that reinforce the ideas introduced in each section. Answering these questions correctly will ensure that you have mastered the important concepts.

- **Discovery Exercises**—Theoretical, research, or scenario-based projects allow you to expand on your current knowledge of the concepts based on what you learned in the section.

Text and Graphic Conventions

Additional information and exercises have been added to this book to help you better understand what's being discussed in the section. Icons throughout the text alert you to these additional materials. The icons used in this book are described below.

Tips offer extra information on resources, how to attack problems, and time-saving shortcuts.

Notes present additional helpful material related to the subject being discussed.

Each **Exercise** in this book is preceded by the Exercise icon.

Discovery Exercise icons mark the end-of-section case projects, which are scenario-based assignments that ask you to independently apply what you have learned in the section.

On the DVDs

On the DVDs included with this text you will find a copy of SLES VM Ware emulation software for lab setup, the Student Manual PDF, files used for section exercises, and a Self-Study Workbook.

Instructor Resources

The following supplemental materials are available when this book is used in a classroom setting. All of the supplements available with this book are provided to the instructor on a single CD-ROM.

Electronic Instructor's Manual. The Instructor's Manual that accompanies this textbook includes additional instructional material to assist in class preparation, including suggestions for classroom activities, discussion topics, and additional projects.

Solutions. Answers are provided for the end-of-section material, including Review Questions, and, where applicable, Discovery Exercises.

ExamView®. This textbook is accompanied by ExamView, a powerful testing software package that allows instructors to create and administer printed, computer (LAN-based), and Internet exams. ExamView includes hundreds of questions that correspond to the topics covered in this text, enabling students to generate detailed study guides that include page references for further review. The computer-based and Internet testing components allow students to take exams at their computers and also save the instructor time by grading each exam automatically.

PowerPoint Presentations. This book comes with Microsoft PowerPoint slides for each section. These are included as a teaching aid for classroom presentation, to make available to students on the network for section review, or to be printed for classroom distribution. Instructors, please feel at liberty to add your own slides for additional topics you introduce to the class.

Distance Learning. Thomson Course Technology is proud to present online test banks in WebCT and Blackboard to provide the most complete and dynamic learning experience possible. Instructors are encouraged to make the most of the course, both online and offline. For more information on how to access the online test bank, contact your local Thomson Course Technology sales representative.

Minimum Lab Requirements

Hardware   The following hardware is required for the Discovery Exercises at the end of each section and should be listed on the Hardware Compatibility List available at *http://www.novell.com/linux/*:

Component	Requirement
CPU	Pentium CPU (Pentium 4 or later recommended)
Memory	512 MB of RAM (1 GB or more recommended)
Disk Space	4 GB hard disk (20 GB or more recommended)
Video	SVGA or higher resolution monitor
Keyboard	Keyboard
Pointing Device	Linux-compatible pointing device
Drives	A DVD-ROM drive
Networking	Two Linux-supported network interfaces and Internet connectivity are required for some activities

Software   SUSE Linux Enterprise Server 10

Acknowledgments

First, I wish to thank the staff at Course Technology and Novell for an overall enjoyable writing experience. More specifically, I wish to thank my editor Tricia Coia for her coordination and insight, as well as the editorial and production teams at Course Technology, for the long hours spent pulling everything together to transform the text into its current state. As well, I wish to thank Frank Gerencser, of triOS College for freeing me up to write this textbook, and Apple Computer Inc. for the amazing computer I wrote it on.

Finally, I wish to thank Linus Torvalds for starting a revolution that engages my curiosity on a daily basis, and Richard Stallman for making the Hacker Ethic and Open Source Software revolution a reality. And, of course, I must thank my daughter Mackenzie for her ongoing appreciation of Linux as "the coolest operating system ever."

Readers are encouraged to e-mail comments, questions, and suggestions regarding *SUSE Linux Enterprise Server: Security (Course 3075)* to Jason W. Eckert: *jason.eckert@trios.com*.

About the Author

Jason Eckert is currently the Technology Faculty Head at triOS College in Ontario, Canada. A graduate of the University of Waterloo, he also possesses over 30 IT certification designations in the areas of UNIX, Linux, Windows, Novell, Networking, and Computer Programming.

With more than 20 years of experience in IT, and more than 10 years of experience teaching college and corporate courses, Jason brings a variety of skills to the IT courses he teaches at triOS College. In addition to teaching, Jason has written several textbooks for Course Technology on topics including Linux, UNIX, Windows Server 2003, and Windows Vista. He is also a key member in many computing and computing-related research projects at various universities in Southern Ontario.

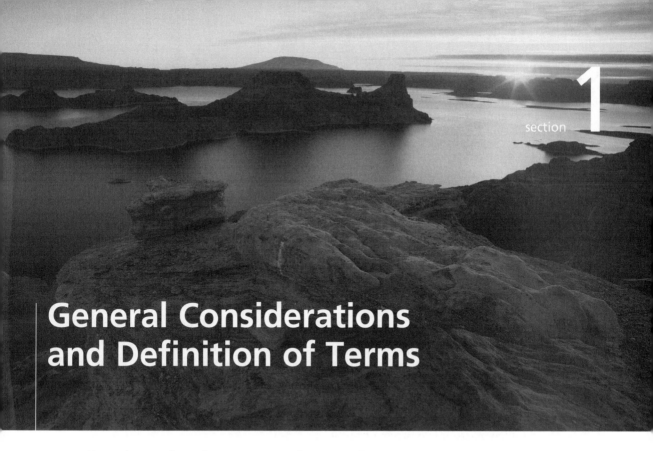

General Considerations and Definition of Terms

Given the number of press reports about attacks on computers, it is not surprising that computer security is being taken more and more seriously. An entire branch of the IT industry is concerned with security. Many security products have been created in recent years. Firewall solutions and antivirus software have become best-sellers, and yet an important component of every security concept—perhaps even the most important component—is being neglected: know-how. Without the appropriate knowledge you cannot recognize and understand security-critical issues in complex IT infrastructures. IT security is by no means an entirely technical matter. Without proper planning and coordination, there is no solution that can be called secure. In this section we will cover preliminary steps to take before implementing technical solutions. It also defines common IT Security terms as they are used in this course.

Objectives

- Create a Security Concept
- Understand Frequently Used Terms

Objective 1—Create a Security Concept

Technical solutions will not achieve their purpose if they are not part of an overall plan stating what level of security is the goal and how it will be achieved.

To create a security concept, you must:

- Understand the Basics of a Security Concept
- Perform a Communication Analysis
- Analyze the Protection Requirements
- Analyze the Current Situation and Necessary Enhancements

Understand the Basics of a Security Concept

"It is easy to run a secure computer system. You merely have to disconnect all dial-up connections and permit only direct wired terminals, put the machine and its terminals in a shielded room and post a guard at the door."

F.T. Grampp and R.H. Morris[*]

It might be possible to operate a computer system in this secure manner, but it's not practical. To deal with network problems in the real world, a different security concept is required.

So what kind of security measures make sense and are reasonable?

In his book *Beyond Fear*, the security expert Bruce Schneier recommends a five-stage evaluation process prior to every security-relevant decision:

- What assets are you trying to protect?
- What are the risks to these assets?
- How well does the security system mitigate those risks?
- What new risks does the security system cause?
- What costs and trade-offs does the security solution impose?

Moreover, you need to consider whether the expected security gain justifies the needed effort and costs.

Actually, security-relevant decisions are made every day. For example, a person may decide to lock or to not lock the door when leaving the house, to install or to not install a certain lock or alarm system, and so forth.

Since there is no single correct answer to the question whether the security gain justifies the effort and the costs, the answer differs from person to person. The answer depends on the individual evaluation of the risk, on the desired security level, and on how much the measures will cost.

In the private sphere, these questions can usually be answered easily. The answer is not so easy for IT managers who need to take numerous factors into consideration.

When we talk about `security strategy`, we mean both the `security policy` and the `security concept`. The security policy defines the basic goals to be achieved in the field of

---

[*]Cited in *"Firewalls and Internet Security: Repelling The Wily Hacker"* by William R. Cheswick and Steven M. Bellovin, Addison Wesley, 1994.

security. The security concept comprises the individual steps for achieving the goals defined in the security policy.

Because information technology has penetrated virtually all business processes and the security policy concerns all employees of a company, the practical implementation can be complex. Therefore, a systematic approach is needed.

As a first step, there are some questions that need to be answered:

- What Assets Do We Want to Protect?
- What Are the Risks to These Assets?
- What Needs to Be Done?

When that is done, you will most likely need further information:

- Information Resources

What Assets Do We Want to Protect? In the field of IT, we need to protect the following:

- Confidentiality
- Availability
- Integrity

The issue of confidentiality includes corporate production, research, development, sales, and marketing secrets. Moreover, personal data, such as the payroll details of the HR department or the patient data of a hospital, are included in this category. Access information like passwords must also be kept confidential.

The issue of availability concerns the question whether the services are available whenever they are needed and if, and to what extent, downtimes can be tolerated.

The issue of integrity comprises questions such as: Have the data been manipulated? Is the system still in the desired state, or has someone gained unauthorized access and manipulated it?

What Are the Risks to These Assets? In this context, many people spontaneously think of hackers, viruses, and worms. However, the assets that need to be protected may be endangered by threats of an entirely different nature. To determine the risk you have to look at the threat, the possible damage, and the likelihood of its occurrence.

Here is a list of some potential risks:

- Natural disasters
- Fires, floods
- Burglary, theft, vandalism
- Fake information (e.g., manipulation of Web pages)
- Denial of service, services cannot be reached due to active attacks or overload (e.g., viruses)
- Data theft (internal, external)
- Misuse (e.g., spam transmission to third parties, taking control of a computer, attacks on third parties)
- User errors (e.g., unintentional deletion of files)

Some of the listed risks require physical measures (e.g., a fire extinguishing system) and cannot be addressed on operating system level. The overall security chain is affected by many factors and is only as good as its weakest link.

Another important and related element of IT security is the data backup concept as discussed in *SUSE Linux Enterprise Server Advanced Administration* (Course 3073).

Following the analysis of the risks, a suitable concept must be developed and implemented to protect the assets in the best way possible against observed or anticipated risks.

What Needs to Be Done?   To answer the last three questions outlined by Bruce Schneier, the goal must be defined precisely. The company management must determine the security policy and formulate concrete goals. The result could be a general rule like "everything that is not explicitly permitted is prohibited" and the determination of the services available at the workplace.

Instead of going into technical details, the goals must be expressed as clearly as possible to prevent liberal interpretations. Therefore, a security policy like "our network should be secure" would make no sense.

The next step is a comprehensive assessment of the current situation and the preparation of a security concept that leads from the current state to the target state.

Such a security concept should also include a discussion about any new problems the security concept could trigger, the costs involved with the implementation, and any remaining risks.

Moreover, the security concept should define processes that ensure that future deviations from the target state are identified and eliminated. Therefore, it is not sufficient to roll out the security concept once and for all; rather, ongoing monitoring is necessary. Thus, the security concept turns into a continuous security process.

The following sections show how such a project could be handled. Based on an imaginary company, projects and subprojects as well as concrete tasks are defined. However, these are not intended as sample solutions that merely need to be adapted to your own situation.

Instead, they show how solutions evolve. The formal procedure presented in this manual has been applied successfully in practice. It helps to identify errors and risks that are not easily discernible, and it provides a good documentation of the overall system.

Information Resources   A very useful and comprehensive information resource which goes far beyond the scope of this training manual is the *IT-Grundschutz Manual* (baseline protection manual) published by the German Federal Office for Information Technology Security *http://www.bsi.bund.de/english/gshb/manual/index.htm*.

Perform a Communication Analysis

Creating a security concept begins with a communication analysis. This includes analyzing the security situation and evaluating the dangers.

Resources are differentiated according to what a user needs and how the access to these resources are controlled.

If users should not have access to certain resources, you can assign different access permissions to individual users.

For example, you can determine which user groups can use a resource or if the user groups can only access the resource during a certain time period.

By answering the following questions, you can get valuable information to use in developing a structured overall picture of your security needs.

- **What information will be exchanged across which barriers and in which direction?**
  A *barrier* can be the virtual barrier between the home directories of two users in a UNIX system or a firewall between two networks.

- **Which data packets will be transported with which protocols to which hosts in the network?**
  The fewer protocols you use, the better security you will have, simply because there are fewer sources of error.

- **What resources are available to individual users and with which access permissions?**
  Consider the resources users will need: printers, files on storage media, the storage media themselves (such as CD-ROMs), sound cards, modems, fax cards, ISDN cards, USB ports, network services (such as FTP or HTTP), and the computing capacity of CPUs.

- **Which resources must be available in each work area?**
  Even in small companies, different departments require different resources.

- **Which data must users have access to and in which way?**
  It does not make sense to organize access to data for each specific user individually. It is better to structure access permissions for user groups.

- **Which external users have external access to company resources, what resources do they use, and how is access controlled?**
  Pay special attention to authenticating external users.

- **Which external resources does the company provide?**
  Usually a company uses Web and mail servers and other Internet services.

- **Should users be charged for resources?**
  Many organizations charge users or departments for expensive resources (such as Internet bandwidth).

- **Which tasks must external service providers be involved in?**
  Determine if it is necessary to exchange any security-relevant data with the external service provider.

- **How do security restrictions affect users, and how open are users to these restrictions?**
  Users are more willing to live with restrictions if they understand why the restrictions are needed.

- **Will you filter transmitted or stored information on gateways between networks or on computers?**
  This applies to virus control, which should take place where the viruses can be reliably detected, on workstations and file servers.
  Scanning e-mail on the mail server is common, but has certain limitations; it is, for instance, not possible to find viruses in encrypted mail.

- **How available do individual resources need to be?**
  Not every file server in the company needs to have a high availability setup. This is why it is important to calculate exactly what costs are incurred if a resource fails.

Important parts of the communication analysis can be represented in tables, also known as *access matrices*.

Table 1-1 shows a simple **access matrix** that lists the accessible ports on servers together with the computers that may access them.

	Proxy Server	Web Server	Mail Server
Workstation Office	8080		
Workstation Web Designer	8080	ssh	
Workstation Sysadmin	8080	ssh	ssh
Mail Server Intranet			smtp

Table 1-1

It is often useful to have two columns for individual protocols, matching the two transport directions (IN or OUT).

Analyze the Protection Requirements

After you have determined the communication demands, you need to analyze the protection requirements for the data.

The expenses for securing individual resources are determined by the amount of potential damage that could be caused by an attack, a faulty operation, or a natural catastrophe.

You should also estimate how often possible damage might occur.

To determine your protection needs, ask yourself the following questions:

- **Which groups of people can access which information?**
  Is some information reserved for management, while other information is available to all employees?

- **Where is protected data located?**
  The degree of data protection needed determines the degree of protection for each individual computer in the corresponding network.

  Also, a security concept for a computer used by multiple users at different times is different from a security concept for an environment in which many different users use multiple computers at the same time.

- **Which zones exist and what security needs do they have?**
  You should create corresponding security zones for computers belonging to the same protection class.

- **What might happen to security zones if security barriers are breached?**
  This question is not difficult to answer if the security zones have previously been clearly defined.

- **Who are potential attackers?**
  You also need to estimate the financial and technical means of the potential attackers.

- **What information is of special interest to others?**
  This question helps you group zones with different security needs.

- **What are the remaining risks when the security concept is implemented?**
  This question can only be asked at the end of the analysis. Consider all questions asked, the relevant answers, and the technical and organizational implementation of the security concept.

Analyze the Current Situation and Necessary Enhancements

A company-wide security policy should guarantee the confidentiality, data integrity, availability, and transparency of a company's business processes and prevent damage.

The security policy determines what security demands are required for specific data and resources. The security policy should include the analysis of the remaining risk. Risks that cannot be removed or can only partially be removed by taking appropriate protective measures should be highlighted.

The security policy always also includes a description of the current state of security. For this, information is needed on who is required to do what to achieve the desired security level.

The following tables show some examples of what topics need to be covered in the security policy and how you could keep track of the various tasks involved in getting from the current state to the target state. The scenario behind the following tables is an imaginary company with subsidiaries in several countries.

Table 1-2 covers aspects of the physical access to the IT infrastructure.

Security of Network Components	How the components and their physical storage areas are secured against unauthorized access
Current state	The network cabinets are freely accessible so that each member of staff can patch his own network connections.
Target state	Technical rooms are locked, so only system administrators have access.
Task	The locks must be checked and keys assigned to system administrators.
Date	2006-02-02
Responsible person	Jenny Doe, head of the System Administration department.
Estimated expense	Approximately 5 days and $3000.
Done/checked	2006-03-01 Henry Boardman, assistant to the board.

Table 1-2

The reasons given in the description of the current state show that:

- Members of the staff need to be told why they can no longer patch their network connections themselves.

- Administrators must be made available to patch the network connections in the future.

 The following examples should not be considered as a template for your own security policy. Every company has its own demands and issues to be solved. The tables should give you an idea of ways to enhance the IT **NOTE** security in your company.

Table 1-3 covers dial-up to and from the internal network.

Security of Network Components	Do connections to other networks or dial-up possibilities to the internal network exist? How are these accesses protected?
Current state	In the departments of the branches located in foreign countries, there is an undefined number of Internet access points. It is not known if the computers used for dial-up are connected to the internal network. A number of administrators are using Windows NT RAS access to administer from home. NT RAS is operated using CHAP and Callback. The situation at the other locations is not known.
Target state	There is no local Internet access. Users who require Internet access can obtain this using the central corporate firewall. If administrators have to access the internal network from the outside, they connect via VPN.
Task	All worldwide locations are connected by VPN to the headquarters in the U.S. in accordance with a board decision. A 2 MB Internet access is used in the headquarters, secured by a three-level firewall with an application-level gateway. Local Internet access is removed.
Date	2006-03-30
Responsible person	Jenny Doe, head of the System Administration department. Management provides Ms. Doe with appropriate powers.
Estimated expense	Approximately 15 days and approximately $200,000.
Done/checked	2006-03-30 Henry Boardman, assistant to the board.

Table 1-3

Table 1-4 covers power failure measures.

Further Security Measures	How are the servers protected against power failure?
Current state	In all technical rooms, a UPS (Uninterruptible Power Supply) is installed so servers automatically shut down in case of a power failure. The UPS and server connecting cables are checked regularly.
Target state	All servers are connected to a functioning UPS. Current state reflects target state.
Task	No action required.
Date	—
Responsible person	—
Estimated expense	—
Done/checked	2006-01-12 Henry Boardman, assistant to the board.

Table 1-4

Table 1-5 covers fire fighting measures.

Further Security Measures	What fire fighting means are available?
Current state	Suitable fire extinguishers are installed in front of all technical rooms. Suitable fire detectors are installed in all technical rooms. The large technical rooms at the U.S. headquarters are equipped with automatic fire extinguishing equipment.
Target state	Technical rooms are equipped with fire detectors and extinguishers outside the doors to the rooms. At the U.S. headquarters technical rooms have automatic sprinklers installed. Current state reflects target state.
Task	No action required.
Date	—
Responsible person	—
Estimated expense	—
Done/checked	2006-01-14 Henry Boardman, assistant to the board.

Table 1-5

Table 1-6 covers data storage issues.

Further Security Measures	How is data security controlled? How are checks made to determine whether the data stored is usable?
Current state	Important servers and workplace machines are equipped with tape drives. Backups take place daily. Responsibility for data backups lies with staff in the technical departments who have been trained for this.
Target state	At each location, backups are made on tape libraries by means of network backup software. The tapes are cloned, regularly recycled, and stored in fireproof safes.
Task	A data backup concept must be drawn up and implemented. An external consultant should be hired.
Date	2006-04-22
Responsible Person	Jenny Doe, head of the System Administration department. Management provides Ms. Doe with appropriate powers.
Estimated expense	A cost estimate will be made by an external consultant.
Done/checked	2006-01-14 Florian Sailer, co-assistant to the board.

Table 1-6

Table 1-7 covers software security updates.

Further Security Measures	How can we guarantee that available software updates to close known security vulnerabilities are tested and installed?
Current state	Installing software updates is left to the judgment of the appropriate administrator, but this is discussed in detail with colleagues and suppliers or vendors.
Target state	Software updates will be recorded, tested, and released company-wide by two accountable members of staff. Security-relevant software updates will be installed, especially on systems in the demilitarized zone (DMZ). Only in exceptional cases, justified in writing, will software updates in the DMZ be delayed. In such cases, the head of System Administration must determine if other kinds of protective measures can be used.
Task	The head of System Administration will assign two system administrators to design a software update concept. These administrators will then be responsible for software updates.
Date	2006-03-30
Responsible person	Jenny Doe, head of the System Administration department.
Estimated expense	Approximately 4 days for designing the concept. The running costs will be included in the concept.
Done/Checked	2006-03-30 Henry Boardman, assistant to the board.

Table 1-7

Table 1-8 covers the virus protection of the IT systems.

Further Security Measures	How are the systems protected from malicious software viruses?
Current state	Virus scanners are only installed on certain workplace computers.

Target state	Virus scanners with a frequent update service are installed on all file servers and workstations. Current virus signatures can be downloaded at any time from the servers of the vendor via the Internet.
	    The virus scanners on workstations get virus signatures from a central server, so new virus signatures only need to be downloaded once.
	    To monitor the file servers, the product of a different vendor than the product monitoring the workstations is used. Overall, an efficient, two-level virus defense concept is implemented.

Task	The head of System Administration assigns two accountable persons who will design a virus defense concept. These administrators will then be responsible for the operation of the virus defense.
Date	2006-03-30
Responsible person	Jenny Doe, head of the System Administration department.
Estimated expense	Approximately 10 days for the product evaluation and concept design. Operating costs will be included in the concept.
Done/checked	2006-03-30 Florian Sailer, co-assistant to the board.

Table 1-8

Table 1-9 covers the documentation of the IT infrastructure.

Further Security Measures	How is the system configuration documented?
Current state	Everyone who has configured a machine on the network writes down or remembers the configuration data.
Target state	All system configurations (hardware and software) are documented centrally in electronic form at the corresponding location. System administrators at the U.S. headquarters can access the documentation from all locations.
Task	The head of the System Administration department will assign two system administrators who will draw up documentation guidelines.
Date	2006-03-30
Responsible Person	Jenny Doe, head of the System Administration department.
Estimated expense	Approximately 20 days to design a concept. The estimated cost of implementing this will be included in the concept.
Done/checked	2006-03-30 Henry Boardman, assistant to the board.

Table 1-9

Objective 2—Understand Frequently Used Terms

The following terms are commonly used in the context of IT security:

- Firewall
- Secure Network
- Insecure N
- Demilitarized Zone (DMZ)
- Packet Filters
- Application-Level Gateway
- Virtual Private Network
- Remote Access Service (RAS)

They are explained here in more detail.

Firewall

The concept of a firewall is taken from architecture: A firewall is a building structure intended to stop a fire from spreading from one part of a building to another one.

In data networks, firewalls link secure networks together with insecure ones. Firewalls consist of different elements, including packet filters and application-level gateways.

A firewall is not so much a piece of hard- and software but the overall concept used to separate one network securely from another, usually comprising several hard- and software elements.

Secure Network

Secure networks are networks that are considered secure because the users are known and trusted. Usually, local company networks are considered secure.

However, even within local company networks, certain subnets, such as those assigned to the research and development department, or Human Resources, could have higher security requirements compared to the rest of the company network.

Insecure Network

Similarly, insecure networks are insecure because the users are not known and thus are considered untrustworthy. As examples of insecure networks, practically all public networks can be mentioned, of which the Internet itself is the most well-known.

Demilitarized Zone (DMZ)

Buffer zones between insecure networks and secure ones are referred to as demilitarized zones (DMZ). Data traffic between public networks and the DMZ is controlled and regulated through packet filters and application-level gateways exactly as data traffic between a DMZ and a secure network is.

Servers operating in a DMZ typically provide services toward public (insecure) networks (such as WWW servers and FTP servers) and are therefore quite visible to potential attackers.

Servers in the DMZ require an increased administration effort compared with systems in a secure network, because they are used by unknown users.

Figure 1-1 shows a typical DMZ setup.

Packet Filters

Packet filters decide by means of rules based on the data of IP, ICMP, TCP, and UDP headers (source address, target address, source port, target port, flags, etc.) what to do with IP datagrams running through them.

The data stream can be regimented on the IP protocol level and the respective transport protocols that are built upon it.

Figure 1-2 shows the ISO/OSI layers involved in routing. While information in layer 3 is used by a packet filter to decide on the fate of a packet, information contained in layer 4 and above is hardly, if ever, taken into consideration by a packet filter.

Screening Router   A packet filtering router placed as the first point of entry to a complex firewall setup is sometimes referred to as a screening router.

Application-Level Gateway

Application-level gateways (sometimes referred to as *application-level firewalls*) are computers on which proxy servers run and that log and check the data traffic running through them. Because proxy servers involve programs that run on the gateway, these are ideally suited for logging and access protection mechanisms.

Application-level gateways with their proxy servers have an essential advantage over packet filters: they do not use IP routing between the networks they connect. The IP datagrams are received by the proxy servers at the application level and the application data will be processed. At this stage all headers of the underlying protocol levels have already been removed.

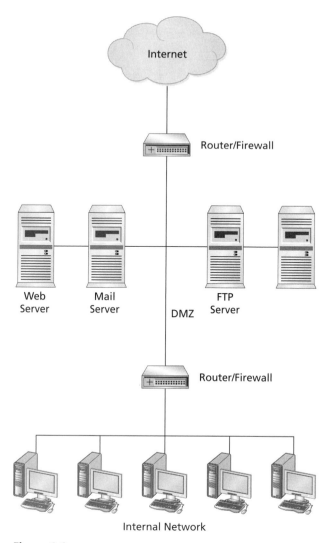

Figure 1-1

The determination of the target is done on the basis of the address data inside the application data (e.g., for e-mail on the basis of the e-mail address, or for HTTP on the basis of the URL).

Before transmitting the data to the actual target host, the application data will be passed through the protocol layers "downward," while each protocol layer builds a new header of its own around the useful data, until finally the packet leaves the physical level of the Application-Level Gateway.

This means that no header data can travel unchanged from one side of the gateway to the other beneath the application level, because they are created each time by the proxy servers before being sent.

Therefore, in the majority of cases malicious headers will be disposed of automatically during the passage through the application-level Gateway.

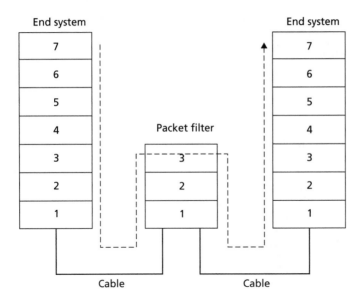

Figure 1-2

Figure 1-3 shows the ISO/OSI layers involved.

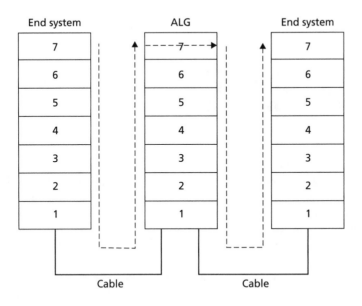

Figure 1-3

Virtual Private Network

Virtual Private Networks (VPNs) are virtual communication channels within public networks created by technical means (such as tunnels, encryption, or encapsulation) as shown in Figure 1-4.

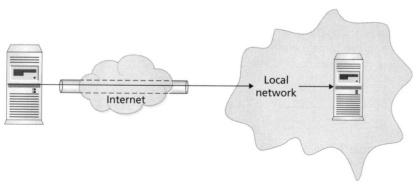

Figure 1-4

Remote Access Service (RAS)

Remote Access Service allows access to resources within a secure network from the outside.
This can be a computer with a modem that provides a dial-in connection via the telephone network, an ISDN router, or a special VPN server for a virtual dial-up through the Internet.

Summary

- All organizations host information that needs protection from potential security threats. This information is typically stored on computer networks that may allow unauthorized access if not secured.

- To secure a computer network, you must carefully plan a security strategy that consists of a security concept and security policy. Before creating a security strategy, you must determine the various types of information resources and assess the level of risk for each.

- An effective security policy lists the current and desired state of security for various information and network resources within an organization.

- The security concept should list the actions necessary to maintain an appropriate level of confidentiality, accessibility and integrity for the resources identified in the security policy.

- To create a security concept, you must first perform a communication analysis that examines the specific information access needs for various users and network components. The results of this communication analysis can be listed using an access matrix to determine which information and network components require the most protection.

- After performing a communication analysis, you can take steps to protect your network using a variety of different methods and technologies.

- Firewalls, packet filters and application-level gateways can prevent unwanted traffic from entering a network.

- Remote Access Service (RAS) servers allow secure access to remote networks.
- Virtual Private Networks (VPNs) may be used to keep information confidential across public networks.
- Demilitarized Zones (DMZs) may be used to provide services without exposing other networks to public access.
- Once you have successfully created a security concept and protected your network resources, you can update your organization's security policy and communicate it to other people within the organization to maintain security.

Key Terms

access matrix   A table that lists the network access needs of various users and computers within an organization as well as the technologies involved.

application-level firewall   See application-level gateway.

application-level gateway   A computer that fully analyzes network traffic passing through a network. They are also called application-level firewalls or proxy servers.

asset   A resource that requires protection within an organization. Company information and computer hardware are two examples of common assets within an organization.

availability   The facet of information security that describes the ease of which information may be obtained.

backup   A copy of data that may be used if the original data is lost or destroyed.

communication analysis   A process whereby an organization's structure and technologies are analyzed to identify security weaknesses.

confidentiality   The facet of information security that describes the level to which information is kept private.

Demilitarized Zone (DMZ)   A network that contains publicly accessed information and network services; because of their public nature, DMZs are a primary focus of network security.

denial of service   A type of threat that prevents normal access to computer resources or information.

firewall   A software or hardware component that restricts access to networks or network applications.

insecure network   A network that contains unknown users. Publicly accessed networks are insecure networks.

International Standard Organization's Open System Interconnect (ISO/OSI)   A model used to describe how computers use protocols to communicate on a computer network.

packet filter   A software component that drops network communication that is addressed to a particular IP address or port number.

proxy server   See application-level gateway.

Remote Access Service (RAS)   A server service that allows remote computers the ability to connect to the local network and access resources.

resources   See asset.

risk   The likelihood that confidential information or network resources will be compromised by a security breach.

screening router   A router that analyzes traffic with packet filters or firewall software before passing it to other networks.

secure network   A network that allows little or no public access.

security concept   A comprehensive security plan for an organization that lists the individual steps that an organization takes to secure computers and information from potential security breaches.

security policy   The goals that an organization needs to achieve in order to secure its computers and information.

security strategy   The plan that an organization takes to secure its computers and data. This plan uses the steps outlined in the organization's security concept to achieve the organization's security policy.

security zone   A set of computers or networks that have similar security requirements.

Virtual Private Network (VPN)   A technology that encrypts communications between two different networks or between a host and a remote network.

Review Questions

1. Which of the following security terms describes the procedures used to secure various resources on the network?

    a.   Security concept

    b.   Security strategy

    c.   Security policy

    d.   Security zone

2. Which of the following features of information and network resources require protection? (Choose three answers.)

    a.   Confidentiality

    b.   Accessibility

    c.   Integrity

    d.   Availability

3. Which of the following are potential risks to an organization's information resources? (Choose all that apply.)

    a.   Floods

    b.   Falsified information

    c.   Information theft

    d.   Viruses

4. Which of the following considerations are appropriate when performing a communication analysis? (Choose all that apply.)

    a.   Should users be charged for resources?

    b.   Who are potential hackers?

    c.   What resources must be available in each work area?

    d.   Where is protected data located?

5. Which of the following considerations are appropriate when analyzing protection requirements? (Choose all that apply.)

    a.   What information is of special interest to others?

    b.   Which zones exist and what security needs do they have?

    c.   Which groups of people can access which information?

    d.   What external resources does the company provide?

6. Which of the following would you normally see outlined in a security policy change document? (Choose all that apply.)

    a.   Current State

    b.   Target State

    c.   Estimated downtime

    d.   Responsible person

7. What type of network resides between the internal network and the Internet?

    a.   Secure network

    b.   Insecure network

    c.   Demilitarized network

    d.   Virtual private network

8. What type of network security device completely analyzes all data that passes through the network at Layer 7 of the ISO/OSI model?

    a.   Application-layer gateway

    b.   Firewall

    c.   Virtual private network

    d.   Packet filter

9. What type of network security device analyzes data that passes through the network up to Layer 3 of the ISO/OSI model?

    a.   Remote Access Server

    b.   Virtual private network

    c.   Application-layer gateway

    d.   Packet filter

10. A DMZ is considered a (an) _____.

    a.   Secure network

    b.   Virtual private network

    c.   Insecure network

    d.   Remote access network

Discovery Exercises

Analyzing Risk

Time is a valuable asset in the corporate environment. As a result, it is important to focus your time on those resources that have the highest risk of a security breach in order to make effective use of your time. Although risk is not easy to calculate since is not easily quantifiable, many security organizations define risk using the following equation:

$$\text{Risk} = P \times C$$

Thus risk is equivalent to P (the probability that security will be breached) multiplied by C (the cost of a security breach to an organization). P is typically given a value from 0 to 1 where 0 indicates a low probability of security breach and 1 represents a high probability of security breach. C is typically given a value from 1 to 10 where 1 indicates a low cost to the organization in the event of a security breach and 10 indicates a high cost to the organization in the event of a security breach.

Using this equation, estimate P and C to calculate the relative risk for each of the following servers. When finished, indicate which servers will require the majority of your time when securing company resources.

1. A Web server that is located in the DMZ. The Web server contains nutritional product information for the food products that your company produces and does not participate in e-Commerce.

2. A file server that is located in the internal private company network. The file server contains sensitive data such as trade secrets and order information. Salespersons within the organization often connect remotely to these servers using VPNs to place orders while traveling.

3. Two e-mail servers that are located in the DMZ. Nearly all internal and external communication is performed by these e-mail servers.

Comparing Firewall Types

Most networks today typically use packet-filtering firewalls or application-layer firewalls (proxy servers) to restrict traffic passing in and out of the network. Use the Internet or other resources to compare the benefits and disadvantages of using packet-filtering firewalls as opposed to proxy servers and summarize your findings in a short memo.

Creating a Security Policy

Using the information provided in this chapter, create a sample security policy document for your school, company, or organization. Ensure that you perform a communication analysis, analyze the protection requirements, and prepare an access matrix to summarize the users, servers, clients and connection technologies used.

Host Security

Host security is achieved by general system administration with security in mind. It starts when the machine is being set up and continues with routine system administration and keeping the security patches installed. This section covers the various aspects involved with host security. Some topics are covered only briefly here, as they have been covered already extensively in the SUSE Linux Enterprise Server Administration courses (3071, 3072, and 3073).

Objectives

- Limit Physical Access to Server Systems
- Partitioning and File System Security
- Limit the Installed Software Packages
- Configure Security Settings with YaST
- Stay Informed about Security Issues
- Apply Security Updates
- Test and Document the Configuration
- Use Logging and Accounting

Objective 1—Limit Physical Access to Server Systems

If a server is not protected from unauthorized physical access, even the best software configuration cannot prevent someone from misusing it.

By rebooting a system from a floppy or CD, or by passing boot parameters to the Linux kernel, someone can access the server without knowing the root password.

To prevent unauthorized users from physically accessing the server, do the following:

- Place the Server in a Separate, Locked Room
- Secure the BIOS with a Password
- Secure the GRUB Boot Loader with a Password

Place the Server in a Separate, Locked Room

The best way to prevent physical access to a server is to lock the server in a dedicated server room. We highly recommend that you do this for every production system.

The server room should be locked with a solid door, and only system administrators should have access. The room should be protected against fire and equipped with an automatic fire extinguishing system.

What can be done depends on the size of the company and on the available financial resources. We recommend a separate, locked room for all servers at the very least.

Secure the BIOS with a Password

For test systems or workstations that are not placed in a secure room, there are some things you can do to make it more difficult to access a system without an account.

One of these is to set a password for the BIOS setup.

The BIOS represents the lowest level of software and lies underneath the operating system. Modern BIOS versions give you the option of protecting the boot process with a password.

You can also protect the BIOS settings and prevent the system from booting from media like floppy disks or CDs.

 The exact procedure for protecting the BIOS depends on the BIOS vendor and version. For more details on this, please consult your vendor documentation.

By preventing the system from booting from a different medium, only the installed system can be started. This system is password protected and cannot be accessed without other effort.

For example, a BIOS password can be reset by removing the CMOS battery for some time or temporarily setting some jumpers on the mainboard. Some older BIOSes even have master passwords which render a BIOS password completely useless.

Due to the above, BIOS passwords give only minor improvements of security. BIOS passwords are never a replacement for a dedicated server room.

Secure the GRUB Boot Loader with a Password

Another way to misuse physical access to a Linux system is to reboot and pass additional parameters (such as init=/bin/bash) to the kernel. This makes it possible to start and access the system as root without entering a password.

The GRUB boot loader can be configured to prompt for a password before any parameters can be entered. To do this, you need to create an encrypted password with the following command:

```
grub-md5-crypt
```

This command asks for a password that needs to be confirmed once and outputs a hashed string. This string looks like the following:

```
$1$SEVCUO$S.7WQLO5kHiK4VKDsKtfIO
```

The password hash needs to be added to the GRUB configuration file:

```
/boot/grub/menu.lst
```

You will find the global section at the beginning of the configuration file. The password needs to be placed in that section as shown in the following example:

```
color white/blue black/light-gray
default 0
timeout 8
gfxmenu (hd0,5)/boot/message
password --md5 $1$SEVCUO$S.7WQLO5kHiK4VKDsKtfIO
```

GRUB is covered in depth in course 3072, **SUSE Linux Enterprise Server 10 Administration**.

Objective 2—Partitioning and File System Security

After a user has logged in to the system, what she can or cannot do is mainly determined by the partitioning, the way the file systems are mounted, and the security settings of the file system.

In UNIX systems like Linux, file system security is especially important because every resource available on the system is represented as a file.

For example, when a user tries to access the sound card to play back audio data, the access permissions of the sound card are determined by the permission settings of the corresponding device file in the /dev directory.

To ensure basic file system security, you need to know the following:

- Hard Disk Partitioning
- The Basic Rule for User Write Access
- The Basic Rule for User Read Access
- How Special File Permissions Affect System Security

Hard Disk Partitioning

The standard installation provides for a swap partition and one partition for the entire "/" directory. This is quite comfortable because the entire space is available for all directories, and you do not need to worry about partitioning.

However, this approach has some disadvantages.

For example, the /var/ directory might be full with log files and occupy the entire hard disk space, leaving no room for users to store files in their home directories. Or a user could consume all of the hard disk space with files in his home directory or in /tmp/, thus preventing other users from working with this machine (Denial of Service).

You can prevent some of these problems by distributing parts of the file system to separate partitions.

Also, using LVM (Logical Volume Manager) results in more flexibility than using a single partition for the entire file system. LVM allocates the available hard disk space to a logical volume group, which in turn is split into several logical volumes.

Similar to hard disk partitions without LVM, each of these logical volumes can hold parts of the file system. However, logical volumes are much easier to resize than native hard disk partitions.

Depending on the purpose of the respective machine, you may want to place some of the following directories in separate partitions:

- /var/ (or individual subdirectories of this directory)
- /tmp/
- /usr/
- /opt/
- /srv/ (or individual subdirectories of this directory)
- /home/

The size of the individual partitions also depends on the purpose: on a mail server, the partition containing /var/spool/mail/ needs most of the space; on a Web server, the partition containing /srv/www/ needs most of the space.

If the file system is distributed to partitions in this way, log files or mail could still fill the respective partition but not the other partitions.

Certain properties of individual partitions can also be modified using mount options in the file /etc/fstab.

Depending on the server's purpose, you may want to mount /home/ and /tmp/ with the options noexec, nosuid, and nodev.

The option ro could be useful for /usr/ and /opt/.

SUSE Linux Enterprise Server 10 also offers the option to encrypt entire partitions. This is especially useful on notebooks to minimize the risk of data getting into the wrong hands when a notebook is lost or stolen. The minimum length of the passphrase required by YaST is 8 characters, but to have a passphrase equivalent in strength to the 128-bit encryption key used to encrypt the partition, you should use 20 random characters.

Partitions, LVM, and file systems, as well as their administration are covered in detail in course 3072, **SUSE Linux Enterprise Server 10 Administration**.

The Basic Rule for User Write Access

The file systems used in Linux are structurally UNIX file systems.

They support the typical file access permissions (such as read, write, execute, sticky bit, SUID, and SGID).

Apart from additional standard functionalities, such as various time stamps, the access permissions can be administered separately for file owners, user groups, and the rest of the world (user, group, and other).

The administration of file ownership and permissions is covered in course 3071, **SUSE Linux Enterprise Server 10 Fundamentals**.

As a general rule, a normal user should only have write access in the following directories:

- The home directory of the user

- The /tmp directory to store temporary files

Depending on the purpose of a computer, other directories can be writable for users.

For example, if you install a Samba file server, a writable share needs a directory that is also writable for the Linux user the connection is mapped to.

Some device files (like those for sound cards) might also be writable for users since applications need to send data to the corresponding devices.

The Basic Rule for User Read Access

Some files in the system should be protected from user read access. This is important for files that store passwords.

No normal user account should be able to read the content of such files. Even when the passwords in a file are encrypted, the files must be protected from any unauthorized access.

The following lists some files containing passwords on a Linux system:

- /etc/shadow—This file contains user passwords in an encrypted form. Even when LDAP is used for user authentication, this file contains at least the root password.

- /etc/samba/smbpasswd—This file contains the passwords for Samba users.

- *Files with Apache passwords*—The location of these files depends on your configuration.
  They contain passwords for the authorized access to the Web server.

- /etc/openldap/slapd.conf—This file contains the root password for the openLDAP server.

- /boot/grub/menu.lst—This file can contain the password for the GRUB boot loader.

This list is not complete. There can be more password files on your system, depending on your system configuration and your software selection.

Some password files can be readable for a non-root account. This is normally the account (user ID) under which the service daemon that needs to access the file is running. For example, the Apache Web server runs under the user ID wwwrun. For this reason, the password files must be readable for the user wwwrun.

In this case you have to make sure that only this daemon account and no other user can read the file.

How Special File Permissions Affect System Security

Three file system permissions influence the security in a special way:

- *The SUID bit*—If the SUID bit is set for an executable, the program starts under the user ID of the owner of the file.

   In most cases, the SUID bit is set to allow normal users to run applications with the permissions of the root users.

   This bit should only be set for applications that are well tested and if there is no other way to grant access to a specific task.

   An attacker could get access to the root account by exploiting an application that runs under the UID of root.

- *The SGID bit*—If this bit is set, it lets a program run under the GID of the group the executable file belongs to.

   It should be used as carefully as the SUID bit.

- *The sticky bit*—The sticky bit can influence the security of a system in a positive way. In a globally writable directory, it prevents users from deleting other users' files that are stored in this directory.

   Typical application areas for the sticky bit include directories for temporary storage (such as /tmp and /var/tmp). Such a directory must be writable by all users of a system.

   However, the write permissions for a directory do not only include the permission to create files and subdirectories, but also the permission to delete these, regardless of whether the users have access to the content of these files and subdirectories.

   If the sticky bit is set for such a writable directory, deleting or renaming files in this directory is only possible if one of the following conditions is fulfilled:

   - The effective UID of the deleting or renaming process is that of the file owner.
   - The effective UID of the deleting or renaming process is that of the owner of the writable directory marked with the sticky bit.
   - The effective UID of the deleting or renaming process is that of the system administrator root.

In SUSE Linux Enterprise Server 10, the files /etc/permissions.* are used to set or remove these bits on executables and directories.

You can use POSIX ACLs (Access Control Lists) to control access to files in more detail.

These are covered in **SUSE Linux Enterprise Server 10 Administration** (Course 3072).

Objective 3—Limit the Installed Software Packages

Every software package that is installed on a system but is not needed by that system, should be removed from a production server.

The more software is installed, the more possible security problems can occur. For example, it does not make sense to install an X Server and graphical applications on a system that is exclusively used as a Web server.

To set up a production system, you can use the minimal system as a base for the software selection during the installation. Then you can manually add just those software packages that are needed.

This rule is especially true for network daemons. A server should never offer any network services that are not needed. For example, if a server is used as a dedicated file server, it is not necessary to run a Postfix mail server on the same system.

You can use the following command to check which services are configured to start in which runlevel:

```
chkconfig -l
```

The command displays a line for every service installed on the system. The following line shows the configuration of the Samba server:

```
smb 0:off 1:off 2:off 3:on 4:off 5:on 6:off
```

After the service name, the configuration for all seven runlevels is displayed. On means the service is configured to be started in the corresponding runlevel; off means the service will not be started.

You can use the following command to prevent a service from being started in any runlevel:

```
insserv -r service_name
```

Removing a service from the runlevel configuration does not stop an already running daemon. A daemon that is already running needs to be stopped manually or the system needs to be rebooted to start with the new runlevel configuration.

Objective 4—Configure Security Settings with YaST

The package bastille offers comparable options to set security parameters. We do not recommend to use bastille, as it might interfere with the settings made by YaST and YaST might interfere with the settings made by Bastille.

However, it gives some useful information on host and network security integrated into its configuration dialog, so it might be worth mentioning.

YaST offers a module to configure certain system settings that affect the local security. You can access the module from the YaST Control Center by selecting `Security and Users > Local Security`.

With the module you can easily change the following settings of the system configuration:

- The password settings
- The boot behavior of the system
- The login behavior
- The user ID limitations
- General file system security

Because this YaST module is already covered in detail in course 3072, *SUSE Linux Enterprise Server 10 Administration*, we decided not to cover it again, despite the fact that its subject matter is relevant for this course as well.

In view of the fact that this module covers various security settings, you might want to review the respective section of the 3072 course.

Objective 5—Stay Informed about Security Issues

One of the most important security tasks for an administrator is to stay informed about current security issues.

Damage can be prevented only when security patches are installed as quickly as possible.

Once you register SUSE Linux Enterprise Server 10 to become part of the Maintenance Program, you are informed by e-mail once security patches are available.

Additionally, you can use the following resources to gather information about SUSE Linux-related security issues:

- *http://www.novell.com/linux/security/securitysupport.html*

    This Web site is the central security information site of SUSE. All security issues affecting SUSE products are announced here.

    You will also find information about security and OpenSource software and the SUSE security team.

- *http://www.suse.com/us/private/support/online_help/mailinglists/index.html*

    This Web site offers an overview of all SUSE-related mailing lists.

    There are two security-related mailing lists that you can subscribe to for further security information:

    - *suse-security*—This mailing list is intended for security-relevant discussions.
    - *suse-security-announce*—This mailing list announces security issues and fixes. This mailing list is read only. For discussions please use suse-security.

    To subscribe to a mailing list, select the check boxes by the name of the list, enter your mail address at the bottom of the page, and then select OK.

Resources on general security issues (Linux and otherwise) are widely available on the Internet. For instance:

- *http://www.securityfocus.com/*
  This Web site is about general IT security. It also offers various security-relevant mailing lists.
  There are many more security resources available on the Internet.

- *http://www.linuxsecurity.com/*
  This site publishes security advisories for several Linux distributions and articles on various Linux topics.

Exercise 2-1: Subscribe to the SUSE Security Announcements

Time Required: 5 minutes

Objective: In this exercise, you subscribe to the SUSE security mailing list. This means that Novell/SUSE will inform you by e-mail about current security issues of SUSE Linux products.

Description: If you don't want to receive these messages, skip this exercise.
Do the following:

1. Start a Web browser of your choice.

2. In the address bar of the browser, enter the following:
   http://www.suse.com/us/private/support/online_help/mailinglists/index.html

3. Scroll down to the entry `suse-security-announce`; then select the check box for that entry.

4. Scroll down to the bottom of that page. In the e-mail Address field, enter *your e-mail address*.

5. Subscribe to the list by selecting `OK`.

6. Close the Web browser window.

Objective 6—Apply Security Updates

SUSE Linux Enterprise Server 10 is sold with system maintenance. This system maintenance includes updates and security patches.

Software updates can be managed with the YaST Online Update (YOU) module. This YaST module downloads and installs software updates and security patches.

To apply security updates, you need to do the following:

- Configure the Novell Customer Center
- Use the YaST Online Update

Configure the Novell Customer Center

To access the configuration of the Novell Customer Center, start the YaST Control Center and select `Software > Novell Customer Center Configuration`. You can also start the dialog directly from a terminal window as root by entering `yast2 inst_suse_register`. The dialog is the same as that offered during installation for this purpose as shown in Figure 2-1.

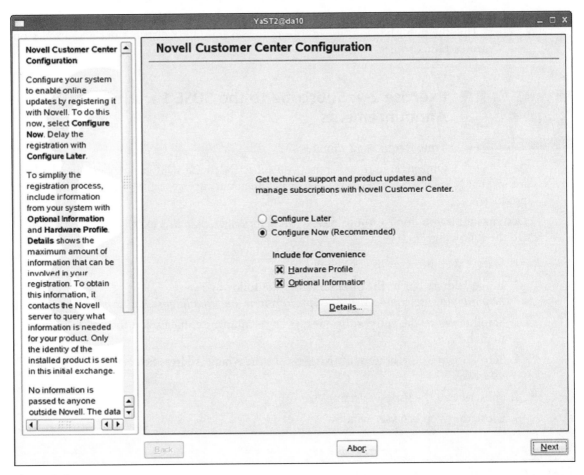

Figure 2-1

Selecting Details shows what information is being collected and sent.

With a browser, the Novell Customer Center can be accessed at *http://www.novell.com/center/*. After you have created a Novell account, you need to register your product with the registration code delivered with the SUSE Linux Enterprise Server 10 product.

The SUSE Linux Enterprise Server 10 DVD you received as part of your student kit does not include maintenance. Visit the Novell Customer Center for information on how to take part in the SUSE Linux Enterprise Server 10 Maintenance Program.

Only registered products with a valid maintenance contract can be updated with the YOU module.

Use the YaST Online Update

The following is a quick guide to applying software updates with YOU.

Start the YOU module from the YaST Control Center by selecting `Software > Online Update`. See Figure 2-2.

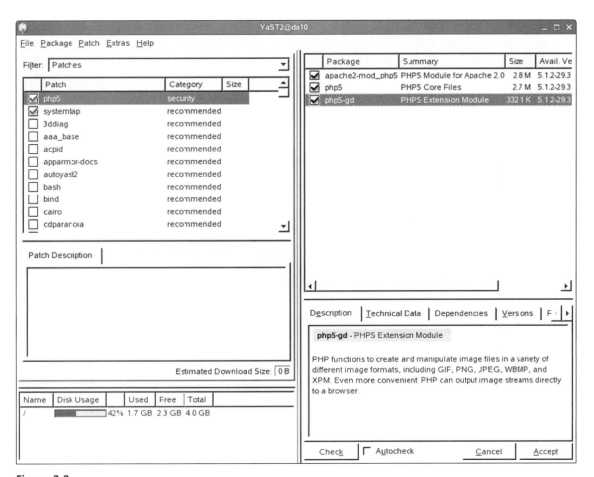

Figure 2-2

On the top left side of the dialog all available patches are displayed. Select an entry to see details for the update on the right side of the dialog. To have an update installed in the next step, select the check box next to the corresponding entry.

Select `Accept` to start the update process.

Depending on your selection an `Automatic Changes` dialog appears as shown in Figure 2-3.

Accept the changes by selecting `Continue`; the patches are transferred from the update server and installed.

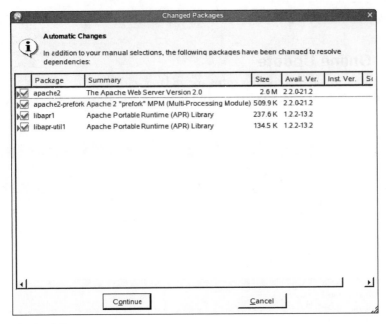

Figure 2-3

During the installation process YOU displays the dialog shown in Figure 2-4.

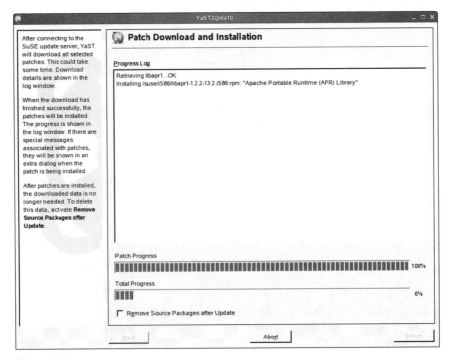

Figure 2-4

Sometimes additional information is displayed for some updates. These dialogs need to be confirmed to install the corresponding software package.

Once all updates have been downloaded and installed, select `Finish` to close the dialog.

Objective 7—Test and Document the Configuration

Before the installed system goes into production, the configuration should be tested. While it is useful if a trusted third party audits the configuration, this is not always feasible. However, you can test the configuration to find errors that might otherwise go by undetected. The results of such scans should become part of the documentation.

The most common open source tools for testing the security configuration are:

- netstat
- ethereal
- nmap
- nessus

netstat

`netstat` is a tool which can be used to check which network sockets are currently used by a system. Additionally you can determine the status of a socket. The command can be invoked with various parameters as shown in Table 2-1.

Parameter	Meaning
-p	Show the PID and the name of the program which owns the socket.
-a	Show both listening and non-listening sockets.
-t	Show TCP sockets.
-u	Show UPD sockets.
-n	Do not resolve IP addresses into host names.
-e	Display more detailed information.

Table 2-1

A very useful parameter combination is `netstat -patune`. It lists UDP and TCP connections, shows the processes involved, and does not resolve names.

The following is an example output of such a netstat call:

```
Proto Recv-Q Send-Q Local Address Foreign Address State  User Inode
PID/Program name
tcp    0      0      0.0.0.0:631   0.0.0.0:*       LISTEN 0    4526
2916/cupsd
tcp    0      0      :::22         :::*            LISTEN 0    3306
2425/sshd
```

From left to right, netstat outputs the following information:

- *Proto*—The used transfer protocol. This can be `tcp`, `udp`, or `raw`.
- *Recv-Q*—The count of bytes not copied by the user program connected to this socket. This value should usually be 0.
- *Send-Q*—The count of bytes not acknowledged by the remote host. This value should usually be 0.
- *Local Address*—The IP address and port number of the local end of the socket. If you don't use the -n option, the addresses are resolved into DNS host names. If the socket is in `LISTEN` state, the IP address 0.0.0.0 or `:::` stands for any local IP address.
- *Foreign Address*—The IP address and port number of the remote end of the socket. If you don't use the -n option, the addresses are resolved into DNS host names. If the socket is in `LISTEN` state, the IP address 0.0.0.0 or `:::` stands for any remote IP address.
- *State*—The state of the socket. Since there are no states in udp and raw mode, this column may be left blank.
  The following is an overview of the possible states:

  - `ESTABLISHED`: The socket has an established connection.
  - `SYN_SENT`: The socket is actively attempting to establish a connection.
  - `SYN_RECV`: A connection request has been received from the network.
  - `FIN_WAIT1`: The socket is closed, and the connection is shutting down.
  - `FIN_WAIT2`: The connection is closed, and the socket is waiting for a shutdown from the remote end.
  - `TIME_WAIT`: The socket is waiting after close to handle packets still in the network.
  - `CLOSED`: The socket is not being used.
  - `CLOSE_WAIT`: The remote end has shut down; waiting for the socket to close.
  - `LAST_ACK`: The remote end has shut down, and the socket is closed. Waiting for acknowledgement.
  - `LISTEN`: The socket is listening for incoming connections. Such sockets are not included in the output unless you specify the –listening (-l) or –all (-a) option.
  - `CLOSING`: Both sockets are shut down, but some of the data has not been sent.
  - `UNKNOWN`: The state of the socket is unknown.

- *User*—The username or the user ID (UID) of the owner of the socket.
- *Inode*—The inode of the socket.
- *PID / Program name*—The PID and the Program name of the process that owns the socket. You need to run netstat as root to see this information for all sockets. For sockets which are owned by kernel processes, this column is blank.

ethereal

Ethereal is a graphical network analyzer. It allows you to capture and analyze network packets. To use ethereal on SUSE Linux Enterprise Server 10, you need to install the package `ethereal`.

Ethereal requires root privileges. Therefore, you need to switch to root using the `su -` command. Then you can start ethereal simply by typing `ethereal`.

After starting ethereal, the window shown in Figure 2-5 appears.

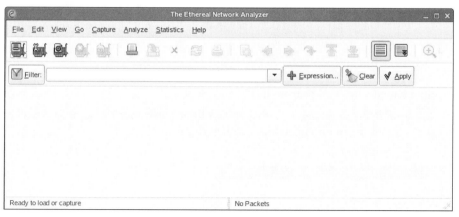

Figure 2-5

To start capturing packets, select `Capture > Options` to select the interface as shown in Figure 2-6.

Figure 2-6

The most important options are:

- *Interface*—This determines which network interface ethereal should use to capture packets. By selecting any, packets from all interfaces are captured.

- *Capture packets in promiscuous mode*—By enabling this option, all packets on the physical layer are captured, rather than just those which are addressed for the machine ethereal is running on.

- *Update list of packets in real time*—If this option is enabled, captured packets are directly displayed in the packet list of ethereal. Otherwise, the packet list would only be loaded after capturing has been stopped.

- *Capture Filter*—With these filters you can limit the amount of captured packets to those you are really interested in. See Figure 2-7.

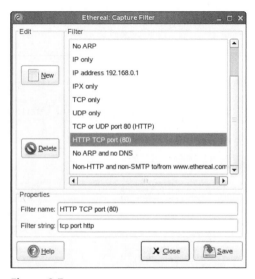

Figure 2-7

There are already several filters in the list. You can create new filters by selecting New.

A filter consists of two parameters, a Filter name and a Filter string. The Filter name is just an identifier and you can basically choose any string you want. The Filter string is an expression which is passed to the underlying capture process. The filter expression determines which packets are captured.

In the example above, the selected filter captures only packets which are sent from or to port 80. This is done with the filter expression tcp port http.

For a full description of all possible filter expressions, have a look at the manpage of tcpdump.

By selecting `Start` in the capture dialog, the capture process starts and ethereal displays a dialog with some packet statistics. By selecting `Stop` in this dialog, the capture process can be terminated.

After the capture process has been finished, ethereal displays the captured packets. See Figure 2-8.

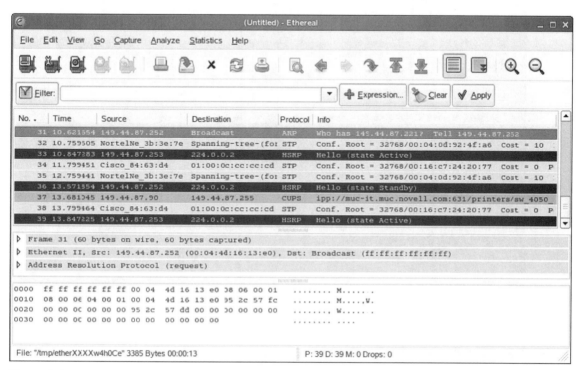

Figure 2-8

The window has three display frames. In the upper frame all captured packets are displayed in a list. In the middle frame, the structure of the selected packet is displayed. And in the lower frame the data of the packet is displayed in Hex and ASCI format.

At the bottom of the window you can add filter expressions, which work on the already captured packets. These filters are also called display filters.

 This was just a quick overview of ethereal. You can find the complete manual on the site of the ethereal project: *http://www.ethereal.com/docs*

nmap

nmap (*http://www.insecure.org/*) is a sophisticated port scanner with many options.

You can use it to determine which ports are open, which services are actually running on those ports, and which operating system is being used by the host you are scanning.

Calling nmap without options shows the main options:

```
da10:~ # nmap
Nmap 4.00 ( http://www.insecure.org/nmap/ )
Usage: nmap [Scan Type(s)] [Options] {target specification}
TARGET SPECIFICATION:
  Can pass hostnames, IP addresses, networks, etc.
  Ex:scanme.nmap.org,microsoft.com/24,192.168.0.1;10.0.0-255.1-254
  -iL <inputfilename>: Input from list of hosts/networks
  -iR <num hosts>: Choose random targets
  --exclude <host1[,host2][,host3],...>: Exclude hosts/networks
  --excludefile <exclude_file>: Exclude list from file
HOST DISCOVERY:
  -sL: List Scan - simply list targets to scan
  -sP: Ping Scan - go no further than determining if host is online
  -P0: Treat all hosts as online -- skip host discovery
  -PS/PA/PU [portlist]: TCP SYN/ACK or UDP discovery to given ports
  -PE/PP/PM: ICMP echo, timestamp, and netmask request discovery probes
  -n/-R: Never do DNS resolution/Always resolve [default: sometimes]
  --dns-servers <serv1[,serv2],...>: Specify custom DNS servers
  --system-dns: Use OS's DNS resolver
SCAN TECHNIQUES:
  -sS/sT/sA/sW/sM: TCP SYN/Connect()/ACK/Window/Maimon scans
  -sN/sF/sX: TCP Null, FIN, and Xmas scans
  --scanflags <flags>: Customize TCP scan flags
  -sI <zombie host[:probeport]>: Idlescan
  -sO: IP protocol scan
  -b <ftp relay host>: FTP bounce scan
...
```

You only need to use the basic options to verify your installation.

Usually you want to find out which ports are open, offering services, and decide if this matches the output of netstat and the list of services you want to offer on this computer.

A TCP connect and an UDP scan should suffice.

```
da10:~ # nmap -sU -sT da20.digitalairlines.com

Starting Nmap 4.00 ( http://www.insecure.org/nmap/ ) at 2006-07-05
12:50 CEST
Interesting ports on da20.digitalairlines.com (10.0.0.20):
(The 3144 ports scanned but not shown below are in state: closed)
PORT        STATE          SERVICE
22/tcp      open           ssh
111/tcp     open           rpcbind
111/udp     open|filtered rpcbind
123/udp     open|filtered ntp
137/udp     open|filtered netbios-ns
138/udp     open|filtered netbios-dgm
139/tcp     open           netbios-ssn
445/tcp     open           microsoft-ds
631/tcp     open           ipp
32768/udp open|filtered omad
MAC Address: 00:11:11:C2:35:F4 (Intel)

Nmap finished: 1 IP address (1 host up) scanned in 1471.627 seconds
```

The scan of UDP ports takes some time. If you scan all the ports (-p 1-65535), expect the scan to be quite time-consuming.

nmap also allows you to scan other hosts with spoofed IP sender addresses interspersed, different settings of TCP flags (like none set - null - or all set - xmas). Which options you use depends on what you want to find out.

You can use nmap to find hosts on a particular network and the services they are offering, or to try to get information about hosts behind a firewall.

You can also run an idle scan which scans a host without sending any packets to that host directly. It uses another machine (the zombie) for this purpose. Idle scans are described in *http://www.insecure.org/nmap/idlescan.html*. This Web page also explains how to defend against such a scan.

The site also lists popular security tools at *http://www.insecure.org/tools.html*.

As a general note of caution: While a port scan is basically nothing to really worry about, some administrators consider it as a kind of attack in itself, or as a first stage of an attack. Also, some ISPs have rules forbidding port scans and reserve the right to terminate service for those violating that rule. So before you start scanning a machine, get permission to do so.

nessus

nessus (*http://www.nessus.org/*) is a vulnerability scanner. Its main purpose is to give you an overview of the vulnerabilities existing in your network.

When you are in charge of many different computers, it is hard to keep track of the vulnerabilities and which computer has been patched against what. nessus can help you with this task.

The scanning itself is done by the nessus daemon, while the nessus client controls and launches the scans. nessus scales well to larger networks, because it is possible to have nessusd running in subnets, avoiding the need to scan across routers, and to control the daemons from one client.

To prevent random users from using nessusd to scan hosts, the client has to authenticate with the server. Certificates are used for this purpose.

Several steps are needed to launch a scan:

1. As root, issue the following command and answer any dialogs with appropriate information:

```
nessus-mkcert
nessus-adduser
rcnessusd start
nessus
```

2. In the graphical user interface, use the login you created with the nessus-adduser script, and the corresponding password.

3. Choose the target, wait a few minutes, and view the result.

Everything is explained with comprehensive descriptions and recommendations, so that you can decide what to do about it. For documentation purposes, the report can be saved as HTML, XML, or Latex.

Because new flaws are being discovered and published every day, new nessus plug-ins are written every day both by the nessus vendor Tenable Network Security and the user community.

You can use the command `nessus-update-plugins` to download the latest nessus plug-ins to your system. Plug-ins are immediately available for direct feed customers and seven days later to registered feed users. See *http://www.nessus.org/plugins/* for details.

A nessus scan can crash services or entire hosts under certain conditions. Don't scan without permission and coordinate with system administrators to avoid server downtimes and upsets.

Documentation

After installation and testing, you should document what has been done. There is no hardbound rule how this is to be done. We suggest to archive at least the following on paper:

- Output of `fdisk -l`
- /etc/fstab
- Configuration files that were changed from the installation defaults
- Output of `rpm -qa`
- Output of `netstat -patune`
- Output of `chkconfig -l`
- Output of `sitar`
- Output of an nmap scan
- Which tests were done and their results

You should also have a backup of the directory /etc/.

Depending on the available storage space, you should consider taking a full image of the installation.

Exercise 2-2: Use nmap and nessus

Time Required: 10 minutes

Objective: In this exercise, you perform a portscan with nmap and scan a computer for vulnerabilities with nessus. You will work with a partner in this exercise.

Description: In the first part of the exercise, scan the computer of your partner with nmap, using a TCP connect scan. Use ethereal to watch your partner scan your computer.

Time Required: 15 minutes

Description: In the second part, set up nessusd and nessus client to scan hosts in the network. Perform a nessus scan on your partner's computer.

Detailed Steps to Complete this Exercise:

- Part I: Use nmap to Scan for Open Ports
- Part II: Run a nessus Scan

Part I: Use nmap to Scan for Open Ports

To use nmap to scan for open ports, do the following:

1. Open a terminal window and `su -` to root with a password of `novell`.
2. Install nmap and ethereal by entering `yast -i nmap ethereal`.
3. Perform a TCP connect scan on your partner's computer by entering the following command:

   `nmap -sT <host_of_partner>`

   Compare the result with the output of `netstat -patune` on his or her computer.

4. Start Ethereal by typing `ethereal`.
5. Select `Capture > Interfaces`; then select `Capture` next to the interface used for capturing packets, for instance, eth0.
6. Let your partner scan your computer with nmap.
7. Select `Stopp` in the ethereal capture dialog.
8. Have a look at the packet list in ethereal. Are you able to identify the packets nmap used for the port scan?
9. Close ethereal, select `Continue without Saving`.

Part II: Run a nessus Scan

To run a nessus scan, do the following:

1. Open a terminal window and `su -` to root with a password of `novell`.
2. Install nessus by entering `yast -i nessus-core`; yast will install this and some other packages that are needed to resolve dependencies.
3. Create a certificate for the nessusd by entering:

   `nessus-mkcert`

   Accept all suggested values by pressing enter.

4. Add a user who can access nessusd by entering:

   `nessus-adduser`

   Use *geeko* as login, accept the default when asked for the authentication, and use *novell* as password. When prompted to enter rules within the adduser-script, press CTRL-D without entering any rules.

   You are asked if your entries are okay, press enter if they are. Otherwise press n and correct any errors.

5. Start nessusd by entering:

   `rcnessusd start`

6. Start the user interface by entering:

   `nessus`

7. Log in as `geeko` with the password you provided within the script.

8. Accept the SSL certificate by selecting the second option in the dialog; click `OK`.

9. A message appears, warning you that certain plugins can crash the target host; click `OK`.

10. Select the `Target` tab and enter the IP address of your partner's computer as the target host; start the scan by selecting `Start the scan`. The scan will take some time.

11. View the report by selecting the entries shown in the report window.

Objective 8—Use Logging and Accounting

While you might consider it the worst case when a computer gets hacked despite all your efforts to prevent that, there is one thing even worse: Getting hacked and never finding out about it.

To reduce this risk, use the wide range of logging and accounting facilities of SUSE Linux Enterprise Server 10.

The system administrator must look at these logs regularly or use tools that can automate the process. For example, some tools mail a digest of the relevant parts of log files to the administrator.

The main topics in this objective are:

- Logging
- Process Accounting
- Tools to Automate Checking of Log Files and Other Information

Logging

Following the installation of the system, well-known log files like `/var/log/messages`, `/var/log/mail`, and `/var/log/wtmp` are available. However, Linux and SUSE Linux Enterprise Server 10 also offer other less well-known logging and accounting options, some of which need to be explicitly installed and activated.

From the aspect of security, these options can be used to detect unusual system activities (such as unusual system load or increased network traffic), or determine when certain activities took place.

System Activity

SUSE Linux Enterprise Server 10 comes with various tools which help you to monitor the system activity. Table 2-2 is an overview of the most important ones.

Tool	Purpose
sysstat	The sysstat package contains tools for documenting system activity. Two cron jobs that are defined in the file /etc/cron.d/sysstat (created by `rcsysstat start`) make sure that the scripts sa1 and sa2 in /usr/lib/sa/ are executed at regular intervals. These, in turn, run the programs sadc and sar in the same directory with suitable options.
sadc	sadc (the System Activity Data Collector) is run every 10 minutes by the sysstat cron job. The system activity is appended to the file /var/log/sa/sa.*currentDate* in a binary format. This directory contains a file for every day the computer was run.
sar	Every 6 hours, the activity recorded up to the designated time on the designated day is converted to a human-readable format by the sar (System Activity Report) utility. The result is saved in the file sar.*currentDate* in the same directory in ASCII format. This file contains a number of values for every 10 minutes, including the processes per second, the CPU load, the amount of data transmitted per second, information on the memory and swap usage, and so on. The sar utility can also be started from the command line. In this case, it shows the CPU load on the designated day. The output can be modified by means of various options. For example, -A displays all available information. The man pages (man sar) describe the other options.
isag	The graphical output of the isag utility is even more informative. The format of the file names in the directory /var/log/sa/ is specified with -m sa.*. The desired system activity parameter can be selected under the menu item Chart. 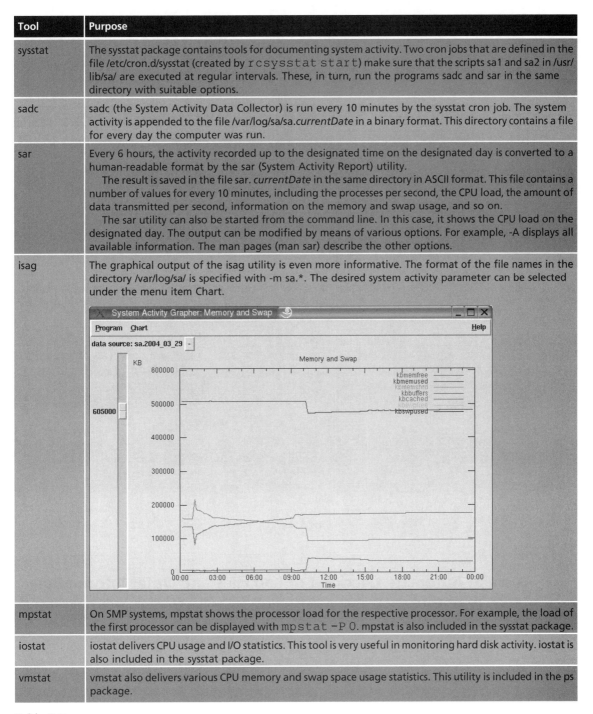
mpstat	On SMP systems, mpstat shows the processor load for the respective processor. For example, the load of the first processor can be displayed with `mpstat -P 0`. mpstat is also included in the sysstat package.
iostat	iostat delivers CPU usage and I/O statistics. This tool is very useful in monitoring hard disk activity. iostat is also included in the sysstat package.
vmstat	vmstat also delivers various CPU memory and swap space usage statistics. This utility is included in the ps package.

Table 2-2

Process Accounting

Process accounting is another aspect of system monitoring. It focuses on process and user activity. The following tools shown in Table 2-3 are available on SUSE Linux Enterprise Server 10.

Tool	Purpose
last	By default, every Linux system logs user logins and logouts in the file /var/log/wtmp. last displays the content of /var/log/wtmp in human-readable form.
package acct	The detailed logging of all processes started on a machine is rather uncommon, mainly because the information is usually not needed and also because of the substantial amounts of data that are generated by such an action. However, special security requirements might dictate the documentation of every single started process. The acct package contains the needed tools.
ac	The ac utility enables an interpretation of the file /var/log/wtmp in terms of login times. For more information, see the man page of ac.
accton	The process accounting is activated by starting accton and specifying the file to which the accounting information is to be written (normally /var/account/pacct). It is stopped by executing accton without any parameters. The script /etc/init.d/acct executes the above-mentioned accton commands without starting any daemons. By entering `insserv acct`, accton is started automatically at boot time.
lastcomm	The lastcomm utility interprets the file /var/account/pacct, which is not human-readable. If executed without any parameters, it displays all previously entered commands listed in the file. If a user name or a command is specified, only the lines containing the user name or the command are displayed.
sa	sa (summarizes accounting) provides a summary of the accounting information. (sa has nothing to do with the above-mentioned utilities sar and sadc.) If you do not use any options, sa delivers summarized information on virtually all executed commands. The option -u lists the users who executed the programs, and -m returns the sum of various values per user.

Table 2-3

Tools to Automate Checking of Log Files and Other Information

The sheer volume of the log files can make it virtually impossible to actually see security-relevant entries. You need tools to sift through the relevant information.

You can write your own scripts or use specialized tools like the following:

- seccheck
- logcheck
- logsurfer

Only seccheck is included with SLES 10. If you want to test the other two tools, you have to get them from the sources mentioned in the text. Detailed instruction on them is not part of this course.

seccheck The package `seccheck` consists of a number of scripts that perform various checks daily, weekly, and monthly. You are informed by mail of bound sockets, SUID programs, loaded modules, devices, and many other aspects that have a security connotation.

It is advisable to install the package.

logcheck `logcheck` (*http://logcheck.org/*) parses system logs and generates e-mail reports based on anomalies.

In the beginning logcheck produces long reports. You have to modify the configuration of logcheck so that harmless entries do not turn up in the report anymore.

After that initial phase, the reports mailed by logcheck should contain only relevant information on security violations and unusual activities.

logcheck should be called regularly via cron to parse log files. logcheck remembers the point to which a log file was scanned previously, so that only the new section is scanned on the next call.

logsurfer The simple parsing of log files line by line has the disadvantage that each line is independent of all other lines. However, you might want additional information when a certain entry is found in the log file.

`logsurfer` (*http://www.cert.dfn.de/eng/logsurf/*) offers this functionality with contexts. Several lines matching a pattern can be stored in memory as a context.

For example, depending on other patterns in the log file, such a context could be mailed to you for inspection or a program could be started.

If this pattern is not found within a certain time or number of lines, the context could be deleted again.

It is also possible to dynamically create or delete matching rules, depending on entries in the log file.

Because logsurfer can be configured in great detail, the configuration is not trivial. However, the advantage is that you can configure very precisely what should happen under what circumstances.

Summary

- Host security consists of several procedures that can be used to increase the security of a SUSE Linux Enterprise server.

- You can physically protect your servers by storing them in a locked room, and implementing BIOS and GRUB passwords.

- By using several partitions and file systems on your system, you reduce the chance that a Denial of Service attack will use all of the free space on the root file system. You can also encrypt individual file systems or mount certain file systems with read-only access to improve security.

- It is good security practice to assign only the necessary permissions for system files and directories. User home directories and the /tmp directory should give write access to the appropriate users, whereas most other files should only grant read access to users. Files that contain passwords should not grant read access to users.

- You can edit the /etc/permissions.* files to refine permissions allowed on system files.

- When applying the SUID and SGID permissions to programs, test your program thoroughly to ensure that no security loopholes exist during execution.

- Use the sticky bit permission on public directories to prevent data loss.

- To reduce the attack surface of your server, ensure that any unnecessary network services are stopped. To prevent a network service from starting when entering a runlevel, you can use the **chkconfig** and **insserv** commands.

- You can use YaST to modify several configuration files that contain security-related information such as password restrictions, boot options and system file permission settings. The YOU module in YAST may be used to obtain important security-related patches from the SUSE update servers.

- There are many Web resources that you can use to stay informed about current security issues.

- You can use several security utilities to analyze your server for vulnerabilities. The **netstat** and **nmap** utilities may be used to determine the sockets, ports and services that are being used by your server. The **ethereal** program may be used to capture and analyze network traffic, whereas the **nessus** program analyzes your server for security vulnerabilities.

- In addition to vulnerability analysis, you should document your system configuration and back up key files to ensure that your system security can be restored to its current state in the future.

- An effective Linux maintenance and security policy requires the auditing of user logins, processes and log files. The **last** and **ac** commands monitor logins, the programs in the **sysstat** package monitor system processes, the **lastcomm** and **sa** commands display the results of process accounting, the **logcheck** and **logsurfer** programs monitor log file entries, and the **seccheck** scripts monitor the overall security of your system.

Key Terms

/boot/grub/menu.lst   The GRUB boot manager configuration file.

/etc directory   Contains most configuration information for a Linux system.

/etc/fstab   A file that lists mount options for file systems.

/etc/openldap/slapd.conf   The file that stores user passwords for the Open LDAP daemon.

/etc/permissions.*   A set of files that list permission restrictions for system files and directories.

/etc/samba/smbpasswd   The file that stores Windows passwords for the Samba file sharing daemon.

/etc/shadow   The file that stores the passwords for local user accounts in SUSE Linux.

/home directory   The directory that stores most user home directories. It is commonly mounted to its own file system.

/opt directory   The directory that typically stores optional software programs. It is commonly mounted to its own file system.

/srv directory   The directory that stores the content used by most network services. It is commonly mounted to its own file system.

/tmp directory   The directory that stores temporary files. It is commonly mounted to its own file system.

/usr directory   The directory that usually stores most system software programs. It is commonly mounted to its own file system.

/var directory   The directory that stores most log files and spool files. It is commonly mounted to its own file system.

/var/account/pacct   The process accounting log file.

/var/log/wtmp   A data file that lists successful login attempts.

ac command   Displays the amount of time users have been logged into the system.

accton command   Starts the process accounting daemons.

Basic Input Output System (BIOS)   The program stored in the CMOS chip on a computer mainboard that is responsible for starting a computer and maintaining device access.

chkconfig command   Used to list and configure services that are started in each system run level.

Complimentary Metal Oxide Semiconductor (CMOS)   The chip on a computer mainboard that stores configuration information and passwords for the BIOS.

ethereal   A packet-sniffer utility that can be used to capture and display network traffic.

fdisk command   Creates and lists hard drive partitions.

GRand Unified Bootloader (GRUB)   The default boot manager for SUSE Linux. It is responsible for loading the Linux operating system kernel during system initialization.

grub-md5-crypt command   Used to generate an MD5 encrypted password for use in the GRUB configuration file.

insserv command   Used to configure system services to start in certain system run levels.

iostat (input output statistics command)   Displays read and write statistics for system storage devices.

isag (interactive system activity grapher) command   Displays a graph of the performance statistics stored in the in the /var/log/sa directory.

last command   Displays the most recent users who have logged in to the system from entries in /var/log/wtmp.

lastcomm command   Displays the process accounting log file.

logcheck   A utility that may be used to locate and extract anomalies in log files.

logging   The process whereby system events are saved to a file for later analysis.

logsurfer   A utility that may be used to check log files for patterns and perform tasks when certain patterns are found.

mpstat (multiple processor statistics) command   Displays processor and system load statistics.

nessus   A program that may be used to monitor security settings on network computers.

nessus-update-plugins command   Downloads the latest plugins for use with nessus.

netstat command   Displays network statistics and open sockets.

nmap command   Probes for and displays open network ports on network computers.

process accounting   A system that logs information about running processes to a file for later analysis.

rpm command   Used to install, remove, and find information on RPM software packages.

sa (summarize accounting) command   Displays a process accounting report based on certain criteria.

sadc (system activity data collector) command   Collects system performance information and logs it to the /var/log/sa directory.

sar (system activity report) command   Monitors the performance of a Linux system.

seccheck   A package that contains a series of scripts that may be used to check for security vulnerabilities on your system.

Set Group ID (SGID)   A special permission set on executable files and directories. When you run an executable program that has the SUID permission set, you become the group owner of the executable file for the duration of the program. On a directory, the SGID sets the group that gets attached to newly created files.

Set User ID (SUID)   A special permission set on executable files. When you run an executable program that has the SUID permission set, you become the owner of the executable file for the duration of the program.

sitar command   Creates a report of system configuration information.

Sticky bit   A special permission that is set on directories that prevents users from removing files they do not own.

su (switch user) command   Used to change the current user account.

sysstat package   Contains system monitoring utilities such as **vmstat** and **sar**.

vmstat (virtual machine statistics) command   Displays process, memory and paging statistics.

YaST Online Update (YOU)   A YaST module that may be used to obtain patches for SLES from the SUSE Web servers.

Yet Another Setup Tool (YaST)   The graphical system configuration utility in SUSE Linux.

Review Questions

1. What special permission should be set on public directories to prevent users from deleting files that other users have contributed? _____

2. Which of the following are good security practices? (Choose all that apply.)

   a. Assigning only necessary file system permissions

   b. Ensuring that system services are started using the root user account

   c. Disabling unused network services

   d. Updating network software

3. You wish to log and monitor the processes being run on your server at a certain time of the day using process accounting. Which command may be used to turn on process accounting? _____

4. Which of the following is the safest practice when securing servers against unauthorized local access?

   a. Updating network software

   b. Securing the BIOS with a boot password

   c. Securing the GRUB boot manager with a boot password

   d. Controlling access to the servers by locking them in a server closet

5. Which of the following may be used to check your system for weak passwords? (Choose all that apply.)

   a. nessus

   b. security –check

   c. seccheck scripts

   d. who -a

6. What command could you use to create an encrypted password for use in the /boot/grub/ menu.lst file? _____

7. Which of the following directories would normally be mounted to a separate file system? (Choose all that apply.)

   a. /var

   b. /etc

   c. /tmp

   d. /home

8. What program in the sysstat package may be used to view CPU usage and hard disk usage? _____

9. Which of the following commands may be used to view open TCP sockets on a SUSE Linux server?

   a. netstat -t

   b. nmap -t

   c. netstat -p

   d. nmap -p

10. What option to the **chkconfig** command lists the system services and the runlevels that they are started in? _____

11. Which of the following directories should a normal user have write access to? (Choose all that apply.)

   a. /etc

   b. /home/username

   c. /tmp

   d. /var

12. What security risk arises from using the SUID and SGID bits on executable programs?
    _____

13. You wish to capture certain types of traffic on your network using the ethereal program for later analysis. What should you do? (Choose all that apply.)

    a. Create a capture filter that matches the traffic that you wish to analyze

    b. Select a NIC that you wish to capture packets on

    c. Choose the type of promiscuous mode that you wish to use

    d. Create a display filter that matches the traffic that you wish to analyze

14. What do you need in order to use YOU to obtain patches for SLES?_____

15. Which of the following utilities monitors log files and alerts you if a certain pattern is found?

    a. logwatch

    b. logsurfer

    c. logmonitor

    d. seccheck

Discovery Exercises

DISCOVERY EXERCISES

Securing SUSE Linux

Using the information and procedures outlined in this chapter, secure your local SLES computer as much as possible without restricting access to information that you require. More specifically, perform the tasks listed below:

1. Physically secure the location of your computer

2. Physically secure the BIOS and boot manager

3. Ensure that unnecessary services are stopped in runlevel 5

4. Verify that any files that use the SUID and SGID bits are either part of the SLES operating system or have been thoroughly tested

5. Ensure that no unnecessary permissions have been granted to regular users for system files and directories

6. Ensure that your software components are updated to the latest versions

Configuring Local Security using YaST

Several security-related parameters may be changed using the Security Settings module under Security and Users in YaST. Use this module to set custom security settings for your computer that perform the following actions:

1. Requires that passwords be a minimum of 8 characters long, be checked against dictionary words and be difficult to guess

2. Stores passwords using the Blowfish encryption algorithm

3. Expires passwords every 42 days. Users should be warned 5 days before expiry

4. Restricts the ability to shut down the system from the KDM to the root user

5. Records failed login attempts, and sets a delay after 2 invalid login attempts

6. Sets secure file permissions

7. Allows the current directory in the path statement for all users

Monitoring SUSE Linux System

Once you have secured your SUSE Linux system using the procedures outlined in this chapter, you should audit your system periodically to ensure that your system is secure and locate areas for improvement. On your SLES system, perform the following actions to monitor the security of your system:

1. Ensure that unnecessary ports and services are stopped using the **netstat** and **nmap** utilities

2. Use **nessus** and **seccheck** to identify any security vulnerabilities

3. Use **logcheck** and **logsurfer** to analyze your log files for irregularities that may be the result of security breaches

4. Set up and use process accounting to ensure that unnecessary processes are not running on your system

Security Documentation

One of the key security practices that is often overlooked is system and configuration documentation. By documenting the configuration of your server and the configuration parameters that you have changed, you allow others to easily change and troubleshoot your server in the future. Ensure that you document the changes that you made to your system in the previous Discovery Exercises, as well as the following key areas of your system:

1. Partition and file system configuration

2. Installed software packages and the runlevel(s) they are set to start and stop in

3. Network configuration

4. Network service configuration (including the configuration files located in /etc)

AppArmor

Novell AppArmor is a mandatory access control scheme that lets you specify on a per program basis which files the program may read, write, and execute. AppArmor secures applications by enforcing good application behavior without relying on attack signatures, so it can prevent attacks even if the attacks are exploiting previously unknown vulnerabilities.

Objectives

- Improve Application Security with AppArmor
- Create and Manage AppArmor Profiles
- Control AppArmor
- Monitor AppArmor

Objective 1—Improve Application Security with AppArmor

While you can keep your software up to date, you can still be hit with an attack that exploits a vulnerability that is not yet known or for which there is no fix yet.

The idea of AppArmor is to have the kernel limit what a software program can do. In addition to the limitations set by the usual user and group permissions, limitations are imposed based on a set of rules for a specific program.

Often an intruder does not directly gain root privileges. By exploiting a vulnerability in, for instance, a Web server, she might be able to start a shell as the user running the Web server. With that unprivileged access, she exploits yet another vulnerability in some other software program to gain root access.

With AppArmor, even if an intruder manages to find a vulnerability in some server software, the damage is limited due to the fact that the intruder may not access any files or execute any programs beyond what the application is allowed by AppArmor's rule set to access or execute in routine operation.

This concept is not limited to normal accounts; it also limits to a certain extent what an application running with root privileges may do. A confined process cannot call certain system calls, even if running as root. Thus even if an attacker gained root privileges, she would still be limited in what she might be able to do.

The AppArmor kernel modules (apparmor and aamatch_pcre) hook into the Linux Security Modules Framework of the kernel.

Profiles in `/etc/apparmor.d/` are used to configure which application may access and execute which files.

AppArmor has to be activated before the applications it controls are started. Applications already running when AppArmor is activated are not controlled by AppArmor, even if a profile has been created for them. Therefore, AppArmor is activated early in the boot process by `/etc/init.d/boot.apparmor`.

In a default installation of SUSE Linux Enterprise Server 10, AppArmor is actively protecting several services using a set of profiles provided by Novell. Using the provided YaST modules or command line tools, you can easily adapt these to your needs and create new profiles for additional applications you want to protect.

As a general rule, you should confine programs that grant privilege, i.e., programs that have access to resources that the person using the program does not have:

- Network agents—programs that have open network ports
- Cron jobs
- Web applications

At some points in the documentation of AppArmor you will find AppArmor's former name, Subdomain.

Objective 2—Create and Manage AppArmor Profiles

SUSE Linux Enterprise Server 10 comes with AppArmor Profiles for various applications, such as named, ntpd, nscd, and others.

The profiles are contained in /etc/apparmor.d/. The filename of the profile represents the filename of the application including the path, with "/" being replaced by a ".": The profile for /usr/sbin/squid would be contained in /etc/apparmor.d/usr.sbin.squid.

A profile can include other files with an #include statement. The directory /etc/apparmor/ abstractions/ contains several files that are intended to be included in profiles, depending on the kind of program to be protected by AppArmor. There are abstractions for files that should be readable or writable by all programs (base), for nameservice-related files like /etc/passwd (nameservice), for files related to console operations (console), and others.

The profiles are plain text files and it is therefore possible to create and modify them with any text editor. However, command line tools as well as a YaST module greatly simplify the process of creating profiles.

In addition to the active profiles in /etc/apparmor.d/, several profiles are already prepared in /etc/apparmor/profiles/extras/ that you can customize to your needs and copy to /etc/apparmor.d/ to activate them.

To successfully administer AppArmor, you need to:

- Understand Profiles and Rules
- Administer AppArmor Profiles with YaST
- Administer AppArmor Profiles with Command Line Tools

Understand Profiles and Rules

Novell AppArmor profiles contain two types of AppArmor rules: path entries and capability entries. Path entries specify what a process can access in the file system. AppArmor, by default, limits the capabilities a process is given (see man apparmor). Capability entries are used to specify specific POSIX capabilities (man 7 capabilities) a process is granted, overriding the default limitation.

Other files containing AppArmor rules can be pulled in with #include statements.

As an example, let's have a look at the profile for /sbin/klogd, the kernel log daemon (/etc/apparmor.d/sbin.klogd):

```
 1   # Profile for /sbin/klogd

     #include <tunables/global>

 5   /sbin/klogd {
       #include <abstractions/base>

       capability sys_admin,

10     /boot/System.map*     r,
       /proc/kmsg            r,
       /sbin/klogd           rmix,
       /var/log/boot.msg     rwl,
       /var/run/klogd.pid    rwl,
15   }
```

Comments (as in line1) start with a # sign, #include (as in line 3 and 6) is not interpreted as a comment, but is used to include rules from other files. The path as given above is relative to /etc/apparmor.d/.

/etc/apparmor.d/tunables/global (line 3) is used to include definitions that should be available in every profile. By default, it just includes /etc/apparmor.d/tunables/home, which defines the variables @{HOMEDIRS} and @{HOME}. These variables are used in various profiles.

The directory /etc/apparmor.d/abstractions/ contains files with general rules grouped by common application tasks. These include, for instance, access to files all applications need (base), access to authentication mechanisms (authentication), graphics environments (kde, gnome), name resolution (nameservice), and others. Instead of having these redundantly specified in several profiles, they are defined at one point and included in the profiles that need them.

Line 5 in the example above gives the absolute path to the program confined by AppArmor. The rules, as well, as any included rules, follow within the curly braces { }.

Line 8 enables the capability sys_admin for this program. Any other capabilities needed would be listed in separate lines starting with capability.

The remaining lines list files and directories, and the access permission granted.

Within lines listing files and directories, the following wildcards can be used:

- *—Substitutes any number of characters, except /.

- **—Substitutes any number of characters, including /. Use ** to include subdirectories.

- ?—Substitutes any single character, except /.

- [abc]—Substitutes a, b, or c.

- [a-d]—Substitutes a, b, c, or d.

- {ab,cd}—Substitutes either ab or cd.

The permissions granted can be

- r—Allows the program to have read access to the resource. Read access is required for scripts, and an executing process needs this permission to allow it to dump core or to be attached to with ptrace.

- w—Allows the program to have write access to the resource. Files must have this permission if they are to be unlinked (removed).

- l—Link mode mediates access to symlinks and hardlinks and grants the privilege to unlink (remove) files.

- m—Allow executable mapping. This mode allows a file to be mapped into memory using mmap(2)'s PROT_EXEC flag. This flag marks the pages executable; it is used on some architectures to provide non-executable data pages, which can complicate exploit attempts. AppArmor uses this mode to limit which files a well-behaved program (or all programs on architectures that enforce non-executable memory access controls) may use as libraries, to limit the effect of invalid -L flags given to ld(1) and LD_PRELOAD, LD_LIBRARY_PATH, given to ld.so(8).

- `ix`—Inherit Execute Mode. The executed resource inherits the current profile.

- `px`—Discrete Profile Execute Mode. This mode requires that a profile be defined for the resource executed. If there is no profile defined, access is denied.

- `Px`—Discrete Profile execute mode—scrub the environment. `Px` allows the named program to run in `px` mode, but AppArmor will invoke the Linux Kernel's unsafe_exec routines to scrub the environment, similar to setuid programs. (See man 8 ld.so for some information on setuid/setgid environment scrubbing.)

- `ux`—Unconstrained Execute Mode. Allows the program to execute the resource without any Novell AppArmor profile being applied to the executed resource. ***This should only be used in rare exceptions.***

- `Ux`—Unconstrained execute—scrub the environment. As ux, it should only be used in rare exceptions.

The last five, ix, px, Px, ux, and Ux, cannot be combined.
The manual page covering the syntax of the profiles is man 5 apparmor.d.

Administer AppArmor Profiles with YaST

The profile for /sbin/klogd, given in the example above, is a rather short profile. When you browse through the profiles in `/etc/apparmor.d/` or `/etc/apparmor/profiles/ extras/` you will see that these profiles can be much more complex.

AppArmor comes with several tools that help to create and maintain AppArmor profiles. YaST modules exist that provide a graphical interface to those tools.

You can accomplish various tasks with YaST:

- Create a New Profile
- Update a Profile
- Delete a Profile

Create a New Profile To create a new profile, you can:

- Use the New Profile Wizard
- Manually Create a New Profile

Use the New Profile Wizard There is a Wizard to create a new profile. Before calling the Wizard to profile an application, the first step is to stop the application for which you want to create a profile.

To access the Add Profile Wizard, start YaST and select Novell AppArmor as shown in Figure 3-1.

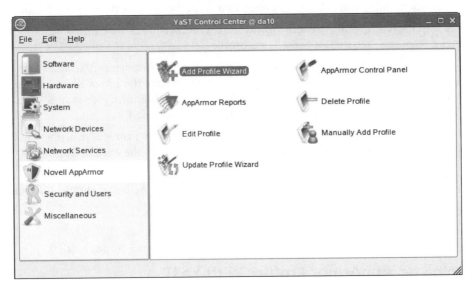

Figure 3-1

Then select the Add Profile Wizard. The first step is to enter the application you want to profile as shown in Figure 3-2.

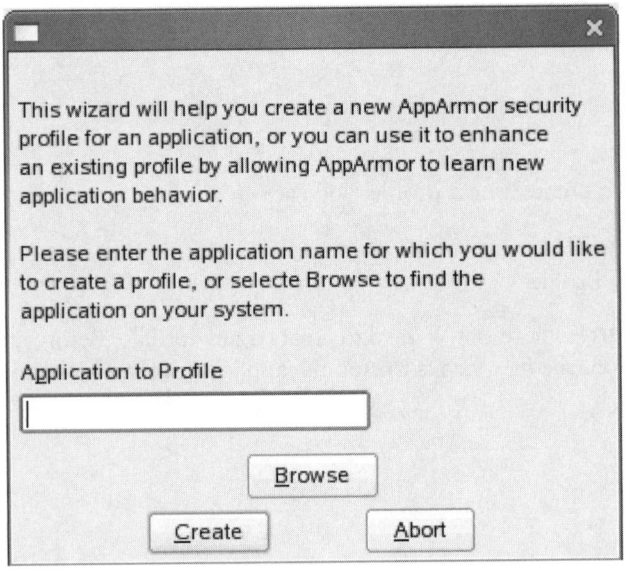

Figure 3-2

If no path is given, the Wizard looks for the binary in the search path (variable $PATH).

The next dialog asks you to start and use the application you want to profile. Use the application in a way that you expect it to be used in production. For instance, if you are profiling a Web server, access it in a way that you expect it to be accessed during normal operation. For a Web browser, use it in a way you expect the users to access Web content.

During this learning phase, any access to files or capabilities needed by the application is granted as well as logged in the log file `/var/log/audit/audit.log`. Because any access is granted, you have to make sure that no attack can happen during this phase of profile creation. AppArmor does not yet protect your application.

Once you feel you have gone through all expected uses of the application, select `Scan system log for AppArmor events` in the YaST AppArmor Profile Wizard dialog.

For each event you are presented with a dialog where you can decide what should happen when this event occurs in the future. The dialog offers different options, depending on the event.

In case of access to a program, the dialog looks similar to Figure 3-3.

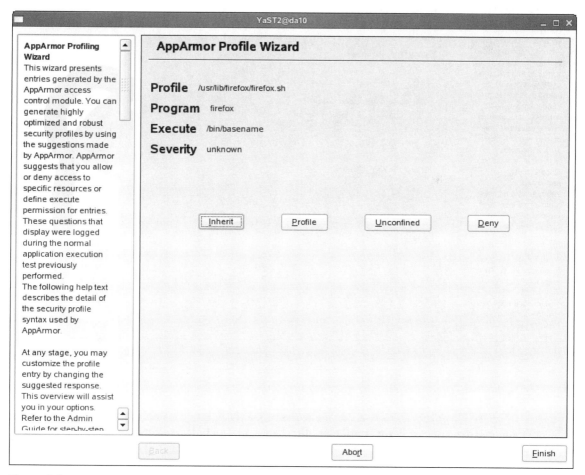

Figure 3-3

The following options are presented:

- *Inherit*—The executed resource inherits the current (parent's) profile.
- *Profile*—Requires that a specific profile exist for the executed program.
- *Unconfined*—Executes the program without a security profile. Do not run unconfined unless absolutely necessary.
- *Deny*—The execution of the program will be denied.

In case of file access, the dialog offers different options as shown in Figure 3-4.

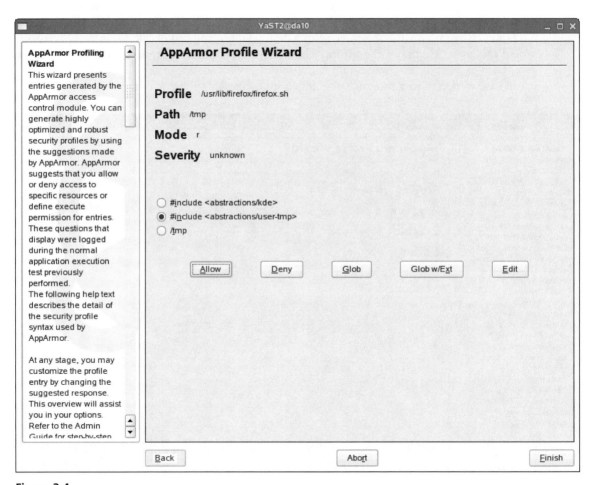

Figure 3-4

The Add Profile Wizard suggests an access mode (r, w, l, or a combination of them). If more than one item appears in the list of files, directories, or #includes, select the radio button in front of the appropriate one, and then select one of these buttons:

- *Allow*—Grants the program access to the specified directory path.
- *Deny*—Prevents the program from accessing the specified file or directory.

Sometimes the suggested files or directories do not fit your needs. In this case, you can modify them:

- *Glob*—Selecting Glob once replaces the filename with an asterisk, including all files in the directory. Selecting Glob twice replaces the file and the directory it resides in by **, including all directories and files of that level in the directory tree. Selecting Glob again goes up one level in the path.

- *Glob w/Ext*—Selecting Glob w/Ext once replaces the filename with an *, but retains the file name extension: text.txt becomes *.txt. Selecting Glob w/Ext twice replaces the file and the directory it resides in by **, retaining the file name extension: /a/b/c/ text.txt becomes /a/b/**.txt.

- *Edit*—Enables editing of the highlighted line. The new (edited) line appears at the bottom of the list.

After you have modified the line, select Allow or Deny. Go through each learning mode entry in this way.

Once all entries have been processed, you are returned to the AppArmor Profile Wizard dialog that asked you to run the application. You can run the application again, and then run through any additional entries generated by this.

Once you conclude you are done, select `Finish`. The profile is written and activated.

If you want to discard your selections, select `Abort`.

Manually Create a New Profile   When selecting `YaST > Novell AppArmor > Manually Add Profile,` you are prompted to select a file for which you want to create a profile. Subsequently the AppArmor Profile Dialog opens. See Figure 3-5. There you can Add, Edit, and Delete entries to the profile by selecting the respective buttons.

The advantage of the YaST module is its syntax check. However, you can also use any text editor, like vi, to create and edit profiles.

Update a Profile   To update a profile, you have two choices:

- Run the Add Profile Wizard Again
- Run the Update Profile Wizard

Run the Add Profile Wizard Again   When you run the Add Profile Wizard on a program for which a profile already exists, the profiling does not start from scratch, but uses the existing profile as a basis.

You go through the same steps as if generating a new profile, but most likely you will have to answer fewer questions than on the first run.

This method is suitable to update a specific profile, especially for client applications that run a finite amount of time.

Run the Update Profile Wizard   When you want to update several profiles, or profiles for applications that run over a longer period of time, using the Update Profile Wizard is the better choice.

Even though the Update Profile Wizard is a YaST module, you may need to take some preparatory steps with command line tools.

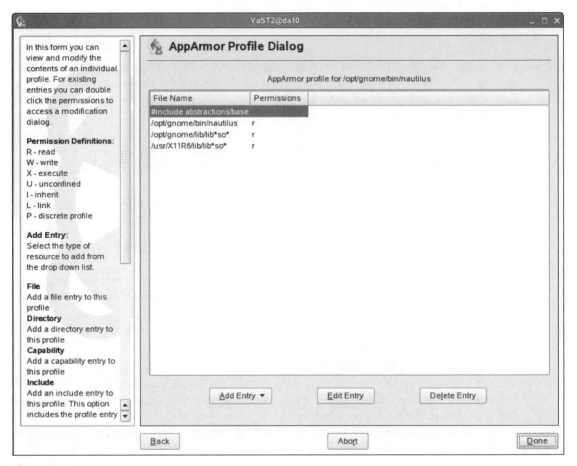

Figure 3-5

The first step is to decide which application profiles you want to update, and to put AppArmor into complain (also called learning) mode with regard to these applications. (If there is no profile yet for an application you want to profile, you have to create one first, using autodep *program*.)

The command complain is used to activate learning or complain mode. You can either use the program or the profile as the argument: For instance, both, complain firefox and complain /etc/apparmor.d/usr.lib.firefox.firefox.sh work to change AppArmor to learning mode for Firefox.

If you want to turn on learning mode for all applications confined by AppArmor, use complain /etc/apparmor.d/*.

In profiles that are in complain mode, the path to the application being confined is followed by flags=(complain):

```
# Profile for /sbin/klogd
#include <tunables/global>
/sbin/klogd flags=(complain){
...
}
```

Then actually use your application(s) to create events in the log file.

The next step is to start the Update Profile Wizard by starting YaST and selecting `Novell AppArmor > Update Profile Wizard` as shown in Figure 3-6.

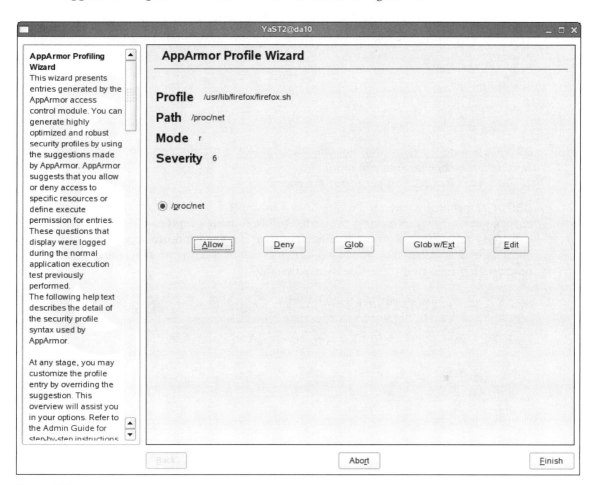

Figure 3-6

The interface is almost identical to the Add Profile Wizard interface; also the choices you are presented do not differ.

However, as you are updating different profiles, you have to pay special attention to the profile in the first line to be sure that your decision on allowing or denying fits the respective profile.

Once the log file has been processed, select `Finish`. The profiles will be reloaded, but AppArmor is still in complain mode.

To have AppArmor again enforce the rules, use the command enforce, which has the same syntax as complain: `enforce /etc/apparmor.d/*` puts all profiles in enforce mode.

Delete a Profile To delete a profile, start YaST and select `Novell AppArmor > Delete Profile`. Select the profile to delete; then select Next. After you select `Yes` in the confirmation dialog, the profile is deleted and the application is no longer confined by AppArmor.

Administer AppArmor Profiles with Command Line Tools

There are various tools to create and maintain AppArmor profiles. These are:

- autodep
- genprof
- logprof
- vim

autodep autodep generates a profile skeleton for a program and loads into the Novell AppArmor module in complain mode.

The syntax is `autodep` *program1 program2* ...

genprof genprof (Generate Profile) is used to create a profile for an application. Stop the application you want to create a profile for before running genprof.

genprof runs autodep on the specified program if there is no profile yet, puts the new or already existing profile in complain mode, marks the log file, and prompts the user to start the program to profile and to exercise its functionality.

```
da10:~ # genprof firefox
Setting /usr/lib/firefox/firefox.sh to complain mode.

Please start the application to be profiled in
another window and exercise its functionality now.

Once completed, select the "Scan" button below in
order to scan the system logs for AppArmor events.

For each AppArmor event, you will be given the
opportunity to choose whether the access should be
allowed or denied.

Profiling: /usr/lib/firefox/firefox.sh

[(S)can system log for SubDomain events] / (F)inish
```

Once the user has done that and presses s in the terminal window where genprof is running, genprof calls logprof to run against the system log from where it was marked when genprof was started.

In case of access to a program, the dialog looks similar to the following:

```
Reading log entries from /var/log/audit/audit.log.
Updating subdomain profiles in /etc/apparmor.d.

Profile:  /usr/lib/firefox/firefox.sh
Program:  firefox
Execute:  /bin/basename
Severity: unknown

[(I)nherit] / (P)rofile / (U)nconfined / (D)eny / Abo(r)t
/ (F)inish
```

In case of access to a file or directory, the dialog looks similar to this:

```
Complain-mode changes:
Profile:  /usr/lib/firefox/firefox.sh
Path:     /dev/tty
Mode:     rw
Severity: 9

 1 - #include <abstractions/consoles>
[2 - /dev/tty]

[(A)llow] / (D)eny / (G)lob / Glob w/(E)xt / (N)ew /
Abo(r)t / (F)inish
```

Press the number to switch lines as applicable, then press the letter in parenthesis corresponding to what you want to do. The options offered are the same as those within YaST; New corresponds to a certain extent to edit in YaST.

Once all log entries have been processed, you are returned to genprof, where you can start a new scan or Finish the profile generation.

```
Writing updated profile for /usr/lib/firefox/firefox.sh.

Profiling: /usr/lib/firefox/firefox.sh

[(S)can system log for SubDomain events] / (F)inish
```

logprof logprof is a tool used to scan the log /var/log/audit/audit.log for entries created by AppArmor for profiles in learning mode, and to interactively create new profile entries.

The choices you have are the same as those described under genprof.

If you want logprof to start scanning from a certain point in the log file, you can pass a string that describes that point. The following is an entry in the log file:

```
type=APPARMOR msg=audit(852099290.789:1103): PERMITTING w
access to /root/.mozilla/firefox/uwgzf7zy.default/prefs.js
(firefox-bin(8770) profile /usr/lib/firefox/firefox.sh
active /usr/lib/firefox/firefox.sh)
```

Using the option -m: logprof -m "852099290.789:1103", you can start the scan of the log file from that point, ignoring earlier entries.

vim The profiles can be changed using any text editor.

Compared to other editors, vim has the advantage that AppArmor includes a syntax highlighting description that enables vim to highlight syntax elements in profiles.

When confining Apache2, you can create subprofiles (also called hats) that use a different security context, for instance for pages using mod_php5. To make use of such subprofiles, an application has to be made "hat-aware." For Apache2 this is achieved with module mod_change_hat that comes with AppArmor on SLES10. For details on hats, see man `change_hat` and section 5 of the ***Administration Guide*** in /usr/share/doc/manual/ apparmor-admin_en/apparmor-admin_en.pdf. Subprofiles are part of the profile for the application itself and are administered with the same tools (genprof, logprof).

Exercise 3-1: AppArmor

Objective: In this exercise, you create, test, and improve a profile for the Firefox browser. This exercise has four parts.

Description: In the first part create a profile for the Firefox browser. While using Firefox to generate log entries for the initial profile, just surf the Web; do not access local files with Firefox.

In the second part, use Firefox to access a local file, such as /usr/share/doc/packages/apparmor-docs/apparmor.7.html. AppArmor should prevent you from viewing the file. Change the profile to allow access. You could use YaST, genprof, or complain and logprof for this purpose.

In the third part, install the Java browser plug-in package java-1_4_2-sun-plugin. Restart Firefox and use it to access a page containing a Java applet.

http://java.sun.com/products/plugin/1.4/demos/plugin/applets.html links to various demos. Firefox will not be able to show these. Change the profile again to be able to run Java applets. Use another method to do so than the method used in part two above.

In the fourth part, compare the profile you generated with those in /etc/apparmor/profiles/ extras/ for Firefox. Find out if your profile is more restrictive or more permissive compared with those profiles.

Detailed Steps to Complete this Exercise

- Part I: Create a Profile for the Firefox Browser
- Part II: Modify the Profile for Firefox to Allow Read Access to the Local File System
- Part III: Use a Browser Plug-in
- Part IV: Compare the Profile You Created with Those From SLES 10

Part I: Create a Profile for the Firefox Browser

Do the following:

1. Start `Yast`, enter the root password (`novell`).
2. Select `Novell AppArmor > Add Profile Wizard`.
3. At the prompt: `Application to Profile`, enter `firefox`.
4. Start Firefox by pressing `Alt+F2`, entering `firefox` and selecting `Run`. View some Web pages. Close Firefox again.
5. In the YaST AppArmor Profile Wizard dialog, select `Scan system log for AppArmor events`.
6. Now you create the profile and need to answer several questions. Note that the application Firefox is quite complex and accesses several executables and files on the system.
   a. Select `Inherit` for /bin/basename and other executed programs.
   b. For files and directories, choose an appropriate option, such as an #include, a filename, a directory, or a path with place holders, and select `Allow`.

7. When you are returned to the AppArmor Profile Wizard dialog, select Finish.

8. Make sure that the Firefox profile is in enforce mode by looking at /sys/kernel/security/apparmor/profiles using cat. There must be an entry /usr/lib/firefox/firefox.sh (enforce). If it is not, execute enforce firefox.

Part II: Modify the Profile for Firefox to Allow Read Access to the Local File System

Do the following:

1. Open a terminal window and su - to root (password novell).

2. Enter tail -f /var/log/audit/audit.log.

3. Start Firefox by pressing Alt+F2, entering firefox and selecting Run. Try to view the file /usr/share/doc/packages/apparmor-docs/apparmor.7.html. (You should not be able to do so.)

4. View the log file in the terminal window. You should see a reject message.

5. Stop viewing the log file by pressing Ctrl+c.

6. In the terminal window, enter complain firefox.

7. In Firefox, try again to access /usr/share/doc/packages/apparmor-docs/apparmor.7.html. You should now be able to access the file.

8. Start Yast, enter the root password (novell).

9. Select Novell AppArmor > Update Profile Wizard.

10. You are presented with the same interface as in Part I, where you can choose Allow, Inherit, Deny, etc. Make sure you are updating the Firefox profile, not some other profile.
    Sooner or later you should see an entry for the path /usr/share/doc/packages/apparmor-docs/apparmor.7.html. By selecting the Glob button three times, you can create a suggestion /usr/share/doc/**. Allow it by selecting Allow.

11. When all entries in the log file have been processed, select Finish.

12. Put the Firefox profile back in enforce mode by entering enforce firefox in the terminal window.

13. In Firefox, try to access files beneath /usr/share/doc/, like /usr/share/doc/packages/. You should be able to access them. However, accessing files elsewhere in the file system should not be possible.

14. Close Firefox and YaST.

Part III: Use a Browser Plug-in

Do the following:

1. Open a terminal window and su - to root (password novell).

2. Install the Java Browser Plug-in by entering (as root):

```
yast -i java-1_4_2-sun-plugin
```

Insert the appropriate media when prompted. Do not close the console window after the installation.

3. Start Firefox by pressing `Alt+F2`, entering `firefox` and selecting `Run`.

4. Visit *http://java.sun.com/products/plugin/1.4/demos/plugin/applets.html* and select one of the demos. (The demo should not work.)

5. In the console window, enter:

```
genprof firefox
```

When asked to exercise the functionality of your application, select one of the demos again as in the previous step. The demo should work now.

6. Close Firefox.

7. Go back to the console window and press `s` to scan the logfile. Select `i` for inherit when the entry for java_vm is shown.

8. Answer the subsequent questions with `Glob` and `Accept`, as applicable.

9. When all questions have been answered, press `f` to finish.

10. Start Firefox again and select another Java demo available at the URL given in Step 4. This should work now, despite the profile being in enforce mode again.

Part IV: Compare the Profile You Created with Those From SLES 10

Do the following:

1. Open a console window and view the profile /etc/apparmor.d/usr.lib.firefox.firefox.sh just created with cat.

2. Open another console window and view the profiles /etc/apparmor/profiles/extras/usr.lib. firefox.firefox*, using cat.

3. Compare the files. Note any differences and decide whether or not they are more restrictive than the one you created.

Objective 3—Control AppArmor

AppArmor can be controlled using the script `/etc/init.d/boot.apparmor` or the link to this script, `/sbin/rcapparmor`. This script takes the usual parameters start, stop, etc, but because AppArmor is not a daemon, their significance is slightly different.

To control AppArmor, you have to know how to:

- Start and Stop AppArmor
- View AppArmor's Status
- Reload Profiles

Start and Stop AppArmor

To confine an application, AppArmor has to be active before the application starts. Therefore, AppArmor is usually activated early in the boot process.

If you do not want AppArmor to confine your applications any longer, use `rcapparmor stop`. This unloads the profiles, but the AppArmor kernel modules apparmor and aamatch_pcre remain loaded. `rcapparmor kill` unloads the kernel modules as well. In both cases, applications are no longer confined.

`rcapparmor start` activates AppArmor. However, only applications started after the activation of AppArmor are confined. Even if, for instance, a profile for Squid exists, Squid will not be confined if it was already running before you started AppArmor. To include Squid in AppArmor's protection, you need to restart Squid after activating AppArmor.

View AppArmor's Status

`rcapparmor status` gives you a general overview of profiles and processes:

```
da10:~ # rcapparmor status
apparmor module is loaded.
50 profiles are loaded.
49 profiles are in enforce mode.
1 profiles are in complain mode.
Out of 69 processes running:
5 processes have profiles defined.
5 processes have profiles in enforce mode.
0 processes have profiles in complain mode.
```

To emphasize the point that, after restarting AppArmor, processes need to be restarted to be again confined, have a look at the following:

```
da10:~ # rcapparmor stop
Unloading AppArmor profiles                    done
da10:~ # rcapparmor start
Loading AppArmor profiles                      done
da10:~ # rcapparmor status
apparmor module is loaded.
50 profiles are loaded.
49 profiles are in enforce mode.
1 profiles are in complain mode.
Out of 62 processes running:
0 processes have profiles defined.
0 processes have profiles in enforce mode.
0 processes have profiles in complain mode.
```

Restarting one of the processes for which there is a profile changes the output of `rcapparmor status`:

```
da10:~ # rcnscd restart
Shutting down Name Service Cache Daemon        done
Starting Name Service Cache Daemon             done
da10:~ # rcapparmor status
apparmor module is loaded.
50 profiles are loaded.
49 profiles are in enforce mode.
1 profiles are in complain mode.
Out of 62 processes running:
1 processes have profiles defined.
1 processes have profiles in enforce mode.
0 processes have profiles in complain mode.
```

The output of AppArmor does not contain specific data regarding the profiles or the processes being confined.

A list of the profiles loaded is kept in /sys/kernel/security/apparmor/profiles. It might look like the following:

```
da10:~ # cat /sys/kernel/security/apparmor/profiles
/usr/sbin/traceroute (enforce)
/usr/sbin/squid (enforce)
/usr/sbin/sendmail (enforce)
/usr/sbin/postqueue (enforce)
...
/usr/lib/postfix/bounce (enforce)
/usr/lib/firefox/firefox.sh (complain)
/usr/bin/ldd (enforce)
...
```

The command unconfined lists processes that have bound sockets but have no profiles loaded:

```
da10:~ # unconfined
2659 /sbin/portmap not confined
2659 /sbin/portmap not confined
2694 /usr/lib/zmd/zmd-bin not confined
2756 /usr/sbin/slpd not confined
2756 /usr/sbin/slpd not confined
2756 /usr/sbin/slpd not confined
2756 /usr/sbin/slpd not confined
2756 /usr/sbin/slpd not confined
2756 /usr/sbin/slpd not confined
2831 /usr/sbin/cupsd not confined
2831 /usr/sbin/cupsd not confined
2874 /usr/sbin/sshd not confined
2905 /usr/sbin/sshd not confined
2905 /usr/sbin/sshd not confined
3040 /usr/lib/postfix/master not confined
3040 /usr/lib/postfix/master not confined
```

This does not give information about processes with profiles that are not confined because they were running already when AppArmor was activated. To spot those, you would have to compare the output from ps with the content of /sys/kernel/security/profiles and restart any processes that should be confined.

Reload Profiles

If you have changed profiles in /etc/apparmor.d/ manually with an editor (not by using the AppArmor tools like logprof), you have to reload the profile or profiles concerned. The command to use is rcapparmor reload. rcapparmor restart is equivalent to reload; it does not stop and then start AppArmor, but it does reload the profiles. Processes that were confined before rcapparmor reload was issued remain confined (unless you deleted their profile or changed their status from enforce to complain).

The commands `enforce` and `complain` toggle the status from enforce to complain and vice versa, and reload the profiles concerned.

Objective 4—Monitor AppArmor

There are two ways to monitor AppArmor:

- Security Event Report
- Security Event Notification

Security Event Report

The YaST module to configure and view AppArmor security event reports can be launched by starting YaST and selecting `Novell AppArmor > AppArmor Reports`. It can also be launched directly from a console window as root by entering `yast2 SD_Report`.

The dialog that opens up shows when security event reports are generated as shown in Figure 3-7.

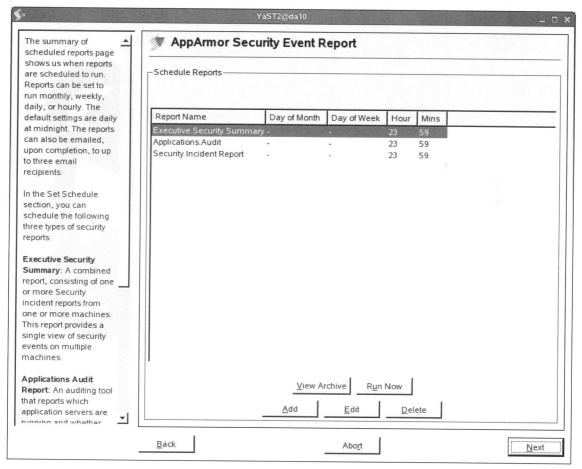

Figure 3-7

By default these are created once a day at midnight.

Using the buttons `Add`, `Edit`, or `Delete`, you can schedule new security incident reports, edit the existing ones, for instance, to set the e-mail address that should receive the report, or delete event reports.

Selecting a report and then selecting `Run Now` either shows the result directly, or, in the case of the Security Incident Report, first opens a dialog where you can fine tune the content of the resulting report. See Figure 3-8.

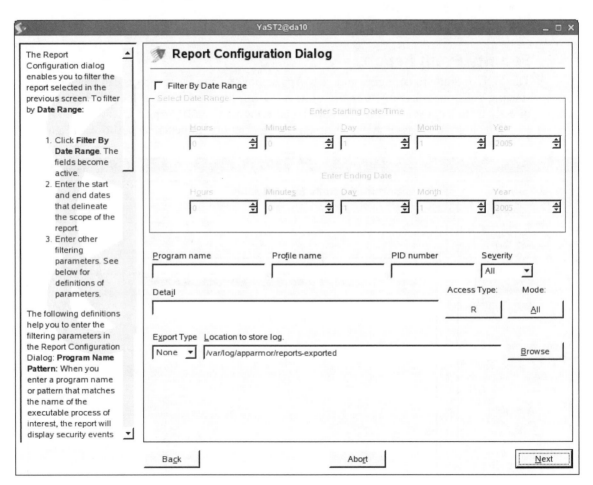

Figure 3-8

The help text on the left explains the available options. Once you configured what you want to have included in your report, select `Next`. The report is displayed in Figure 3-9 showing the security events:

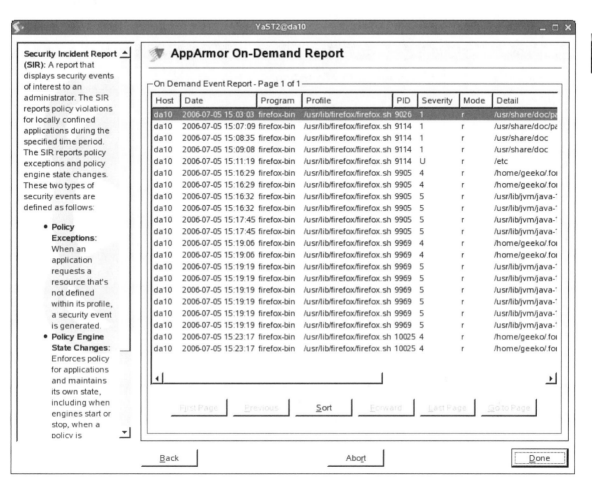

Figure 3-9

Depending on your configuration in the previous dialog, it is also saved to disk, by default in the directory /var/log/apparmor/reports-exported/.

Security Event Notification

To configure the security event notification, start YaST and select Novell AppArmor > AppArmor Control Panel, or start the module directly from a console window as root by entering yast2 subdomain. See Figure 3-10.

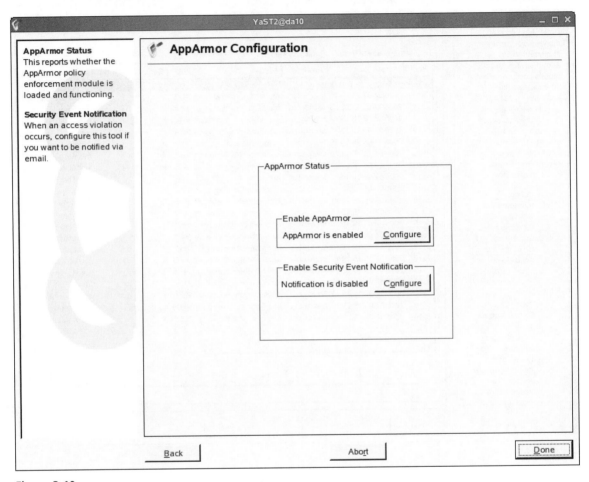

Figure 3-10

Select `Configure` in the `Enable Security Event Notification` box shown in Figure 3-10. A dialog opens up where you can configure the frequency of the notifications, e-mail addresses, and the severity levels the reports should cover as shown in Figure 3-11.

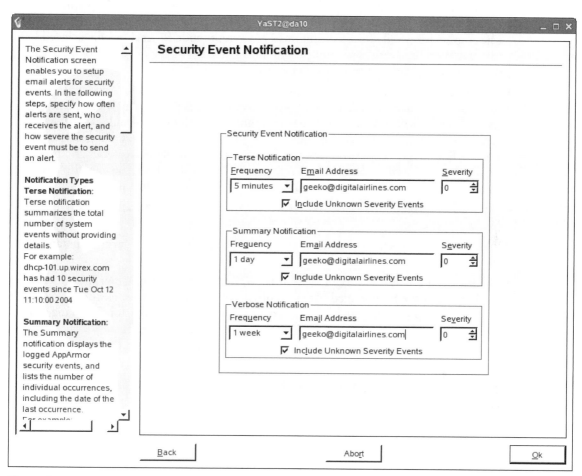

Figure 3-11

Select `Ok` to save your configuration. Close the AppArmor configuration window by selecting `Done`.

Summary

- AppArmor prevents intruders from gaining unauthorized access to your system by exploiting existing software programs. AppArmor kernel modules are used to restrict the actions of existing programs using information stored in AppArmor profiles.

- Each application on your Linux system can have an AppArmor profile that contains path rules that specify file system restrictions and capability rules that specify process restrictions.

- SUSE Linux Enterprise Server 10 comes with several default AppArmor profiles in the /etc/apparmor.d directory that are used to restrict key system services.

- AppArmor profiles are in one of two modes: complain mode and enforce mode. Complain mode allows you to monitor program actions and edit the AppArmor profile, whereas enforce mode allows AppArmor to enforce the restrictions within the AppArmor profile for the program. The current mode for each profile is listed in the /sys/kernel/security/apparmor/profiles file. You can change the mode of a profile using the complain and enforce commands.

- To create an AppArmor profile automatically, you can use the AppArmor module of YaST or the genprof command (which runs the autodep and logprof commands). A default profile will be created for your program in complain mode and you will be prompted to run the application while AppArmor is logging the files and processes that the application accesses. Following this, you can select the files, directories and processes that will be allowed or denied using AppArmor. During selection, you can also choose to include rules from other files, or use globs to select multiple files or processes.

- AppArmor profiles may also be created manually in the /etc/apparmor.d directory using a text editor.

- You can edit AppArmor profiles after creation using YaST, the logprof command or a text editor.

- AppArmor only affects programs that are started after the AppArmor kernel modules and profiles have been loaded. After modifying AppArmor profiles, ensure that you restart the appropriate programs that are restricted by AppArmor for the changes to take effect.

- The rcapparmor command may be used to unload and reload AppArmor kernel modules and profiles, as well as display AppArmor profile statistics.

- After implementing AppArmor, you should audit it periodically to ensure that it is protecting your programs.

- You can use YaST to produce reports on AppArmor activity or notify administrators when AppArmor detects a certain number of restricted access events.

- To see which running programs are not restricted by AppArmor, you can use the unconfined command.

Key Terms

/etc/apparmor.d directory   The location of AppArmor profiles.

/etc/apparmor.d/abstractions directory   Contains files that define generic program restrictions for use within AppArmor profiles.

/etc/apparmor.d/profiles/extras directory   Contains sample AppArmor profiles.

/etc/init.d/boot.apparmor   A file used to load AppArmor kernel modules and profiles at system initialization.

/sys/kernel/security/apparmor/profiles   A file that lists all AppArmor profiles and their current mode.

/var/log/apparmor/reports-exported directory   The default location for reports generated by the AppArmor module of YaST.

/var/log/audit/audit.log   The file that AppArmor uses to store program-related events for later use when creating AppArmor profiles.

AppArmor   A technology that restricts the actions an application program can take on a Linux system.

AppArmor Control Panel   A utility in the AppArmor module of YaST that may be used to start and stop AppArmor kernel modules or configure AppArmor notifications.

AppArmor Reports   A utility in the AppArmor module of YaST that may be used to produce usage and incident reports about application programs that are restricted by AppArmor.

autodep command   Creates a default AppArmor profile for an application and sets the profile to complain mode.

capabilities   An AppArmor term that refers to the ability of an application program to access other processes on the system.

complain command   Sets a program that has an AppArmor profile to complain mode.

complain mode   For application programs that have an AppArmor profile, it refers to the state where the restrictions within the AppArmor profile are not enforced and any program actions are logged to the /var/log/audit/audit.log file.

enforce command   Sets a program that has an AppArmor profile to enforce mode.

enforce mode   For application programs that have an AppArmor profile, it refers to the state where the restrictions within the AppArmor profile are enforced by the AppArmor kernel modules.

genprof (generate profile) command   Creates a new profile for an application and sets the application to complain mode.

glob   A process whereby multiple file names may be specified using wildcard characters such as asterisk (*).

learning mode   See complain mode.

logprof (log profile) command   Analyzes the entries in the /var/log/audit/audit.log file for a particular application and allows you to create entries in an AppArmor profile based on them.

profile   A file that lists AppArmor restrictions for an application program.

rcapparmor command   Used to start and stop the AppArmor kernel modules, load and unload AppArmor profiles, and view the status of AppArmor.

rule   A line within an AppArmor profile that lists the access an AppArmor-controlled program has to other processes and files.

Security Event Notification   A feature of AppArmor that can be configured in YaST to notify administrators when certain AppArmor-related events occur.

Security Event Report   A list of AppArmor-related events that can be generated by the AppArmor module of YaST.

unconfined command   Lists active programs on the system that are not controlled by AppArmor.

vim (vi improved) command   Used to start the interactive vi text editor available on nearly all UNIX and Linux systems.

Review Questions

1. What program is used to load AppArmor at boot time? _____

2. Which of the following files would contain AppArmor restrictions for /usr/bin/myprogram?

   a.   /etc/apparmor.d/usr/bin/myprogram

   b.   /etc/apparmor.d/usr.bin.myprogram

   c.   /etc/apparmor.d/myprogram

   d.   /etc/apparmor.d/profiles/myprogram

3. Which of the following programs are likely to be confined by AppArmor? (Choose all that apply.)

   a.   Network agents and services

   b.   Text editors

   c.   Cron jobs

   d.   Web applications

4. You are manually modifying an AppArmor profile for a new program that you have added to your Linux system. You would like to add the default restrictions that apply to most programs on the system. What lines would you add to the AppArmor profile? (Choose two answers.)

   a.   #include <tunables/global>

   b.   #include <abstractions/nameservice>

   c.   #include <capabilities/system>

   d.   #include <abstractions/base>

5. What command can you use to view the syntax rules for AppArmor profiles?

   _____

6. When manually modifying an AppArmor profile, what permissions for a particular file allow the program to delete the file? (Choose all that apply.)

   a.   r

   b.   w

   c.   l

   d.   Ux

7. You have manually modified the settings within an existing AppArmor profile. What command could you run in your shell to reload all AppArmor profiles such that the changes take effect? (Choose all that apply.)

   a.   enforce /etc/apparmor.d

   b.   complain /etc/apparmor.d

   c.   rcapparmor restart

   d.   rcapparmor reload

8. You wish to create a custom AppArmor profile for the BIND daemon based on a default configuration. What directory contains sample AppArmor profiles in SUSE Linux? _____

9. Which of the following occurs when a program is set to complain mode? (Choose all that apply.)

    a. The settings in the AppArmor profile for the program are enforced

    b. Program actions are logged to /var/log/audit/audit.log

    c. The contents of /var/log/audit/audit.log are automatically copied to the AppArmor profile

    d. The AppArmor kernel modules do not enforce the restrictions within the AppArmor profile

10. When using the AppArmor Profile Wizard, you are prompted to choose the appropriate permission for the file /usr/local/program/chrome.rdf. However, you would like to apply the same permission to all files in the /usr/local/program directory. What button would you select?

    a. Allow

    b. Allow All

    c. Glob

    d. Glob w/Ext

11. What utility in the AppArmor module of YaST allows you to update an AppArmor profile after creation? (Choose all that apply.)

    a. Add Profile Wizard

    b. Update Profile Wizard

    c. Modify Profile Wizard

    d. Manually Create Profile Wizard

12. Which of the following utilities will not allow you to modify entries in an AppArmor profile?

    a. genprof

    b. logprof

    c. vim

    d. autodep

13. What command would you enter in your shell if you wanted to unload all AppArmor profiles without unloading the AppArmor kernel modules? _____

14. Which of the following commands will allow you to view the number of AppArmor profiles that are currently being enforced? (Choose all that apply.)

    a. rcapparmor status

    b. rcapparmor profiles

    c. unconfined

    d. less /sys/kernel/security/apparmor/profiles

15. You have created and loaded AppArmor profiles for most network services on your Linux system. What command will allow you to see any remaining network services that are currently running on your system without an AppArmor profile? _____

Discovery Exercises

DISCOVERY EXERCISES

Securing Network Services with AppArmor

Nearly all security breaches that occur across a network involve an intruder that interacts with an existing network service in an undesirable way. As a result, it is important to protect your services with AppArmor to minimize the chance that a network intruder will be able to access information using the network service itself.

To greater familiarize yourself with locking down network services using AppArmor, download and install a small network service program and use the appropriate utilities in this chapter to create and enforce an AppArmor profile for it. A large Open Source repository that includes several network services is found on the Internet at *http://www.sourceforge.net*.

Also note that some network services create temporary files that may be detected by AppArmor when it scans the /var/log/audit/audit.log file and will be incorporated into the AppArmor profile in the /etc/apparmor.d directory. If this is the case, the rcapparmor reload command will report that certain lines in the AppArmor profile could not be parsed because the file no longer exists. In that case, simply remove those lines from the AppArmor profile using a text editor and re-run the **rcapparmor reload** command.

Testing AppArmor Protection

After creating an AppArmor profile for a network service, it is important to ensure that AppArmor is providing adequate protection. For the network service that you secured with AppArmor in the previous Discovery Exercise, interact with the network service from a client computer on your network and attempt to access unauthorized areas of your system.

If you were able to gain access to unauthorized information, set your AppArmor profile to complain mode and repeat your steps. When finished, use the appropriate utilities to extract the information from the /var/log/audit/audit.log and create rules in the AppArmor profile that prevent the unauthorized access in the future.

Monitoring AppArmor

Most network services come with their own security features and AppArmor adds to this functionality. However, new network-based attacks may arise over time and exploit these services. As a result, network security is only effective when it is monitored. Configure AppArmor to notify you of any unauthorized access attempts for the network service that you protected with AppArmor in the previous Discovery Exercises. Next, attempt to gain unauthorized access to your system by interacting with this network service from a client computer and observe any notifications.

Following this, use YaST to print a security report that lists the attempted access and use it to identify the activities you took from your client computer.

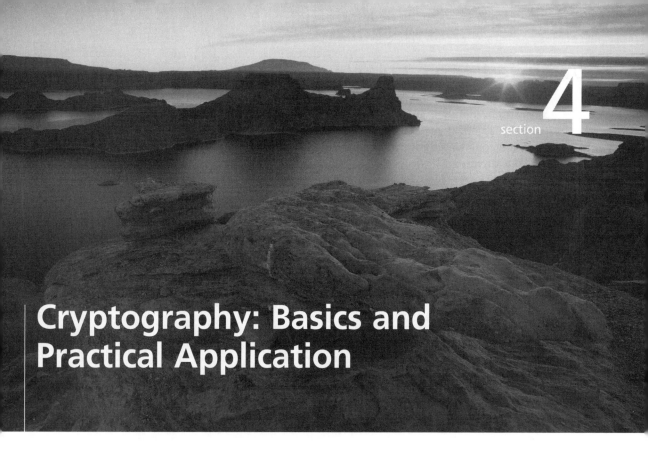

Cryptography: Basics and Practical Application

Until 30 years ago, cryptographic techniques were not in broad public use, but were limited to government agencies like the military. This has remarkably changed with the publication of public key cryptography and other cryptographic techniques that were developed in the mid-1970s. Today, e-commerce and many other applications rely heavily on cryptography. Indeed many applications would not work without it. The fact that strong cryptography is readily available for every citizen has various social and political implications. This section covers cryptography in general as well as practical aspects.

Objectives

- Cryptography Basics
- Create a Certification Authority (CA) and Issue Certificates with CLI Tools
- Create a Certification Authority (CA) and Issue Certificates with YaST
- GNU Privacy Guard (GPG)

Objective 1—Cryptography Basics

Cryptography is the mathematical science that deals with the development of cryptographic algorithms and their analysis.

In its practical application, cryptography is used to prevent unauthorized individuals from viewing confidential information, to electronically sign documents, and to authenticate individuals or various devices.

Among other things, cryptography deals with:

- Encryption and Decryption
- Cryptographic Hash Algorithms and Digital Signatures

Encryption and Decryption

The information required to encrypt and decrypt data is referred to as the `key`. The original message is referred to as `cleartext`, whereas the encrypted version is called `ciphertext`. The mathematical method to transfer cleartext into ciphertext using the key is referred to as `cryptographic algorithm`.

There are two classes of encryption procedures:

- Symmetric Encryption
- Asymmetric Encryption

Symmetric Encryption   In symmetric encryption, the same key is used for encryption and decryption. Figure 4-1 shows encryption.

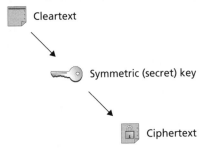

Figure 4-1

This key needs to be kept secret. If this key is known, all data encrypted with that key can be decrypted, as shown in Figure 4-2.

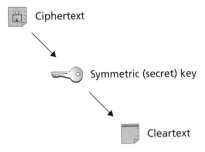

Figure 4-2

The encryption algorithm should be known and published, so that competent cryptographers are able to review it. As a rule, you should never use a procedure where the manufacturer claims that the security of the procedure depends on the algorithm being kept secret. In other words, the secrecy of your message should only depend on the key being kept secret. If it depends on the algorithm being kept secret, your message is most likely not secured at all.

An important characteristic of an encryption procedure is the length of the key. A symmetric key with a length of 40 bits can be broken with brute-force methods (trying every possible key) in a very short time: 40 bits correspond to "only" 1,099,511,627,776 possibilities. Key lengths of 128 bits or more are currently considered secure.

Some common symmetric procedures are:

- DES (Data Encryption Standard)
- Triple DES
- IDEA (International Data Encryption Algorithm)
- Blowfish
- AES (Advanced Encryption Standard)

DES (Data Encryption Standard) DES was standardized in 1977 and is the foundation of many encryption procedures (such as UNIX/Linux passwords). The key length is 56 bits.

However, in January 1999 the EFF (Electronic Frontier Foundation) decrypted a text encrypted with DES in 22 hours using brute force (trying one possible key after the other). Therefore, a key with a length of 56 bits is no longer secure, because messages protected with such a key can be decrypted in a short time.

Triple DES Triple DES is an extension of DES, using DES three times. Depending on the variant used, the effective key length offered is 112 or 168 bits.

IDEA (International Data Encryption Algorithm) IDEA is an algorithm with a key length of 128 bits. This algorithm has been patented in the USA and Europe (its noncommercial use is free).

Blowfish This algorithm has a variable key length of up to 448 bits. It was developed by Bruce Schneier; it is unpatented and license-free. It can be freely used by anyone.

AES (Advanced Encryption Standard) AES is the successor to DES. In 1993 the National Institute of Standards and Technology (NIST) decided that DES no longer met today's security requirements and organized a competition for a new standard encryption algorithm. The winner of this competition was the Rijndael algorithm, which supports key lengths of 128, 192, or 256 bits.

Asymmetric Encryption
The main problem with symmetric algorithms is how to securely transmit the secret key to your communication partner. Some governments use couriers for this purpose. Another approach is to use asymmetric encryption procedures.

To use asymmetric encryption you need to know some theory and understand asymmetric encryption's strengths and weaknesses.

- Theory of Asymmetric Encryption
- Caveats of Asymmetric Encryption

Theory of Asymmetric Encryption In an asymmetric encryption, also often called public key cryptography, there are two keys: a private key and a public key. See Figure 4-3.

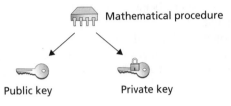

Figure 4-3

It is not possible to derive the private key from the public key. Data that was encrypted with the public key can only be decrypted with the private key as shown is Figure 4-4 and Figure 4-5.

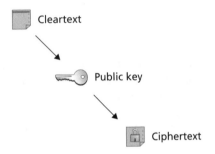

Figure 4-4

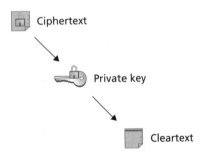

Figure 4-5

In the same way, data encrypted with the private key can only be decrypted with the public key.

The private key has to be kept secret. However, the public key can be distributed freely to everyone. Unlike symmetric encryption, there is no need to keep the key that was used to encrypt a message secret.

The key lengths used with asymmetric encryption are typically much longer than those used with symmetric encryption. The key length currently considered secure for an RSA key is 2048 bit.

Some important asymmetric encryption procedures are:

- RSA
- DSA
- Diffie-Hellman

RSA The name RSA is derived from the surnames of its developers, Rivest, Shamir, and Adleman. Its security is mainly based on the fact that it is easy to multiply two large prime numbers, but it is difficult to regain the factors from this product.

DSA The DSA (Digital Signature Algorithm) is based on a cryptographic procedure developed by ElGamal. It is a US Federal Government standard for digital signatures.

Diffie-Hellman The Diffie-Hellman key exchange describes a method to establish cryptographic keys securely without having to send the keys across insecure channels. Such a key can then be used as a secret key in symmetric encryption.

Caveats of Asymmetric Encryption Since anyone can create a private/public key pair and distribute it as the key of John Doe, the main problem with asymmetric encryption is how to determine the public key actually belongs to the person with whom you want to exchange encrypted communication.

The best solution is to personally exchange the keys. When personal exchange of keys is not feasible, the answer is to use a certificate by a trusted third party that guarantees that a certain public key belongs to a certain person or legal entity. This topic is covered later in this section.

Another problem of asymmetric procedures is their low speed. Symmetric procedures are much faster. Therefore, symmetric and asymmetric procedures are often combined: A key for symmetric encryption is transmitted through a channel encrypted asymmetrically. The information is then encrypted using a symmetric procedure and the key that was just transmitted. This is how the secure shell, SSL, and other protocols work.

Cryptographic Hash Algorithms and Digital Signatures

This topic contains the following:

- Hash Algorithms
- Digital Signatures
- Use of the Private Key to Encrypt Messages

Hash Algorithms A cryptographic hash algorithm is a mathematical procedure that takes data (a file of any length containing a message or binary data) as input and creates as output a string (the cryptographic hash) of a fixed length that is different for different input.

Ideally, no two messages ever have the same hash. In practice, such a collision is not absolutely impossible, but with hash algorithms currently in use the probability of such a collision is considered negligible for practical purposes.

Various cryptographic algorithms are used to produce hashes from messages. They differ in the algorithm and the length of the hash. Common ones are MD5 (Message Digest Algorithm 5, developed by Ron Rivest, 128-bit hash), SHA1 (Secure Hash Algorithm, developed by the National Institute of Standards and Technology in collaboration with the National Security Agency, 160-bit hash), or Ripe160 (developed within an EU project, RACE Integrity Primitives Evaluation, 160-bit hash).

Cryptographic hash algorithms are used when messages are digitally signed.

Digital Signatures A good example for digital signatures are the SUSE RPM packages. They are signed with the SUSE Build Key. You can verify the integrity of a package with the command: `rpm -K <rpm_package>`. The public key to check the signature is shipped with SLES9. To check packages from other sources, you need to import the required public key with the command: `rpm --import <PUBKEY>`.

Sometimes it is not really important to keep a message secret, while it might be crucially important to be sure that a message actually comes from a certain person and has not been altered, for example, during transmission.

When a document is digitally signed, not the actual document is signed, but a hash derived from that document using a cryptographic hash algorithm is signed.

Use of the Private Key to Encrypt Messages

When using asymmetric encryption to keep a message secret, the public key is used to encrypt the message. The private key is used to decrypt the message.

When digitally signing data, the private key is used to encrypt a cryptographic hash of the message. See Figure 4-6.

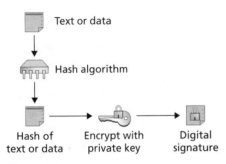

Text or data

Hash algorithm

Hash of   Encrypt with   Digital
text or data   private key   signature

Figure 4-6

The original message and encrypted hash are then sent together to the recipient.

The corresponding public key is used to decrypt the hash. This decrypted hash is then compared to a hash of the message generated by the same procedure by the recipient. If the two hashes—the newly calculated one and the decrypted one—are the same, it is assumed that the owner of the corresponding private key signed the message and that it has not been altered as shown in Figure 4-7.

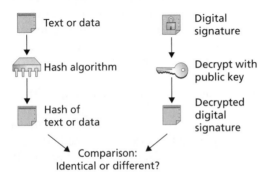

Text or data   Digital signature

Hash algorithm   Decrypt with public key

Hash of   Decrypted
text or data   digital signature

Comparison:
Identical or different?

Figure 4-7

For example, this principle is applied when signing e-mail with GPG.

It is also used to create a certificate. In this case, a data structure containing a public key and some identity, like an e-mail address or a name, is signed with the private key of a certification authority, thus stating that the public key and name belong together.

Another application is the signature created with the SUSE build key, which is contained in RPM packages from SUSE. The integrity of these RPM packages can be verified using the key in /root/.gnupg/suse_build_key.

Objective 2—Create a Certification Authority (CA) and Issue Certificates with CLI Tools

Certification authorities (CA) and certificates are a solution to the problem of determining if a certain public key actually belongs to a certain person.

As long as keys are only exchanged personally between a few people within an office or a town, a CA is not needed. But as soon as the number of people involved increases or the distance gets too large, a CA markedly facilitates key exchange and management.

The CA acts as a trusted third party that checks the identity of an entity (person or company) and issues a certificate that basically states: The public key in this certificate belongs to the identity given in here. It implies that the identity owns the corresponding private key.

Certificates are either issued by a commercial CA offering this service, or by a CA you set up on your own. Whether a commercial CA or one created within the company is used depends to a large degree on the use of the certificates and the security standards set by the security policy.

When an e-commerce Web site is offering worldwide services, a certificate issued by companies like VeriSign or eTrust is a must. If your security policy has requirements that go beyond a purely software-based public key infrastructure (PKI), you will most likely also turn to an outside company to take care of your certificates.

However, if you do not have such requirements, you do not need an external company to take care of your certificates. You can create your own CA. You can use OpenSSL on the command line for this purpose, and SUSE Linux Enterprise Server 10 comes with a YaST module to create and manage a CA and certificates.

Using your own CA has advantages if, for instance, the whole purpose is to authenticate the staff members of the company when they are remotely accessing the internal network via the Internet. Compared to getting a certificate for each employee from an outside company, it is more flexible and less costly.

To issue a certificate, you have to:

- Create a Root CA with YaST
- Create a Certificate Signed by the CA with YaST

To revoke a certificate, it is necessary to:

- Create a Certificate Signed by the CA with YaST

Create a Root CA

CAs can form a hierarchy. The topmost CA is called the root CA. As there is no agency above it to sign its certificate, the root CA has to sign it itself. The root CA issues certificates for lower CAs or certificates for end users, depending on its policy.

A CA below the root CA would have a certificate validated by the root CA. It could then issue certificates to even lower CAs or end users.

The package OpenSSL includes all you need to create a CA and issue certificates. OpenSSL keeps certificates and keys in separate directories, that have to be created before you start creating certificates.

Let's say you want to keep the certificates in root's home directory in the directory da10-CA. The following commands create the necessary structure:

```
da10:~ # mkdir da10-CA
da10:~ # cd da10-CA/
da10:~/da10-CA # mkdir certs newcerts private crl
da10:~/da10-CA # chmod 700 private
da10:~/da10-CA # ls -l
total 1
drwxr-xr-x    6 root root   144 Apr 26 16:50 .
drwx------   20 root root  1024 Apr 26 16:49 ..
drwxr-xr-x    2 root root    48 Apr 26 16:50 certs
drwxr-xr-x    2 root root    48 Apr 26 16:50 crl
drwxr-xr-x    2 root root    48 Apr 26 16:50 newcerts
drwx------    2 root root    48 Apr 26 16:50 private
da10:~/da10-CA #
```

`certs` and `newcerts` will hold certificates, while the corresponding private keys are stored in `private`. `crl`, which stands for certificate revocation list, which will be explained in more detail later.

That would already be enough to start creating the root certificate. However, by editing `/etc/ssl/openssl.cnf` to fit your needs before creating the first certificate, you can spare yourself a lot of typing. You should edit HOME and `dir` and some other variables in this file as well as the default values suggested during the certificate creation. The following shows some of the entries you might want to change in italics:

```
# This definition stops the following lines choking if HOME isn't
# defined.
HOME             = /root/da10-CA
...
dir              = /root/da10-CA    # Where everything is kept
certs            = $dir/certs       # Where the issued certs are kept
crl_dir          = $dir/crl         # Where the issued crl are kept
database         = $dir/index.txt   # database index file.
unique_subject   = yes              # Set to 'no' to allow creation
of
                                    # several certificates with same
                                    # subject.
new_certs_dir    = $dir/newcerts    # default place for new certs.
                                                    (Continued)
```

```
certificate    = $dir/da10-cacert.pem    # The CA certificate
serial         = $dir/serial             # The current serial number
#crlnumber      = $dir/crlnumber          # the current crl number
                                          # must be commented out to leave a
V1 CRL
crl            = $dir/da10-crl.pem        # The current CRL
private_key    = $dir/private/da10-cakey.pem # The private key
RANDFILE       = $dir/private/.rand       # private random number file
...
[ req_distinguished_name ]
countryName                      = Country Name (2 letter code)
countryName_default              = de
countryName_min                  = 2
countryName_max                  = 2

stateOrProvinceName              = State or Province Name (full name)
stateOrProvinceName_default      = Bavaria

localityName                     = Locality Name (eg, city)
localityName_default             = Munich
...
```

Now you can create the root-CA certificate. The following command creates a self-signed certificate (valid for 10 years) in X509 format, and the corresponding (2048-bit RSA) private key. PEM (Privacy-Enhanced Electronic Mail) denotes the format used for the certificate:

```
da10:~/da10-CA # openssl req -newkey rsa:2048 -x509 -days 3650 \
               -keyout private/da10-cakey.pem -out da10-cacert.pem
Generating a 2048 bit RSA private key
...........+++
.+++
writing new private key to 'private/da10-cakey.pem'
Enter PEM pass phrase:
Verifying - Enter PEM pass phrase:
-----
You are about to be asked to enter information that will be incorporated
into your certificate request.
What you are about to enter is what is called a Distinguished Name or a
DN.
There are quite a few fields but you can leave some blank
For some fields there will be a default value,
If you enter '.', the field will be left blank.
-----
Country Name (2 letter code) [de]:
State or Province Name (full name) [Bavaria]:
Locality Name (eg, city) [Munich]:
Organization Name (eg, company) [Digitalairlines]:
Organizational Unit Name (eg, section) [Training]:
Common Name (eg, YOUR name) []:RootCA on da10
Email Address []:ca-admin@digitalairlines.com
da10:~/da10-CA #
```

The private key is encrypted using 3DES. The passphrase is of paramount importance. If someone gets a private key and can figure out your passphrase, he can create certificates for your CA. Of course, that would completely defeat its whole purpose.

If you want to use a different encryption algorithm for your private key, you have to first generate a public/private key pair:

```
openssl genrsa -aes256 -out private/da10-
cakey.pem 2048
```

and then create the certificate:

```
openssl req -new -x509 -days 3650 -key
private/da10-cakey.pem \
-out da10-cacert.pem -set_serial 1
```

You can view the certificate using:

```
da10:~/da10-CA # openssl x509 -in da10-cacert.pem -text
Certificate:
    Data:
        Version: 3 (0x2)
        Serial Number:
            ba:45:1c:b0:81:e1:20:0c
        Signature Algorithm: sha1WithRSAEncryption
        Issuer: C=de, ST=Bavaria, L=Munich,
O=Digitalairlines, OU=Training, CN=RootCA on
da10/emailAddress=ca-admin@digitalairlines.com
        Validity
            Not Before: Apr 19 04:44:09 2006 GMT
...
```

For more information on the openssl options available when creating certificates, see man x509.

Create a Certificate Signed by the Root CA

Using your root CA, you can now create certificates to authenticate your Web servers, mail servers, VPN gateway, or notebooks.

OpenSSL keeps track of the issued certificates in a text file. Each certificate gets a serial number, and the next number to be issued is kept in an ASCII file as well. You must create both files:

```
da10:~ # cd /root/da10-CA
da10:~/da10-CA # touch index.txt
da10:~/da10-CA # echo 01 > serial
```

Getting a certificate consists of creating a certificate signing request and then actually signing it with the private key of the root CA.

The following is an example of creating the key pair and the certificate signing request:

```
da10:~/da10-CA # openssl req -new -keyout private/server_prv_key.pem \
                           -out certs/server_req.pem -days 365
Generating a 1024 bit RSA private key
..............................+++++
.....+++++
writing new private key to 'private/server_prv_key.pem'
...
```

You are again asked for the information such as country and company. (You do not need to provide anything for the last two questions that ask for a challenge password and an optional company name.)

If the certificate is used for a server, the common name has to be the DNS domain name used to contact it, like *www.digitalairlines.com*. If you use something else, the users get error messages that the certificate does not match the server contacted.

The certificate in this case is valid for one year.

For more information on other openssl options available when creating certificate signing requests, see man req.

This certificate signing request is then signed by the CA. The option -policy policy_anything refers to the respective section in /etc/ssl/openssl.cnf and defines which parts of the distinguished name have to be the same as those of the CA and which may differ (see man ca for more details). The command to enter looks like this:

```
da10:~/da10-CA # openssl ca -policy policy_anything -notext \
            -out certs/servercert.pem -infiles certs/server_req.pem
Using configuration from /etc/ssl/openssl.cnf
Enter pass phrase for /root/da10-CA/private/da10-cakey.pem:
Check that the request matches the signature
Signature ok
Certificate Details:
        Serial Number: 1 (0x1)
        Validity
            Not Before: Apr 19 05:00:05 2006 GMT
...
keyid:15:90:C7:E1:F6:1D:51:27:EE:12:8C:1A:67:B8:F1:FF:70:55:BE:74

Certificate is to be certified until Apr 19 05:00:05 2007 GMT (365 days)
Sign the certificate? [y/n]:y


1 out of 1 certificate requests certified, commit? [y/n]y
Write out database with 1 new entries
Data Base Updated
da10:~/da10-CA #
```

For more information on other openssl options available when signing certificates, see `man ca`.

In addition to the certificate in the directory `certs`, a copy of the certificate is in `newcerts`. The number in the file `serial` has been increased by one and the file `index.txt` contains some information about the certificate (validity, timestamp, serial number, DN).

```
da10:~/da10-CA # cat index.txt
V        070419050005Z           01        unknown
/C=de/ST=Bavaria/L=Munich/O=Digitalairlines/OU=Training/CN=da10.
digitalairlines.com/emailAddress=ca-admin@digitalairlines.com
```

There is an alternate command to sign the certificate request, but it does not update the database in index.txt:

```
openssl x509 -req -in certs/server_req.pem -out
certs/servercert.pem \
-CAda10-cacert.pem-CAkey private/da10-cakey.pem\
-CAserial serial
```

The certificate request, certs/server_req.pem in our example, can be deleted because it is no longer needed.

Create a Certificate Revocation List (CRL)

Sometimes it is necessary to revoke a certificate. This would be the case if the passphrase for the secret key had been compromised. You would also, for instance, want to revoke the certificate used to authenticate a notebook at the VPN gateway if the notebook is lost or stolen.

A certificate revocation list is a database that lists the certificates that are no longer considered valid despite the fact that their expiration date has not been reached.

Two steps are necessary to revoke a certificate:

- Revoke the certificate:

```
da10:~/da10-CA # openssl ca -revoke  certs/servercert.pem
Using configuration from /etc/ssl/openssl.cnf
Enter pass phrase for /root/da10-CA/private/da10-cakey.pem:
Revoking Certificate 01.
Data Base Updated
```

- Create the certificate revocation list (crl/da10-crl.pem in the following example):

```
da10:~/da10-CA # openssl ca -gencrl -out crl/da10-crl.pem
Using configuration from /etc/ssl/openssl.cnf
Enter pass phrase for /root/da10-CA/private/da10-cakey.pem:
da10:~/da10-CA #
```

If you get one or both of the following error messages:

```
/root/da10-CA/crlnumber: No such file or directory
error while loading CRL number
```

it means that you did not put a comment symbol in front of the line:

```
crlnumber = $dir/crlnumber
```

in /etc/ssl/openssl.cnf (see page 88–89).

You have two choices: Either put the comment symbol there, or create the missing file using:

```
echo 01 > /root/da10-CA/crlnumber
```

In the latter case, you create CRL in Version 2 format, which some applications might not be able to use.

This changes the entry in the file index.txt for that certificate. Note the change from V (valid) to R (revoked) and the additional time stamp showing the time the certificate was revoked:

```
da10:~/da10-CA # cat index.txt
R       0704190500005Z  060419051137Z    01        unknown
/C=de/ST=Bavaria/L=Munich/O=Digitalairlines/OU=Training/CN=da10.
digitalairlines.com/emailAddress=ca-admin@digitalairlines.com
```

The CRL needs to be published for others to check the validity of certificates. How this is done depends on the security policy of the CA. In some cases, it might be enough just to copy the file to an application directory: in other cases, it will be published on a Web site or in a directory service like LDAP.

Cryptography, public key infrastructures, CAs, and certificates are a broad subject. There are many publications on the subject. A search for cryptography in any online bookstore will result in a long list of books. The OpenSSL Web site is at *http://www.openssl.org/*.

Exercise 4-1: Create a Root CA and Certificates on the Command Line

Objective: The purpose of this exercise is to familiarize you with the openssl command.

Description: Following the steps outlined in this objective, create a root CA and a certificate for your computer da*xx*.digitalairlines.com. Create another certificate for server.digitalairlines.com; then revoke that certificate and create a CRL.

The certificate created in this exercise for your computer will be used in Exercise 5-2 "Use stunnel to Secure POP3 with SSL" on page 140.

Detailed Steps to Complete this Exercise

1. Open a terminal window and su – to root with a password of novell.

2. Create the necessary directory structure in root's home directory (using your hostname instead of da*xx*), and change the permissions for the private directory:

```
mkdir -p daxx-CA/{certs,newcerts,private,crl}
cd daxx-CA
chmod 700 private
```

3. Edit the file /etc/ssl/openssl.cnf with a text editor and change variables and company entries appropriately, for example, /root/da*xx*-CA for dir and Digitalairlines for company.

   The following is an example for the system da10. Replace da10 by the hostname of your computer. The line numbers on the left tell you where you find the variables in /etc/ssl/openssl.cnf. (Note that in line 41 and 143 comment signs have been removed.)

```
      # This definition stops the following lines choking if HOME isn't
      # defined.
  8   HOME              = /root/da10-CA
  ...
 37   dir               = /root/da10-CA   # Where everything is kept
      certs             = $dir/certs      # Where the issued certs are kept
      crl_dir           = $dir/crl        # Where the issued crl are kept
      database          = $dir/index.txt  # database index file.
 41   unique_subject    = yes             # Set to 'no' to allow creation
      of
                                          # several certificates with same
                                          # subject.
      new_certs_dir     = $dir/newcerts   # default place for new certs.
 45
      certificate       = $dir/da10-cacert.pem   # The CA certificate
 47   serial            = $dir/serial     # The current serial number
      #crlnumber        = $dir/crlnumber  # the current crl number
 49                     # must be commented out to leave a V1
 50   CRL
      crl               = $dir/da10-crl.pem  # The current CRL
      private_key       = $dir/private/da10-cakey.pem  # The private key
      RANDFILE          = $dir/private/.rand  # private random number file
  ...
125   [ req_distinguished_name ]
      countryName                    = Country Name (2 letter code)
      countryName_default            = de
      countryName_min                = 2
      countryName_max                = 2
130
      stateOrProvinceName            = State or Province Name (full name)
132   stateOrProvinceName_default    = Bavaria


                                            (Continued)
```

```
         localityName                = Locality Name (eg, city)
         localityName_default        = Munich
143  ...
         organizationalUnitName      = Organizational Unit Name (eg, section)
         organizationalUnitName_default = Training
```

4. To create the self-signed root certificate of your CA, enter:

```
openssl req -newkey rsa:2048 -x509 -days 3650 \
-keyout private/daxx-cakey.pem -out daxx-cacert.pem
```

   Answer the questions appropriately; in most cases the default values can be accepted, as you have set them in /etc/ssl/openssl.cnf according to your needs.

5. To view the certificate, enter:

```
openssl x509 -in daxx-cacert.pem -text
```

6. To create the files index.txt and serial, enter:

```
touch index.txt ; echo 01 > serial
```

7. To create a certificate signing request for your computer, enter:

```
openssl req -new -keyout private/daxx_key.pemdaxx_key.pem \
-out certs/daxx_req.pem -days 365
```

   Answer the questions appropriately; in most cases the default values can be accepted, as you have set them in /etc/ssl/openssl.cnf according to your needs. Be sure to use the fully qualified domain name of your computer in answer to the question, "Common Name (eg, YOUR name)."

   If you wanted to have a certificate issued by a commercial CA, you would have to send this request to that CA for signing.

8. To sign the certificate signing request and create the certificate, enter:

```
openssl ca -policy policy_anything -notext \
-out certs/daxx_cert.pem -infiles certs/daxx_req.pem
```

9. View the files index.txt and serial with cat.

10. Repeat steps 7–9 to create another certificate for server.digitalairlines.com; use different file names, such as servercert.pem, for the key and certificates.

11. To revoke the certificate just created and to create a certificate revocation list, enter:

```
openssl ca -revoke certs/servercert.pem
openssl ca -gencrl -out crl/daxx-crl.pem
```

12. View the files index.txt and serial with cat.

13. Convert the certificate revocation list to DER format in order to be able to import it into Firefox with the following command:

```
openssl crl -in crl/daxx-crl.pem -outform der \
-out crl/daxx-crl.der
```

Objective 3—Create a Certification Authority (CA) and Issue Certificates with YaST

As you learned in the previous objective, openssl is all you need to run your own CA. However, due to the numerous parameters and switches, the commands are somewhat cumbersome.

If you are looking for an alternative, you might want to try the YaST CA management module. It acts as a frontend to openssl and keeps track of your certificates.

The basic steps to create a certificate are the same as with the command line interface. You have to:

- Create a Root CA with YaST
- Create a Certificate Signed by the CA with YaST

To revoke a certificate it is necessary to:

- Create a CRL with YaST

Create a Root CA with YaST

Creating a Root CA with YaST is easy. First, you launch YaST and select the section Security and Users. Figure 4-8 shows the dialog that appears.

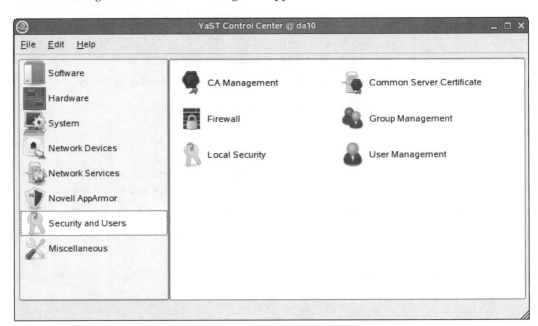

Figure 4-8

Select CA Management.
In the next dialog, select Create Root CA. See Figure 4-9.

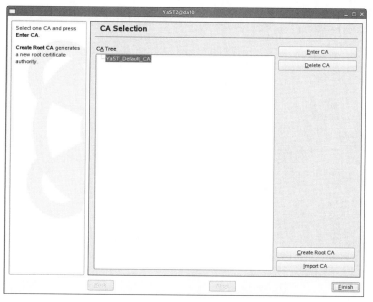

Figure 4-9

A wizard guides you through the necessary steps. Enter the appropriate information; then select Next. See Figure 4-10.

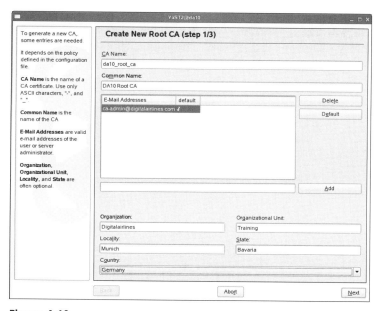

Figure 4-10

The next dialog asks you to enter a password and the period of validity for the CA. In Figure 4-11, it is 10 years.

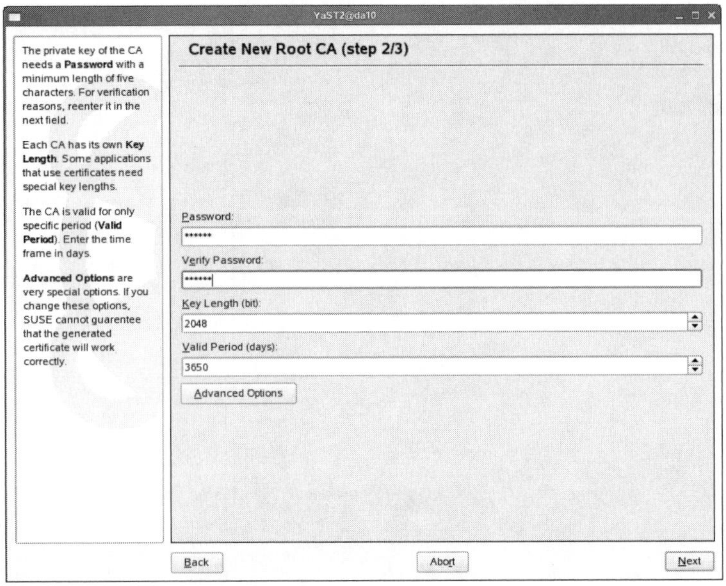

Figure 4-11

In the next dialog, review the values of the various fields. If everything is correct, select Create. See Figure 4-12.

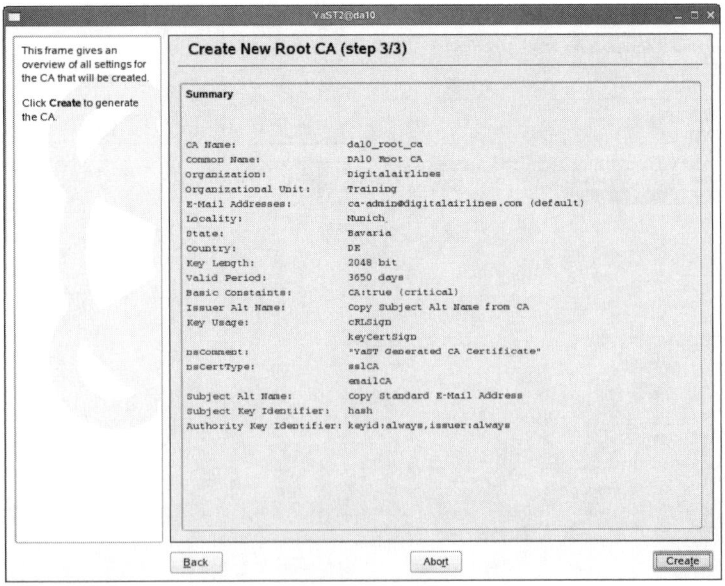

Figure 4-12

Certification authorities can form a hierarchy, and you could decide not to have the root CA issue certificates for servers directly but to use a subCA for this purpose.

After creating the subCA and exporting the certificate of the root CA, you can save the files of the root CA under /var/lib/CAM/ to a backup medium and lock it in a safe (be sure to have the passphrase for the root CA at a secure, but separate location, too).

To create a subCA, enter the root CA (that is, enter the passphrase that unlocks the private key of the root CA) by selecting it and clicking on `Enter CA` in the main dialog of the CA Management module (Figure 4-9).

In the following dialog, which opens up after entering the password, select `Advanced` and `Create SubCA` as shown in Figure 4-13.

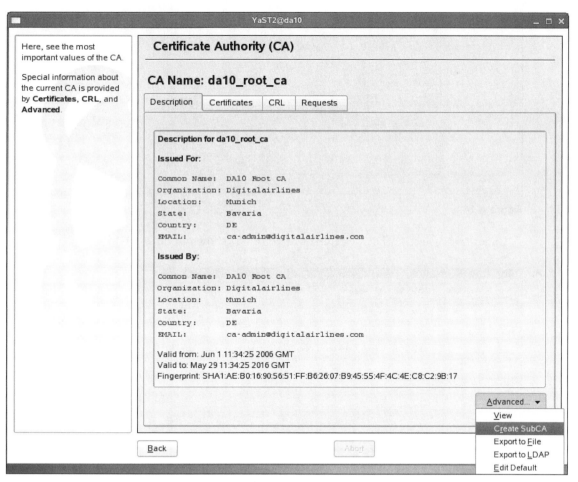

Figure 4-13

Repeat the steps you took to create the root CA now for the SubCA.

You are now ready to issue individual certificates signed by the SubCA for individuals or hosts.

Create a Certificate Signed by the CA with YaST

To create a certificate, do the following:

Enter the SubCA and select the `Certificates` tab as shown in Figure 4-14.

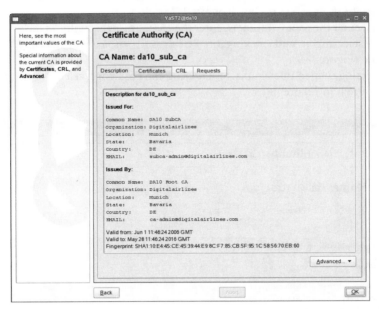

Figure 4-14

Under `Add`, select `Add Server Certificate` as shown in Figure 4-15.

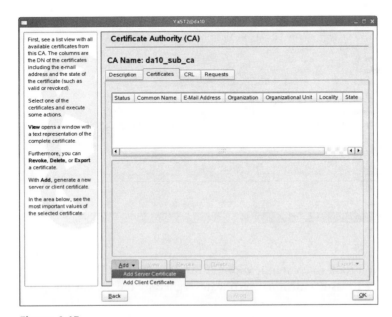

Figure 4-15

The following dialogs are very similar to those used when creating the root CA. See Figure 4-16.

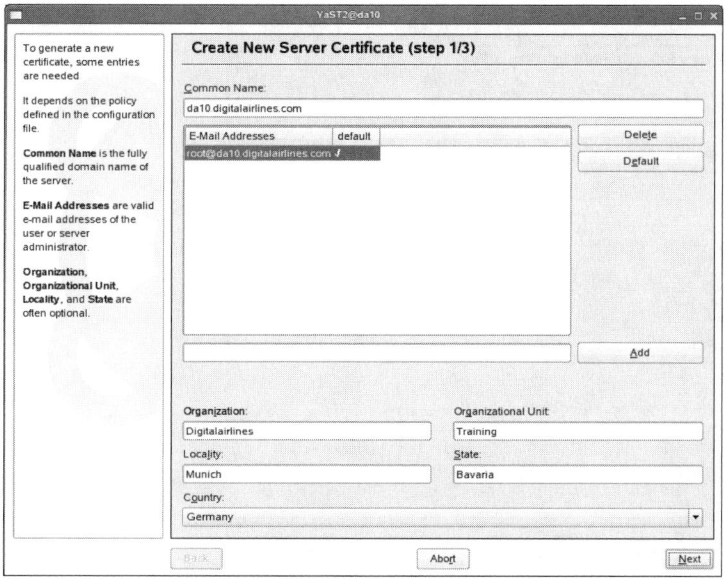

Figure 4-16

It is important to heed the note on the left regarding the common name; otherwise, the certificate won't match the hostname, causing error messages.

Select `Next` to open the following dialog shown in Figure 4-17.

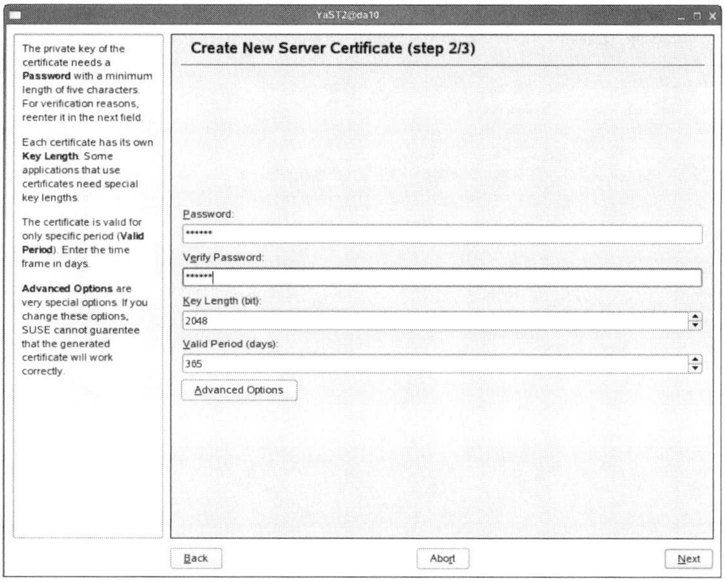

Figure 4-17

Note that the validity of the certificate cannot be longer than that of the CA. After you select Next, the input is summarized. See Figure 4-18.

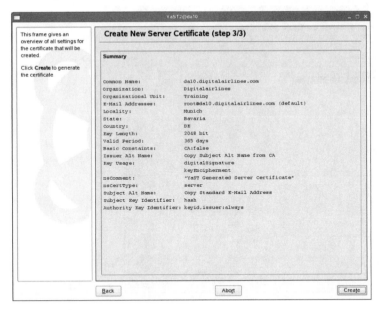

Figure 4-18

If everything is correct, choose Create to create the certificate. The certificate is then listed in the overview dialog of the SubCA as shown in Figure 4-19.

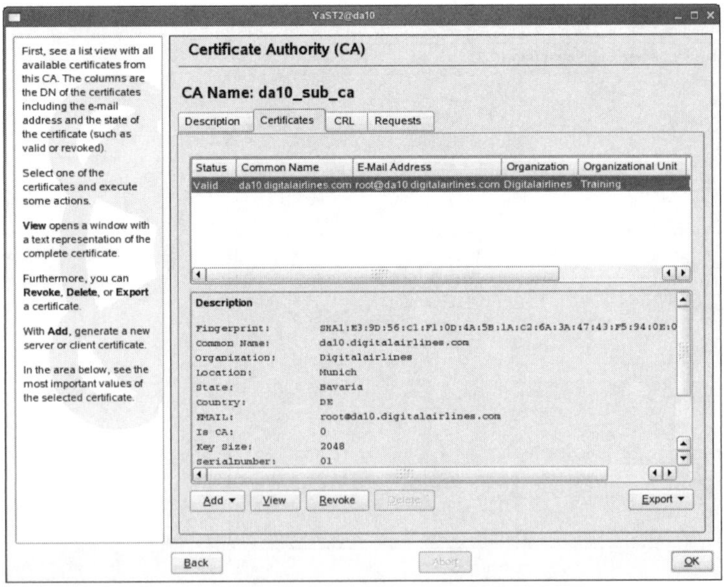

Figure 4-19

To use this certificate on the server it is intended for, you must export it and take it to the server. Select Export to do this and then select the option that fits your needs.

There are various choices to export the certificate and the private key as shown in Figure 4-20. Which one you choose depends on how you want to use it and on the requirements of the software. A private key used by the Apache Web server may be encrypted, but it means that you will be prompted for the passphrase every time Apache is started. Other programs, like stunnel, do not offer a dialog to enter the passphrase when starting up. For such programs you need the private key unencrypted.

Figure 4-20

Create a CRL with YaST

As with the command line, there are two steps to create a certificate revocation list (CRL):

- Revoke the certificate.
- Create the CRL.

To revoke a certificate, do the following:

1. Enter the CA
2. Select Certificates
3. Select the certificate you want to revoke
4. Select Revoke
5. Choose a reason for the revocation and select OK.
   You are returned to the Certificates Overview and the certificate is now marked as revoked.

To create or update the CRL, do the following:

1. Select the CRL tab and then Generate CRL.

2. A pop-up asks you to enter the validity of the CRL. After selecting OK, the CRL is generated.

3. Export the CRL to a file using the Export dialog.

Exercise 4-2: (Optional) Create a Root CA and Certificates with YaST

Time Required: 15 minutes

Objective: The purpose of this exercise is to teach you how to manage a CA using YaST. To keep the exercise simple, no Sub-CA is created.

Description: Using the YaST CA Management module, create a Root CA; export the Root CA certificate to a file. Enter the Root CA and issue a certificate for your computer; export your server certificate to a file.

As Objective 3 outlines the steps in detail, just a rough outline of steps is given here. Do the following:

1. Start a terminal window and su – to root with a password of novell.

2. Start the YaST CA Management module by entering yast2 ca_mgm.

3. Select Create Root CA and follow the steps of the wizard to create a root CA. Use applicable values of your choice to fill in the dialogs.

4. Enter the root CA you just created.

5. Export the CA certificate to a file.

6. Create a server certificate.

7. Export the server certificate.

Objective 4—GNU Privacy Guard (GPG)

Even if you secure the transmission of the e-mail between server and client, this has no effect on the mail message itself. The communication between mail servers in the Internet is unencrypted, as is the e-mail message while it is waiting on the mail server to be picked up.

The only protection from government organizations, nosy administrators, or criminal hackers is to encrypt the e-mail message itself. This is not an imaginary threat. In the past there were actual instances where mail got into the wrong hands with serious impact on a business, like losing a potential contract because the competitor was then able to make a better offer.

PGP (Pretty Good Privacy) is probably the best-known program to encrypt e-mail. SUSE Linux Enterprise Server 10 comes with the compatible open source alternative GNU Privacy Guard. Kmail has built-in GPG support. Support for GPG can be added to Thunderbird, the e-mail client created by the Mozilla project, using the Enigmail plug-in.

With these programs, using encryption is easy. Mail encryption should be used much more often than it is currently.

To use GPG, you have to know how to do the following:

- Create a Key Pair
- Export and Import Public Keys
- Encrypt and Decrypt Files
- Use GPG within Kmail

Create a Key Pair

GPG uses the cryptographic principles outlined in Objective 1, Cryptography Basics. The public key of a public/private key pair is used to encrypt a symmetric session key that is then used to encrypt the message. The encrypted message is then sent to the recipient together with the encrypted session key.

The following shows how to generate an asymmetric key pair:

```
geeko@da10:~> gpg --gen-key
gpg (GnuPG) 1.4.2; Copyright (C) 2005 Free Software Foundation, Inc.
This program comes with ABSOLUTELY NO WARRANTY.
This is free software, and you are welcome to redistribute it
under certain conditions. See the file COPYING for details.

gpg: directory '/home/geeko/.gnupg' created
gpg: new configuration file '/home/geeko/.gnupg/gpg.conf' created
gpg: WARNING: options in '/home/geeko/.gnupg/gpg.conf' are not yet
active during this run
gpg: keyring '/home/geeko/.gnupg/secring.gpg' created
gpg: keyring '/home/geeko/.gnupg/pubring.gpg' created
Please select what kind of key you want:
   (1) DSA and Elgamal (default)
   (2) DSA (sign only)
   (5) RSA (sign only)
Your selection?
DSA keypair will have 1024 bits.
ELG-E keys may be between 1024 and 4096 bits long.
What keysize do you want? (2048)
Requested keysize is 2048 bits
Please specify how long the key should be valid.
        0 = key does not expire
     <n>  = key expires in n days
     <n>w = key expires in n weeks
     <n>m = key expires in n months
     <n>y = key expires in n years
Key is valid for? (0)
Key does not expire at all
Is this correct? (y/N) y

You need a user ID to identify your key; the software constructs the
user ID
from the Real Name, Comment and Email Address in this form:
    "Heinrich Heine (Der Dichter) <heinrichh@duesseldorf.de>"
                                                  (Continued)
```

```
Real name: Geeko
Email address: geeko@digitalairlines.com
Comment: Chameleon
You selected this USER-ID:
    "Geeko (Chameleon) <geeko@digitalairlines.com>"

Change (N)ame, (C)omment, (E)mail or (O)kay/(Q)uit? O
You need a Passphrase to protect your secret key.
```

Like a password, the passphrase should contain upper- and lower-case characters, and numbers. Special characters can be used, but may be problematic to enter on keyboards with a layout for a different language.

GPG creates the key pair, which can take some time.

```
gpg: /home/geeko/.gnupg/trustdb.gpg: trustdb created
gpg: key 15B847F3 marked as ultimately trusted
public and secret key created and signed.

gpg: checking the trustdb
gpg: 3 marginal(s) needed, 1 complete(s) needed, PGP trust model
gpg: depth: 0  valid:   1  signed:   0  trust: 0-, 0q, 0n, 0m, 0f,
1u
pub   1024D/15B847F3 2006-04-19
      Key fingerprint = 3762 FF45 8BF9 3224 49EF  4257 171A 5A58
15B8 47F3
uid                     Geeko (Chameleon) <geeko@digitalairlines.com>
sub   2048g/3C480751 2006-04-19
```

The private key is written to ~/.gnupg/secring.gpg, the public key to ~/.gnupg/pubring.gpg.

To send you an encrypted message, the sender needs your public key. And similarly, if you want to send an encrypted message to someone, you need his public key.

Export and Import Public Keys

To export the public key just created, use the option --export. If you want to publish the key on a Web page, use the ASCII format with the option -a.

```
geeko@da10:~> gpg --export -a geeko
-----BEGIN PGP PUBLIC KEY BLOCK-----
Version: GnuPG v1.4.2 (GNU/Linux)

mQGiBERF+nIRBAC7hEkguu7nW8CftGr+GfZEA88A/m2KjKFvSop6qug+RuDY6u3d
dQ5DokzSo8yzrvw9HpTWBN0577tgwGiKnQwbEeR4ML8bAO6rTnGb6H1uNmf+eJMY
...
REX7DAIbDAAKCRAXGlpYFbhH81xTAKCYo9uk2c2FGQkdScu2F51rTwf45wCgmulE
TorJ/FjPnRo/7GDBJDjFnqM=
=sHTg
-----END PGP PUBLIC KEY BLOCK-----
```

The key is written to stdout. Redirect the output to a file as needed.
To import keys from others, use the option `--import`:

```
geeko@da10:~> gpg --import /tmp/tux.asc
gpg: key EE82B088: public key "Tux P (The Penguin)
<tux@digitalairlines.com>" imported
gpg: Total number processed: 1
gpg:               imported: 1
```

To view the keys available in your key ring, use `--list-keys`:

```
geeko@da10:~> gpg --list-keys
/home/geeko/.gnupg/pubring.gpg
------------------------------
pub   1024D/15B847F3 2006-04-19
uid                  Geeko (Chameleon) <geeko@digitalairlines.com>
sub   2048g/3C480751 2006-04-19

pub   1024D/EE82B088 2006-04-19
uid                  Tux P (The Penguin) <tux@digitalairlines.com>
sub   2048g/F3971E52 2006-04-19
```

To view the available options, use `gpg --help` or `man gpg`.

Encrypt and Decrypt Files

Now that you have public keys, you can encrypt files. The option to use is `-e`:

```
geeko@da10:~> gpg -e message.txt
You did not specify a user ID. (you may use "-r")

Current recipients:

Enter the user ID.  End with an empty line: tux
gpg: F3971E52: There is no assurance this key belongs to the named
user

pub  2048g/F3971E52 2006-04-19 Tux P (The Penguin)
<tux@digitalairlines.com>
 Primary key fingerprint: 53CE 1FF9 5568 EA63 BC3E  57F8 A283 907F
EE82 B088
      Subkey fingerprint: 297D 148D FE9C 961D 7E74  EC1B A480 8828
F397 1E52

It is NOT certain that the key belongs to the person named
in the user ID.  If you *really* know what you are doing,
you may answer the next question with yes.

Use this key anyway? (y/N) y

Current recipients:
2048g/F3971E52 2006-04-19 "Tux P (The Penguin) <tux@digitalairlines.com>"

Enter the user ID.  End with an empty line:
```

You could specify the recipients on the command line using the option -r: `gpg -r tux -e message.txt`.

The encrypted file in this example is message.txt.gpg. If you use the option `-a`, it would be an ASCII text file and the extension would be .asc instead of .gpg.

Because you do not have the private key corresponding to the recipients public key, you are not able to decrypt the file you just encrypted. If you want to prevent an attacker from reading the clear text file on your hard disk while still being able to read it yourself, you would have to encrypt it to yourself as well:

`gpg -r tux -r geeko -e message.txt`

Then delete the cleartext file using a utility like shred that overwrites the file before it deletes it. (Note that shred and other such utilities have limitations on journaling file systems; see `man shred` for details.)

You have to confirm using the key because there is no CA certifying that this key belongs to the ID tux (in the above example). You have to certify that yourself or rely on other users to do so.

Each key has a so-called key fingerprint. You can view the fingerprint using the option `--fingerprint username`:

```
da10:~ # gpg --fingerprint geeko
pub   1024D/15B847F3 2006-04-19
      Key fingerprint = 3762 FF45 8BF9 3224 49EF  4257 171A 5A58 15B8
47F3
uid                     Geeko (Chameleon) <geeko@digitalairlines.com>
sub   2048g/3C480751 2006-04-19
```

To ensure that a certain key belongs to a certain person, you can view the fingerprint of the key you have in your possession with the command shown above, and then find out from the person if that matches the fingerprint of the key in their possession. Some users print the fingerprint on their business card or publish it on their Web site. You could also contact the person personally or by phone to find out. What is acceptable to you as a proof depends on your personal security needs and policies.

Once you are convinced the key belongs to the person named in the user ID, you can sign the key:

```
geeko@da10:~> gpg --edit tux
gpg (GnuPG) 1.4.2; Copyright (C) 2005 Free Software Foundation, Inc.
This program comes with ABSOLUTELY NO WARRANTY.
This is free software, and you are welcome to redistribute it
under certain conditions. See the file COPYING for details.

pub 1024D/EE82B088 created: 2006-04-19 expires: never    usage: CS
                   trust: unknown       validity: unknown
sub 2048g/F3971E52 created: 2006-04-19 expires: never    usage: E
[ unknown] (1). Tux P (The Penguin) <tux@digitalairlines.com>

Command> sign

pub 1024D/EE82B088  created: 2006-04-19 expires: never   usage: CS
                   trust: unknown       validity: unknown
 Primary key fingerprint: 53CE 1FF9 5568 EA63 BC3E  57F8 A283 907F
EE82 B088

     Tux P (The Penguin) <tux@digitalairlines.com>
                                              (Continued)
```

```
Are you sure that you want to sign this key with your
key "Geeko (Chameleon) <geeko@digitalairlines.com>" (15B847F3)

Really sign? (y/N) y

You need a passphrase to unlock the secret key for
user: "Geeko (Chameleon) <geeko@digitalairlines.com>"
1024-bit DSA key, ID 15B847F3, created 2006-04-19

gpg: gpg-agent is not available in this session

Command> quit
Save changes? (y/N) y
```

Once you have signed the key, it is used for encryption without having to confirm its use.

Using the option `--edit`, you have several commands at your disposal to administer your key rings. See the gpg man page for details.

A network of key servers exists to facilitate the exchange of keys. You can publish your key there, and also retrieve keys from others. *http://www.cam.ac.uk.pgp.net/pgpnet/wwwkeys.html* lists available servers.

Use GPG within Kmail

With the commands covered so far, you could encrypt files that you could then send as attachments to e-mails. For day-to-day e-mailing this is far too complicated, because hardly anyone would write an e-mail message to a file, encrypt it, and then attach the encrypted file to an otherwise empty e-mail.

Kmail supports encryption of e-mails and attachments with the click of a mouse, making encryption very easy.

To configure GPG for use within Kmail, select `Settings > Configure Kmail > Modify`. In the dialog, select `Identities`, mark the identity you want to configure, and then select `Modify`. In the dialog that opens, click on the `Cryptography` tab and then select `Change` next to OpenPGP signing key. Choose the key you want to use for this identity. See Figure 4-21.

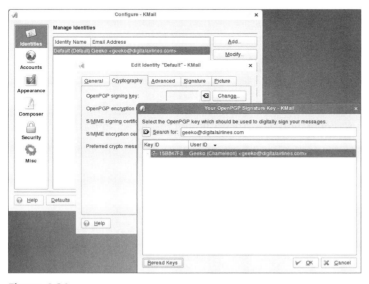

Figure 4-21

Also choose an `OpenPGP encryption key` that is used to encrypt messages to yourself so that you are able to read encrypted messages you sent to others. See Figure 4-22.

Once you have done that, all it takes to encrypt and sign messages is to select the respective buttons when you write an e-mail.

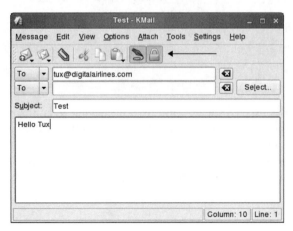

Figure 4-22

Once you are finished writing your e-mail and send it, a dialog asks you to confirm the selection of keys as shown in Figure 4-23.

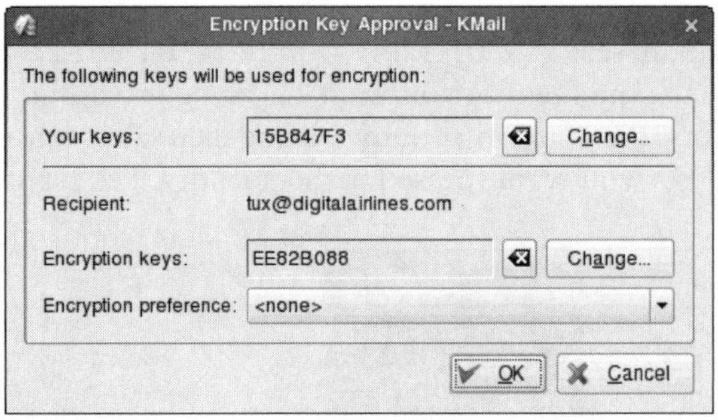

Figure 4-23

You can change the selected keys as needed. When done, select OK. See Figure 4-24.

When receiving an encrypted mail, you are prompted for the passphrase of your private key:

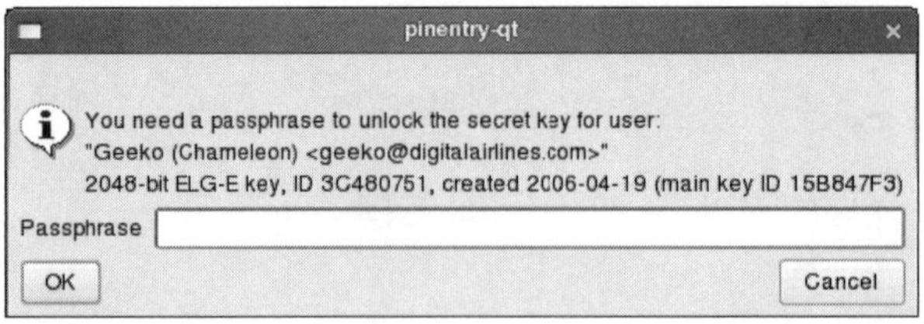

Figure 4-24

Kmail shows the decrypted e-mail, as well as information on any signature.

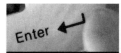

EXERCISE

Exercise 4-3: Work with GPG

Time Required: 20 minutes

Objective: The purpose of this exercise is to familiarize you with some of the features of GPG and with how keys are managed to exchange encrypted mail. You will work with two user accounts, geeko and tux, to exchange keys and exchange encrypted e-mails or files.

Description: Create a public/private GPG key pair for each account, export the public key of one account, and import it to the key ring on the other account. As geeko, encrypt a text file with the public key of tux, and decrypt it again.

Detailed Steps to Complete this Exercise

1. Make sure two user accounts, geeko and tux, are available. If tux is not available, create the second one using useradd (as root). As geeko, open two terminal windows, and in one of them su – to tux.

2. In each of the terminal windows create a public/private GPG-key pair by entering:

   ```
   gpg --gen-key
   ```

   You have to answer several questions; the defaults will do for this exercise.
   Make sure that you remember the Real name you enter during the key creation process.
   If there is a message like "Not enough random bytes available. Please do some other work to give the OS a chance to collect more entropy! (Need 284 more bytes)" move the mouse, enter text on the keyboard or start some application.

3. To export the public key to a file, in both windows enter:

   ```
   gpg -a --export "real name" > /tmp/name.asc
   ```

   Choose reasonable names for the key files.

4. To import the public key of the other account, enter:

   ```
   gpg --import /tmp/name.asc
   ```

   (As geeko you would import the key of tux and vice versa.)

5. As geeko, write a message to a file, such as:

   ```
   echo "Hello Tux, how are you?" > /tmp/msg-to-tux
   ```

6. To encrypt that file, enter:

   ```
   gpg -ea /tmp/msg-to-tux
   ```

   You are prompted to enter a user ID. The name that is part of the key, for instance tux, will do, or use the hexadecimal ID of the key if there are several keys with the same name.

7. View the file /tmp/msg-to-tux.asc using cat.

8. As tux, decrypt the file; enter:

   `gpg /tmp/msg-to-tux.asc`

   You will be asked if you want to overwrite the existing file `msg-to-tux`; type n and then enter a new filename. View the file with:

   `cat /tmp/`***newfilename***

   To view the decrypted file directly on the screen, you can use:

   `gpg -o - /tmp/msg-to-tux.asc`

9. As geeko, sign the file with:

   `gpg --clearsign /tmp/msg-to-tux`

   Overwrite the existing file /tmp/msg-to-tux.asc.

10. Verify the signature with:

    `gpg --verify /tmp/msg-to-tux.asc`

11. Load the file /tmp/msg-to-tux.asc in vi and alter one letter of the message. Save the changes and close vi. Verify the signature again.

Summary

- Cryptography is a process used to ensure that only certain individuals can gain access to sensitive data. It consists of encryption and decryption. Encryption turns cleartext data into ciphertext using a cryptographic algorithm and key. Alternatively, decryption obtains the original cleartext data from ciphertext using a cryptographic algorithm and key.

- Symmetric encryption uses a single key alongside an encryption algorithm to encrypt and decrypt data. Common symmetric encryption algorithms include DES, Triple DES, IDEA, Blowfish and AES.

- Asymmetric encryption uses separate keys for encryption and decryption. A public key is used alongside an encryption algorithm to encrypt data and a private key is used alongside an encryption algorithm to decrypt data. Public keys are typically made available to anyone, whereas private keys are kept on one computer only. Common asymmetric encryption algorithms include RSA, DSA and Diffie-Hellman.

- Longer cryptographic keys are more difficult to attack, but increase the time needed to encrypt and decrypt data.

- Symmetric encryption typically uses keys that are 128-bits in length, whereas asymmetric encryption typically uses keys that are 2048-bits in length. As a result, most technologies use symmetric encryption to encrypt data, and asymmetric encryption to protect the key used for symmetric encryption.

- A hash is a unique, fixed length value for a piece of data that is calculated using a cryptographic hash algorithm. MD5, SHA1 and Ripe160 are common cryptographic hash algorithms.

- Digital signatures consist of a hash that is encrypted using a private key alongside an encryption algorithm. The recipient of the digital signature decrypts the hash using the public key of the sender to verify its authenticity and uses the decrypted hash to verify the contents of the data. Digital signatures are commonly used in e-mail and RPM packages.

- Since public keys are commonly transferred across networks, it is important that you verify the identity of the public key using a certificate from a trusted third party Certification Authority (CA).

- There are several commercial CAs on the Internet that can create certificates. Alternatively, you can create your own CA within your organization. The first CA within an organization is called a Root CA.

- To create a Root CA in SUSE Linux, you can edit the /etc/ssl/openssl.cnf file and run the openssl command to create a CA certificate. Alternatively, you can use the CA Management module of YaST to create a Root CA.

- After a CA has been created, you can use the openssl command or CA Management module of YaST to create and issue certificates.

- CAs publish a Certificate Revocation List (CRL) to advise certificate users of certificates that should no longer be used. To revoke a certificate and create a CRL, you can use the openssl command or CA Management module of YaST.

- GPG is an Open Source implementation of PGP that is commonly used to encrypt e-mail and files that are distributed across the Internet. It uses asymmetric encryption and does not require the use of a CA since both parties must manually import the public key of the other party.

Key Terms

/etc/ssl/openssl.cnf   The main configuration file for the OpenSSL package.

/root/.gnupg/suse_build_key   A public key used to verify the authenticity of SUSE software packages.

~/.gnupg/pubring.gpg   The location of a user's public key for use with GPG.

~/.gnupg/secring.gpg   The location of a user's private key for use with GPG.

AES (Advanced Encryption Standard)   A symmetric encryption algorithm that uses up to 256-bit keys. It was designed to be the successor to DES.

algorithm   See cryptographic algorithm.

asymmetric encryption   An encryption method that uses a public key to encrypt data and a private key to decrypt data.

Blowfish   A freely available symmetric encryption algorithm that uses up to 448-bit keys.

CA Management   A YaST module that can implement and manage certificates and Certification Authorities.

Certificate Revocation List (CRL) A public catalog of certificates that should not be trusted. It is located on a Certification Authority.

Certification Authority (CA) A trusted third party that verifies the identity of a public key using public key certificates.

ciphertext Data that has been encrypted using an encryption algorithm.

cleartext Data that is not encrypted.

cryptographic algorithm A set of steps used with a key to scramble data.

cryptographic hash A fixed length value that is unique to a particular portion of data.

cryptography A system that encrypts sensitive information to prevent anyone who is unable to decrypt the contents from viewing it.

decryption The process of unscrambling data using a cryptographic algorithm and key.

DES (Data Encryption Standard) One of the oldest and most common symmetric encryption algorithms. DES keys are 56-bits long.

Diffie-Hellman The first widely-used asymmetric encryption algorithm.

digital signature A hash that has been encrypted with a private key. Since there is typically only one copy of a private key in existence, you can obtain the associated public key, decode the hash and prove that the digital signature is authentic.

DSA (Digital Signature Algorithm) An asymmetric encryption algorithm that is endorsed by the U.S. Government for use with digital signatures.

encryption The process of scrambling data using a cryptographic algorithm and key.

GNU Privacy Guard (GPG) An Open Source implementation of PGP.

gpg command Generates keys, digitally signs, encrypts and decrypts data using GPG.

hash See cryptographic hash.

hash algorithm An algorithm used to produce a hash. MD5, SHA1 and Ripe160 are common hash algorithms.

IDEA (International Data Encryption Algorithm) A commonly used symmetric encryption algorithm that uses 128-bit keys.

key A random component used alongside an encryption algorithm to make the result of the encryption algorithm difficult to decode. Longer keys result in stronger encryption.

Kmail A common mail client in SUSE Linux that can use GPG keys.

MD5 (Message Digest Algorithm 5) A common hash algorithm that is used to store passwords and verify file contents.

OpenSSL A Linux package that allows for the creation and management of certificates and Certification Authorities.

openssl command The configuration command for the OpenSSL package. It may be used to create and issue certificates as well as manage Certification Authorities.

PGP (Pretty Good Privacy) A widely used implementation of asymmetric cryptography developed in 1991.

private key An asymmetric encryption key typically used to decrypt data encrypted using the associated public key.

public key An asymmetric encryption key typically used to encrypt data.

Public Key Infrastructure (PKI) A system that uses a Certification Authority to verify the authenticity of public keys used for asymmetric encryption.

Ripe160 A strong hash algorithm originally intended to replace MD5.

RSA (Rivest, Shamir, Adleman) An asymmetric encryption algorithm that is widely used in many Web applications.

SHA1 (Secure Hash Algorithm 1) A strong hash algorithm developed by the National Institute of Standards and Technology.

symmetric encryption An encryption method that uses a single key to both encrypt and decrypt data.

Triple DES (3DES) A version of DES that uses keys that are up to three times the length of the original DES keys.

4

Review Questions

1. How many bits must a key be for symmetric encryption to be considered secure by today's standards? _____

2. Which of the following are symmetric encryption algorithms? (Choose all that apply.)

    a. IDEA

    b. RSA

    c. DSA

    d. Blowfish

3. Which of the following statements are true? (Choose all that apply.)

    a. Symmetric encryption uses the same key to encrypt and decrypt data

    b. Asymmetric encryption uses the same key to encrypt and decrypt data

    c. The longer the key used for encryption, the stronger the encryption itself

    d. Triple DES is three times stronger than DES

4. Which symmetric encryption algorithm was designed to be the successor to DES and typically uses 256-bit keys? _____

5. Which of the following statements are true regarding asymmetric encryption between the sender and recipient of data? (Choose two answers.)

    a. Data is typically encrypted by the sender using the recipient's public key

    b. Data is typically encrypted by the sender using the recipient's private key

    c. Data is typically decrypted by the recipient using the recipient's public key

    d. Data is typically decrypted by the recipient using the recipient's private key

6. What is the primary weakness of asymmetric encryption across large networks such as the Internet? _____

7. Which of the following are asymmetric encryption algorithms? (Choose all that apply.)
   a. AES
   b. DES
   c. RSA
   d. Diffie-Hellman

8. Which of the following statements are true regarding the use of digital signatures between the sender and recipient of data? (Choose all that apply.)
   a. A hash of the data is encrypted by the sender using the sender's private key
   b. A hash of the data is encrypted by the sender using the sender's public key
   c. The data hash is decrypted by the recipient using the private key of the sender
   d. The data hash is decrypted by the recipient using the public key of the sender

9. You wish to create a CA within your organization on a SUSE Linux system. What type of CA must you first create? _____

10. What file must you edit within the OpenSSL package to define CA parameters? _____

11. When you generate a public/private key pair for your CA, why are you prompted for a passphrase?
    a. The passphrase is the same password as your user account such that the CA can validate your identity
    b. The passphrase is used to symmetrically encrypt the private key using 3DES
    c. The passphrase is used to validate anyone who wishes to use the public key
    d. The passphrase is used in case you forget your root password when using the CA Management module of YaST

12. When creating a certificate for use with asymmetric encryption, what information is stored within the certificate itself? (Choose all the apply.)
    a. The validity period for the certificate
    b. The serial number of the certificate
    c. The technology that must use the certificate
    d. The distinguished name of the CA that issued the certificate

13. What file in the CA directory lists the certificates that the CA has previously issued?
    a. certs
    b. serial
    c. index.txt
    d. issue

14. A certificate that you have previously issued has been compromised. As a result, you have revoked the certificate on your CA. What must you do now? _____

15. You plan to use GPG to encrypt e-mail attachments between you and a co-worker. Each of you have generated a public/private key pair using the gpg command. What steps must you do next? (Choose two answers.)

   a. Use the gpg command to export your private key to a file and send the file to the other person

   b. Use the gpg command to export your public key to a file and send the file to the other person

   c. Import the private key of the other person using the gpg command

   d. Import the public key of the other person using the gpg command

Discovery Exercises

The Evolution of Modern Cryptography

In this section, you learned of the various symmetric and asymmetric algorithms and technologies used to encrypt data on SUSE Linux systems. However, to put this material in context, you should understand how these technologies established themselves as mainstream cryptography mechanisms.

Using your local public library, read the following book on the history and development of the cryptography mechanisms discussed in this section and summarize your findings in a short memo.

Crypto: How the Code Rebels Beat the Government - Saving Privacy in the Digital Age

by Steven Levy (Viking, New York; 2001)

Exploring Cryptography Technologies

Nearly all technologies today use cryptography mechanisms to protect their data. Using the Internet, research the types of cryptography (asymmetric, symmetric) and the algorithms (DES, RSA, etc.) that are used in the following technologies:

1. Secure Socket Layer (SSL)

2. Smart Cards

3. IP Security (IPSec)

4. Layer 2 Tunneling Protocol (L2TP) Virtual Private Networks (VPNs)

5. Kerberos Authentication

Obtaining Certificates from a Commercial CA

In this section, you configured a Root CA in your organization to issue certificates for use with asymmetric encryption. While this works well for technologies that exist within the organization, it is ill-suited for public technologies such as secure public Web sites using SSL. In those cases, commercial CAs are available to sign certificates for a fee that depends on the certificate's use and validity period.

To request a CA certificate from a commercial CA, you must first generate a public/private key pair and upload the public key to the CA. Once the CA validates your identity, it will digitally sign your public key and create a certificate. You can then download and use this certificate in your technologies. The public keys of all commercial CAs are included with almost all operating systems and Web browsers today. Clients can use these CA public keys (called Trusted Roots) to validate the digital signature on certificates and prove that the certificates were signed by a trusted third party commercial CA.

Most commercial CAs allow you free trial periods for certificates such that you can become familiar with this process. Visit the Verisign commercial CA at *http://www.verisign.com* and request a free trial SSL certificate. Follow their instructions to request and obtain a signed certificate.

Using GPG with Kmail

In this digital age, communication across public networks such as the Internet is very common. Because of this, the need for privacy is also common, and most application programs have the ability to use asymmetric encryption to protect the data they work with.

In this section, you worked with an implementation of asymmetric cryptography called GPG, and used command line utilities to send encrypted messages between the geeko user and the tux user. Using the procedures outlined in this section, configure Kmail to encrypt messages sent between the geeko user and the tux user.

Network Security

When a certain service is being offered to users on the Internet or in the local network, the servers have to be accessible to fulfill their purpose. However, they then are also accessible to people who plan to abuse the service for other purposes, like sending spam, launching distributed denial of service attacks, or gaining access to confidential information. Your task is to prevent abuses while at the same time offering legitimate users all necessary features. This section covers general security aspects of different technologies and protocols. It also discusses general procedures used to secure network services, such as controlling access or using cryptographic means.

Objectives

- Understand Services and Protocols
- Secure Access with TCP Wrapper
- Use SSL to Secure a Service
- Secure Clients

Objective 1—Understand Services and Protocols

Within a network, several different protocols are used to offer all kinds of services. They all have their own security strengths and weaknesses, which are covered briefly in this objective:

- Infrastructure
- Remote Access
- RPC-Based Services
- E-mail
- The World Wide Web
- File Transfer
- Wireless Networks

Infrastructure

Infrastructure refers to services closely associated with running and managing the network itself.

These are:

- DNS
- DHCP
- SNMP
- NTP

DNS DNS (Domain Name System) holds the mapping from names to IP addresses and vice versa. Because of this information, a DNS server is a worthwhile target for a potential attacker, who can create detailed network plans from DNS information.

If someone manages to manipulate address and name allocation in DNS for an attack, an attacker can slip into the role of a friendly system (DNS spoofing) and then possibly be able to use certain services through a firewall (this assumes the firewall relies on name resolution when checking connections). Through DNS spoofing, queries to a Web or mail server can also be diverted to other servers. This is why DNS must be carefully managed.

Care should always be taken that the only information that gets outside is information that is supposed to be there. A DNS server that administers internal zone information and at the same time provides the external zone information is not a good idea—internal DNS and external DNS should remain separate from one another. If you do not want to use two computers, two instances of BIND9 can be started on one computer.

If the Internet connection provides a DMZ for servers that offer services to the outside, the external DNS is positioned inside the DMZ.

DNS servers provide their service on port 53 UDP and TCP. In general, queries from clients are initially made to UDP port 53. The server then answers from UDP port 53 to an unprivileged UDP port (1024 and higher) of the client making the request.

When using a static packet filter, this means all UDP packets with source port 53 addressed to ports 1024 and above have to be allowed.

You can mitigate this by using a stateful packet filter that allows inbound UDP packets only after observing a suitable outbound packet. If you use your own name server as forwarder to the ISP's nameserver, you can create even stricter rules that allow DNS traffic only between your local and the ISP's nameserver. Clients within your network would use your nameserver for name resolution.

If the UDP communication is faulty or down, the DNS protocol makes provisions for an automatic fallback to TCP. While DNS should still function when the high UDP ports are blocked by packet filters, the performance will suffer considerably.

As a remedy to fix the problems of spoofed DNS records, DNSsec was developed. It relies on digitally signed DNS entries and transfers. Due to various unsolved practical aspects, like signing the records of a huge zone like .com, DNSsec is hardly used.

 Configuration of DNS is covered in detail in couse 3074 **SUSE Linux Enterprise Server 10: Networking Services.**

DHCP   DHCP (Dynamic Host Configuration Protocol) ought to be used by every administrator who looks after a network or the computers in a network. It allows you to store, administer, and distribute the network settings (such as IP address, router, and name server) for all clients centrally. Installing a new client means setting DHCP as the default setting for the network interface and everything else will be taken care of automatically each time the machine is rebooted.

DHCP servers should only be reachable from the intranet, because an attacker who accesses the information contained in the DHCP configuration can draw up a very detailed network plan. A DHCP daemon offers its service on UDP port 67 and the client uses port 68; both must be blocked by firewalls to the Internet.

Within the ISC (Internet Systems Consortium, *http://www.isc.org/*) DHCP daemon configuration it is possible to assign host-specific IP addresses based on the MAC address of the network card. Furthermore, it is possible to specify the host name instead of the IP address for a specific host.

This is convenient because, when IP addresses are changed, it is sufficient to maintain the DNS database. The DHCP server will get the corresponding IP addresses for the host name from the DNS server when the DHCP daemon is started. The next time the client requests an IP address, he is assigned the new address.

One danger frequently mentioned in connection with DHCP is the possibility that an intruder could occupy all dynamic addresses of an IP address pool, preventing the clients for which these IP addresses are reserved from reaching the network.

This is a classical denial of service attack. However, it does not work if the clients are assigned their IP addresses depending on their MAC address. Admittedly, MAC address spoofing is also possible, but as an attack it is much less effective—the attacker would have to try too many addresses for his attack to have any effect.

In another scenario, a laptop is connected by a stranger to a data socket in the company and immediately integrated into the network via DHCP without the stranger needing to know anything at all about the network. In this context, it is important to mention that no stranger anywhere in the company should be unaccompanied and able to find a patched data socket to which he could connect a notebook.

If you have a switched network, it is worth thinking about activating port security on the switches so each switch will only accept the same MAC address on the same port.

Configuration of DHCP is covered in detail in couse 3074 **SUSE Linux Enterprise Server 10: Networking Services.**

SNMP   SNMP (Simple Network Management Protocol) (ports 161 and 162) controls various network components—computers, routers, switches, etc. SNMP collects status information, such as configuration or network traffic information, from these devices. It can also be used to change the configuration of these devices, making network management much easier.

The main issue with SNMP is that the widely used version 1 uses no encryption and no authentication. Access depends on the knowledge of the so-called community string, which for read access in many cases is the string "public." Depending on the circumstances, the leaked information might be sensitive. Write access is usually secured with a different community string, but this string is transmitted in cleartext in version 1. Version 3 is much more secure, but not yet in wide-spread use.

Due to these properties of SNMP, it must be blocked at the firewall and can only be used within local networks considered secure.

NTP   NTP (Network Time Protocol) ensures that all computers have the correct time, which is received from an authoritative time source, such as an atomic clock, GPS, or a time server on the Internet.

Various services require synchronized time between computers to function properly. Some depend on it for proper function, like Novell eDirectory, or remote authentication using time-based tokens. Others need it to enforce rules, like allowed logon hours. Having the same time on all machines is also necessary to be able to match events in log files on different computers.

If any of these services are critical for you, then NTP is critical, too. To prevent bogus time sources from changing time settings in your network, ntpd servers can be authenticated using keys.

Configuration of NTP daemon is covered in detail in couse 3073 **SUSE Linux Enterprise Server 10 Advanced Administration.**

Remote Access

In remote access, several techniques are used to access one computer from another, either to log in or to run single commands.

The most common are:

- Telnet
- r-Tools
- SSH

Telnet Telnet provides terminal access to a machine. The user is prompted for a user name and password which are both transmitted in cleartext. The same holds true for the ensuing communication between client and server.

Because cleartext passwords should be avoided as much as possible, disable Telnet on all machines.

If you have to offer telnet for some reason, consider implementing one-time passwords. However, this does not protect the session itself.

r-Tools The r-Tools provide a functionality similar to telnet plus the execution of single commands without a terminal on the remote machine and the copying of files. Under certain circumstances (appropriate entries in the file /etc/hosts.equiv or in a user's ~/.rhosts file), it is not even required to enter a password. All transmissions are unencrypted.

Due to the lack of any security mechanism worth mentioning, the r-Tools should not be used.

SSH SSH (Secure Shell) can and should replace telnet and the r-Tools in any network. It allows you to log in to other hosts and to execute commands (ssh), as well as the secure copying of files (scp). An interface similar to a command line ftp client is also available (sftp).

ssh has many features and options, including:

- Authentication using user name and password or public/private keys
- X11 forwarding
- Port forwarding

ssh is a very powerful tool. You should be aware that it can be used to tunnel practically anything through your firewall. It requires a computer in the Internet where you have ssh access. If your corporate security policy forbids accessing certain Web sites, a user with access to ssh could enter a command like the following:

```
geeko@da10:~> ssh -L 8080:blocked-site.example.com:80
athome.example.net
```

If she then enters in the address field of the browser *http://localhost:8080/* it will bring up the Web pages of blocked-site.example.com. With the option -D *port*, ssh works as a socks proxy.

```
geeko@da10:~> ssh -D 8080 athome.example.net
```

Configuring the browser to use `localhost` **port** as socks proxy allows access to any Website that can be accessed from the computer the ssh tunnel ends on, no matter what the local firewall rules state. In case port 22 is blocked on the firewall, this works through an HTTPS proxy as well, as explained in "Use Squid to Tunnel Connections."

In short, ssh can be used by internal users to overcome most of the restrictions a firewall puts on them. As long as you allow HTTPS and ssh is available, you usually cannot absolutely enforce your limits, short of completely crippling your Internet access.

If your security policy allows internal users to access only a limited number of services on the Internet, you will have to educate your users on the consequences of violating the security policy (including the possible consequences for their employment if there are any); beyond that, you will have to trust them.

The configuration of the ssh daemon and the ssh client is covered in detail in course 3072 **SUSE Linux Enterprise Server 10 Administration.**

RPC-Based Services

Sun's RPC (Remote Procedure Calls) protocol underlies various services, like:

- NIS
- NFS

The portmap daemon plays a central role for RPC services. When an RPC-based server starts, it binds to a port and registers its service and port with the portmapper. A client that wants to connect to a server first connects to the portmapper (port 111) to find out the port of the server. In a second step, it connects to the server itself.

Except for NFS, which usually runs on port 2049, the ports used by RPC-based services are more or less random.

Any host can query the services offered by a server using the command `rpcinfo`. To hide this information from a potential attacker as well as to protect the RPC-based services and their weaknesses, the portmapper, NIS, NFS, and other RPC-based services should never be offered to the Internet and their ports should be blocked on the firewall.

Access to the portmapper can be controlled by TCP wrapper and the files /etc/hosts.allow and /etc/hosts.deny.

NIS NIS (Network Information Service) is used to distribute various databases over the network to the clients. Among these are files like /etc/hosts and /etc/services, but also the files /etc/passwd and /etc/shadow. This allows central user administration, but the password hashes are transmitted over the network. `ypcat passwd` allows you to view the hashes and a password cracker like John (*http://www.openwall.com/john/*) allows dictionary attacks on them.

If you use NIS at all, block it on the firewall. It is best to replace NIS with an LDAP server secured by SSL.

NFS NFS (Network File System) is very common in Linux/UNIX environments. It is possible to limit on the server which clients can access the file system exported by NFS based on the IP of the client, but beyond that there is no authentication.

NFS uses port 2049, but other components of NFS (like nlockmgr and mountd) use random ports. You should limit access to these ports to internal hosts with the firewall blocking any NFS-related traffic.

On the NFS client side, we recommend that you do not trust an NFS server blindly; instead, take the following precautionary measures.

- NFS mounts should always be mounted with the `nosuid` option.

    SUID programs installed on network drives are then much less threatening. nosuid is especially important if the NFS server is administered by another administrator who does not have root permissions on your own systems. She could obtain root privileges on the client via an SUID program installed on the server as root and run as a normal user on the client.

- NFS clients are made even more secure if the remote file systems are mounted with the option `noexec`, because then no programs can be started from the network drive.

    However, this might not always be practical, for example, when the directories /opt or /usr are mounted via the network. In these cases you will have to mount them without noexec.

The essential factor on the NFS server side is the decision whether root on the NFS client is trusted.

- Because no normally maintained system, whether it is a Linux or non-Linux one, can keep normal users away from root privileges with absolute certainty, assume that a user can obtain root privileges without the knowledge of the administrator. root on clients is therefore fundamentally not trusted and, with NFS accesses to NFS servers, root is degraded to the user nobody by means of the option `root_squash` in the file /etc/exports on the server.

- A user who has illegally become root cannot be prevented from assuming every available user ID on the client by using the command su *username*. In certain cases (for example, on installation servers), it makes sense to convert all users to nobody by means of the option `all_squash`.

E-mail

E-mail is one of the most complex services to administer. Several components have to work together to ensure e-mail is delivered properly, errors are cared for, and no mail is lost.

Several protocols and programs are involved:

- SMTP
- POP3 and IMAP
- GPG/PGP

SMTP   SMTP (Simple Mail Transfer Protocol) is used to get e-mail from the mail client to the mail server and from one mail server to the next until the mail server in charge of the recipient's mail is reached. SMTP is a cleartext protocol that does not, at least in its simple form, include authentication. There is no check of the sender's identity—anyone can impersonate anyone.

In the early days of the Internet this was adequate; it even provided some protection from breakdowns. If one mail server was down, another could take over the load. Due to these characteristics, this service is easily abused by spammers. In the past they mainly used open relays, mail servers that accept mail from anyone to anyone, to send their unsavory e-mail.

To solve the obvious problems, several measures were taken. ISPs developed SMTP after POP, allowing customers to send mail only after fetching mail from their account with a user name and password. Furthermore the SMTP protocol was extended to allow authentication with a user name and password. This has now widely replaced the SMTP-after-POP mechanism. Open relays are now usually put on black lists and their administrators are urged to administer their machines properly.

These various actions took care of the open relays, but the spammers found other ways to fill the mailboxes with junk. Today probably most of the spam is sent from home computers infected by worms and under the control of someone else other than the owner.

Thousands of computers form a botnet with a combined bandwidth that is impressive. While these botnets are mostly composed of home computers, this does not mean that the administrator of a corporate network can relax.

Desktop computers can become infected as well, by a virus that comes via e-mail or some infected notebook that is connected to the internal corporate network. Spam sent from a corporate network can be embarrassing and even cause legal problems.

While you might not be able to guarantee such an infection is never going to happen in the network you are in charge of, you can at least prevent the propagation of such viruses or worms. You can:

- Block packets with destination port 25 from the internal network to the Internet.

  Because some ISPs block outgoing traffic to port 25 (with the exception of the ISPs mailserver) for the same reason, your external staff might not be able to access the corporate mail server to send mail while they are travelling. Due to this, you should consider offering SMTP services for them on the submission port (587) and/or SMTPS port (465).

- Use authentication even on your internal mail servers.

- Use TLS and authentication for the e-mail servers accessible from the Internet.

- Use antivirus software on the mail server and the desktops.

- Educate your end users not to open attachments indiscriminately.

POP3 and IMAP   POP3 (Post Office Protocol Version 3) (port 110) and IMAP (Internet Message Access Protocol) (port 143) are used by the recipient to access mail that has been delivered to the destination mail server.

While POP just copies the mail to the client machine (and usually deletes it on the server), mail usually stays on the mail server when the protocol IMAP is being used.

The main issue with both protocols is that the user name and password are transmitted in cleartext. This gives an eavesdropper the opportunity to sniff both. The connection can be secured with TLS (POP3S port 995, IMAPS port 993). Adding TLS (Transport Layer Security) encryption to POP3 is covered later in this section, in the objective Objective 3 Use SSL to Secure a Service. IMAP can be secured in the same way.

GPG/PGP Even if you secure the transmission of the e-mail between server and client, this has no effect on the mail message itself. The communication between mail servers in the Internet is unencrypted, as is the mail while it is waiting on the mail server to be picked up. The solution to this is end-to-end encryption, using GPG or PGP. GPG was covered in the previous section, "GNU Privacy Guard (GPG)" on page 104.

The World Wide Web

For many people, World Wide Web and Internet are synonymous. The popularity of the Internet can largely be attributed to the World Wide Web.

From a security standpoint, you must look at both sides:

- WWW Server
- WWW Client

WWW Server Web servers are a very popular target for several reasons:

- Defacing the main page of a company brings fame to the hacker and embarrassment to the affected company.

- Installing content on Web servers, like manipulated graphic files, that exploit vulnerabilities of client browsers allows criminals to get control of the client computers of those visiting the Web site.

- E-commerce sites are built on databases that contain personal information on their customers, often including credit card details. These are very valuable targets for criminals.

    The information gathered can then be used to abuse the credit card details or to impersonate the customers by using their identity information. In 2005, hundreds of thousands of credit card numbers were stolen. To make things worse, the companies involved often choose to not inform the affected customers to avoid the loss of confidence in their business practices and IT security.

Web servers have shown various vulnerabilities in the past. All commonly used servers (Apache, IIS, and others) were affected at one time or another to some degree. Sometimes it's not the Web server itself that is at fault, but extensions like CGI scripts or extensions or modules like PHP.

WWW Client Clients are a valuable target, too, for various reasons:

- Most home computers are not administered professionally and an intrusion might remain undetected for a longer period of time.

- Personal information (such as financial information and passcodes) that can be abused could be stored on such workstations.

- By controlling thousands of home computers with DSL connectivity, an enormous bandwidth can be harnessed for dubious means, like spamming, or distributed denial of service attacks.

There are vulnerabilities in browsers that allow a program to be installed on a computer without the user doing more than just visiting a Web site. Microsoft's Internet Explorer has gained some notoriety in this respect, but other browsers like Mozilla, Firefox, and Opera have not been immune either.

The programs installed can be anything the criminal behind the attack deems useful. It could be a key logger to gain access to passwords, a backdoor combined with an SMTP engine to send spam, or whatever else he dreams up.

Features, like ActiveX, Java, and JavaScript, can also pose a threat. ActiveX controls are basically programs like any other that run with the privileges of the user running the browser. On Microsoft Windows systems, the user is frequently logged in as administrator, which means that an ActiveX program is not restricted at all. Java and JavaScript have more restrictions regarding what they are allowed to do on a computer, but there were instances in the past of security issues as well.

There is a rather new attack that falls more in the category of social engineering, combining e-mail and the Web: Mail allegedly from a bank, eBay, Paypal, etc., is sent to users, asking them to enter confidential information into some form. However, the form is a fake page that looks like the real one, but resides on some other server. With the information gathered, the criminal tries to loot the account of the user.

Keeping the software on the client computers up to date and educating the users has to be part of the security concept.

File Transfer

Files can be transferred by many different methods. The popular methods are:

- FTP
- Peer-to-Peer Networking

Other methods include, but are not limited to, TFTP (Trivial File Transfer Protocol) and SMB (Server Message Blocks).

FTP FTP (File Transfer Protocol) differs from many protocols, because it uses two connections: The control connection from a high port of the client to port 21 of the server and from port 20 of the server back to a high port of the client (active FTP) or from a high port of the client to a high port of the server (passive FTP).

Active FTP makes the task of protecting the client more difficult. When a rule on the firewall blocks all incoming connection requests, active FTP is not feasible. To allow it, the firewall would have to permit connections from port 20 to high ports of the clients, making all upper ports accessible from port 20.

To solve that issue, passive FTP was developed. With passive FTP the FTP administrator now has a similar problem, as he has to allow connections from any high port to any high port. However, protecting the clients is easier with passive FTP. Browsers "speak" the FTP protocol and use passive FTP.

FTP is widely used for all kinds of file transfers over the Internet. When a company offers drivers, software, or other large binary files, it is usually done by FTP. FTP checks the user name and password, and both are transmitted in cleartext. FTP with SSL support is rarely used; however, ssh offers an FTP-like interface to transfer files securely.

To transfer files without an account, anonymous FTP is used. In this case the user name is *ftp* or **anonymous** and the password is the e-mail address, which is usually not verified. From a security perspective it is important to not allow anonymous uploads and downloads of the same files. Such servers soon get abused to exchange all kinds of illegal files, from music, videos, and pornography to illegal software copies. By the same token it is mandatory to keep the server and its FTP (and other) software up to date, as a hacked server can be abused for the same purpose.

Peer-to-Peer Networking Peer-to-peer networking has become very popular over the past years. It is controversial because most of the files transferred are, according to the music and film industry, illegal copies of music and videos.

On the other hand, there are valuable uses of peer-to-peer networking, like the distribution of ISO images via BitTorrent in the Open Source community.

To keep out of any legal battles, it is advisable for most companies to block peer-to-peer networking on the firewall. Because peer-to-peer networking can also use up bandwidth, it is also economical to block it. Another negative aspect of peer-to-peer networking involves letting unknown peers access files on your computer, which might also violate the security policy. Viruses and worms have spread in the past via peer-to-peer networks as well.

Wireless Networks

WLANs do not really fit in the category of protocols and services because they concern the link layer. However, as their use becomes more and more widespread, their security implications have to be looked at.

The original standard, IEEE 802.11b, included Wired Equivalent Privacy (WEP) to secure the communication. Due to major flaws in the implementation it is possible to defeat the encryption if you capture enough WLAN packets. Depending on the traffic, this number can be reached within a few hours. Due to improvements in the tools to regain the key, this time has been reduced to minutes under certain circumstances.

 A tool used for this purpose is AirSnort, *http://airsnort.shmoo.com/*.

Despite the fact that WEP is no longer secure, several devices still available on the market support only WEP. If you have to use a wireless LAN where only WEP is available, always use additional encryption, like IPSec for all connections, or SSL to protect specific ones.

The IEEE extended the original standard, now called Wi-Fi Protected Access (WPA, and WPA2). It is considered secure, with the only currently known attack being a brute force attack on the key.

Objective 2—Secure Access with TCP Wrapper

The first and foremost measure to take to secure a service against unintended use is to keep the software up to date, as was covered in "Apply Security Updates" on page 29.

There are other general measures that make it harder for a potential attacker to gain control over the machine:

- Minimal software installation.
- No user logins on computers such as Web and mail servers that users do not need to access.
- Hard-to-guess root password that includes upper case and lower case letters, numbers, and special characters, with a minimum length of eight characters.
- Intelligent partitioning of the hard disks and restrictive file system permissions.

These were covered in Section 2, "Host Security" on page 21, and are part of general system administration. Beyond those general measures, you can limit access to a service to limit the number of potential attackers. While the public Web site of a company usually should be accessible from everywhere, it might be possible to limit the hosts from which access to other services is allowed.

Access to individual network services can be restricted with the help of the TCP wrapper. For standalone services, TCP wrapper support must be compiled into the daemon, service, or application. For services started via xinetd, TCP wrapper support is part of xinetd.

To configure TCP wrapper, you need to understand the following:

- The Role of the TCP Daemon
- Configure Access Controls
- Check the TCP Wrapper
- Moles and Trappers

The Role of the TCP Daemon

The TCP wrapper /usr/sbin/tcpd in the case of inetd, or the library libwrap.so.0 in the case of xinetd and programs compiled with TCP wrapper support, acts as a filter and is placed between xinetd or the respective service daemons.

The wrapper checks if the connection is allowed. If it is, the actual service is started. If not, the wrapper writes the name and address of the host requesting the connection to a log file, usually /var/log/messages and, in the case of xinetd, also to /var/log/xinetd.log.

The command ldd can be used to find out if a program is linked against libwrap, as in the following example:

```
da10:~ # ldd /usr/sbin/xinetd
        linux-gate.so.1 =>  (0xffffe000)
        libwrap.so.0 => /lib/libwrap.so.0 (0xb7ee3000)
        libnsl.so.1 => /lib/libnsl.so.1 (0xb7ece000)
        libm.so.6 => /lib/libm.so.6 (0xb7ea9000)
        libcrypt.so.1 => /lib/libcrypt.so.1 (0xb7e76000)
        libc.so.6 => /lib/libc.so.6 (0xb7d56000)
        /lib/ld-linux.so.2 (0xb7f00000)
```

When the connection between the client and the server program is established, the wrapper is deleted from memory and does not create any additional load for the current connection.

However, after an authorized server has started, in some cases it can accept additional connections on its own without consulting the wrapper about whether additional connections should take place. For example, some UDP services remain in memory for a short time after the connection has already been closed in order to receive additional connection requests. These services usually can be recognized by having wait = yes as part of their xinetd configuration.

The configuration of xinetd is covered in course 3073 **SUSE Linux Enterprise Server 10 Advanced Administration.**

Configure Access Controls

You can configure access controls for the TCP wrapper by editing /etc/hosts.allow (for permitted requests) and /etc/hosts.deny (for denied requests).

When receiving a request, tcpd first reads /etc/hosts.allow. If no matching pattern is found, tcpd then reads /etc/hosts.deny.

If you allow access in /etc/hosts.allow, it cannot be restricted again in /etc/hosts.deny.

If tcpd does not find a pattern that matches the request in either of the configuration files, the connection is permitted. The same is true if one or both configuration files are empty or do not exist.

The syntax of both configuration files is the same and consists of the following three fields: *daemon: host [: option : option . . .].*

- *daemon*—The executable of the daemon without its path, like sshd, in.telnetd, vsftpd.
  Note: Because vsftpd is not linked against libwrap, /etc/hosts.allow and /etc/hosts.deny have no effect on ftp connection requests when vsftpd runs as a standalone daemon (without xinetd).

- *host*—A list of host names, IP addresses, subnets, or domains, separated by commas.

- *option*—A list of options.

In addition, tcpd recognizes the keywords ALL and EXCEPT for both the host and option fields, and LOCAL, KNOWN, UNKNOWN, and PARANOID for the host field.

Table 5-1 provides a description of these keywords.

Keyword	Description
ALL	All services and all hosts; exceptions can be defined by EXCEPT.
LOCAL	All host names that do not have a dot in the name—usually all the host names defined in /etc/hosts.
UNKNOWN	All hosts whose names tcpd cannot verify.
KNOWN	All hosts in which the host name matches the given IP address and vice versa.
PARANOID	All hosts in which the host name does not match the given IP address and vice versa.

Table 5-1

The following examples show configurations for hosts.allow and hosts.deny that permit the use of all network services in the local network but deny external computers access to telnet, finger, and ftp:

- `/etc/hosts.allow`:

  `ALL: LOCAL`

- `/etc/hosts.deny`:

  `in.telnetd, in.fingerd, vsftpd: ALL`

The following is an example of a more complex configuration:

- `/etc/hosts.allow`:

  ```
  ALL: da10.digitalairlines.com
  ALL EXCEPT vsftpd: da20.digitalairlines.com
  vsftpd: da30.digitalairlines.com
  ```

- `/etc/hosts.deny`:

  `ALL: ALL`

The first line in /etc/hosts.allow ensures that all network services can be accessed from da10.digitalairlines.com. In the second line, all network services other than ftp are made available for da20.digitalairlines.com. The third line ensures that only ftp transfers are possible from the host da30.digitalairlines.com.

In /etc/hosts.deny, all other hosts are denied all services. ALL also includes services that are not started via xinetd but are run as independent services, and whose access control is also implemented via the files /etc/hosts.allow and /etc/hosts.deny. Because this applies, for instance, to the portmapper, NFS and NIS would also be affected by the above configuration—a possibly unexpected and unwanted effect, which, if you do not consider it, could lead to a long search for the cause of errors. Another example is sshd, which is also linked against libwrap.

If you require more specific control functions, Table 5-2 lists some of the more commonly used keywords for monitoring access.

Keyword	Description
ALLOW or DENY	You can use these keywords to summarize all the access rules in the file /etc/hosts.allow. These options allow or refuse access, respectively.
spawn	Runs the given shell script after the placeholders shown in Table 5-3 are replaced.
twist	The given command is started instead of the daemon specified in the first field. Existing placeholders are replaced first.
rfc931 [timeout]	Identifies users attempting to establish a connection. For this, a client-side RFC931-compatible daemon is required. If the daemon is not present, it can lead to delays in setting up the connection. If no value is given for timeout, the default value (10 sec.) is used.
banners /directory	Searches in /directory for a file whose name matches the daemon to be started. If such a file is found, its contents will be sent to the client after the placeholders have been expanded.
nice [number]	The server process is started with the corresponding nice value. This can be useful to make more resources available to other server processes.
setenv name value	Defines environment variables for the server process. Here, too, a placeholder expansion is executed.

Table 5-2

The following example in /etc/hosts.allow allows telnet access from anywhere:

```
in.telnetd: ALL: banners /etc/tcpd: ALLOW
```

If a file in.telnetd is located in the /etc/tcpd/ directory, its contents will be sent to the client before the telnet service is started.

In the following example, finger is only allowed in the local network:

```
in.fingerd: ALL EXCEPT LOCAL: banners /etc/tcpd: spawn ( echo "finger
request from %h" | mail -s "finger!!" root ) & : DENY
```

Clients not listed in /etc/hosts with their name only (no dots in the hostname) cannot access the finger daemon; they are given the information contained in the /etc/tcpd/in.fingerd file instead. An e-mail to root is generated that contains the host name or IP address of the computer making this request.

The following example starts the ftp daemons with a nice value of 15:

```
vsftpd: ALL: nice 15
```

This enables you to influence the load on a server, for instance, by allocating more resources to other services.

In the following example, the command echo "No one logged in" is started instead of the finger daemon:

```
in.fingerd: ALL: twist ( echo "No one logged in" )
```

The client is informed that no one is logged in.

For more information on these and other options, enter
`man 5 hosts_access` and `man hosts_options`.

Check the TCP Wrapper

Because a command's flexibility can easily lead to configuration errors, you cannot just hope that your network services are secure without testing the configuration first.

The TCP wrapper package offers some tools for troubleshooting as well as for error analysis. However, these only work together with /etc/inetd.conf. xinetd is not supported.

You can review the configuration of tcpd using the `tcpdchk` command. This program reports a multitude of possible problems; these might be network services listed in /etc/inetd.conf that do not really exist, syntax errors in the configuration files, or unknown host names.

However, there are some configurations in which tcpdchk does not find any errors but where tcpd still does not act as expected. In such cases, you can use `tcpdmatch` to provide information about how tcpd would handle various types of access attempts.

With xinetd, you have to test your configuration by actually establishing various connections to see if they are accepted or denied as expected.

Moles and Trappers

You can enter shell commands in the configuration files, which will be executed when the request matches one of the patterns defined in the daemon and host fields.

Because tcpd recognizes the following placeholders that can be used in shell scripts, attempts at accessing certain services can be monitored, as shown in Table 5-3.

Placeholder	Description
%a	IP address of the host making the request.
%c	Information about the host making the request (such as user@host and user@address), depending on the information available.
%d	Name of the daemon.
%h	Name of the host making the request or the IP address, if the name cannot be determined.
%n	Name of the host making the request, unknown, or paranoid.
%p	The process ID of the daemon.
%s	Information about the server (such as daemon@host and daemon@address), depending on the information available.
%u	User name on the host making the request or unknown if the remote host does not possess a user ID as recognized by RFC 931.

Table 5-3

The following example shows a script in the configuration file /etc/hosts.allow that records all successful access attempts to all services in a log file:

```
ALL: ALL: spawn echo "Access of %u@%h to %d" >> \
/var/log/net.log
```

A finger client (/usr/sbin/safe_finger) is also included in the TCP wrapper to provide better protection against defense measures that other computers might have in store when their finger daemons are queried. The idea behind safe_finger is to entrap (using simple methods) possible intruders by uncovering their identities with a `fingerd` query, such as the following:

```
ALL EXCEPT in.fingerd : ALL EXCEPT LOCAL : \
twist /usr/sbin/safe_finger -l @%h >> \
/var/log/unknown.net.log
```

In this example, all query results of access attempts to any network service taking place outside the network, other than finger, are stored in a log file.

Excluding finger itself from this screening process is a measure of caution. If such a trap including finger were set up remotely as well, an endless loop could result, where the finger query of one computer would be followed by a finger query of the other in an endless cycle. The workability of this approach is limited, as few computers have a finger server running these days; the finger server is needed to get an entry in the log file.

Exercise 5-1: Configure the TCP Wrapper

Objective: In this exercise, you configure the TCP wrapper and work with a partner to test each other's configuration. The exercise consists of three parts.

Description: In the first part, install vsftpd and configure xinetd to start vsftpd when ftp connections are made. Then configure the TCP wrapper to prevent ftp connections from your partner's computer while allowing others to connect.

In the second part of the exercise, configure a twist using echo, so that anyone trying to connect receives the message: This service is not accessible from *ip_address*.

In the third part, configure logging using spawn, logging *IP_address* accessed *service* to /var/log/service-access.log.

Detailed Steps to Complete this Exercise

- Part I: Secure the FTP Service
- Part II: Configure a Twist
- Part III: Configure Logging

Part I: Secure the FTP Service

Do the following:

1. Open a terminal window and su – to the root user.

2. Install the package vsftpd by entering yast –i vsftpd.

3. Open the file /etc/xinetd.d/vsftpd with a text editor. Make sure the line disable = yes starts with a # character. Save and close the file.

4. Open the file /etc/vsftpd.conf with a text editor and make sure the parameter listen is set to NO. Save and close the file.

5. Restart xinetd with the command rcxinetd restart.

6. Open the file /etc/hosts.deny in a text editor. Add the following to the end of the file:

   vsftpd : *IP_of_partner*

   Save the file.

7. Have your partner attempt to ftp to your system; then have another student in the classroom attempt to ftp to your host.
   The connection for your partner is closed. However, others can ftp to your server.

8. Place a comment character (#) in front of the line you just added to the file /etc/hosts.deny; then add the following line:

   ALL : ALL

   Save the file and close the editor.

9. Open the file /etc/hosts.allow in a text editor.
   Add the following to the end of the file:

   vsftpd : ALL EXCEPT *IP-of-partner*

   Save and close the file.

10. Have your partner try to ftp to the system; then have another student in the classroom attempt to ftp to your host.
    The results should be the same as in Step 7.

Part II: Configure a Twist

Do the following:

1. Open a terminal window and su to the root user.

2. Edit the ALL:ALL line in /etc/hosts.deny to reflect the following (on one line):

   ALL: ALL: twist (echo "This service is not accessible from %a!")

3. Save and close the file.

4. Have your partner try to ftp to the system to verify that the message is sent.

Part III: Configure Logging

Do the following:

1. Open a terminal window and su to the root user.

2. At the bottom of the file /etc/hosts.allow, change the "vsftpd" line to reflect the following (on one line):

   ```
   vsftpd : ALL : spawn (echo "%a accessed %s" >> /var/log/service-
   access.log)
   ```

3. Save and close the file.

4. Have your partner attempt to ftp to the system to verify that the entry is logged in /var/log/service-access.log.

5. Verify that all of the activity to the services under xinetd have been logged in /var/log/xinetd.log by entering:

   ```
   cat /var/log/xinetd.log.
   ```

6. Remove (or put comment signs in front of) all of the lines you added in /etc/hosts.allow and /etc/hosts.deny to prevent unexpected effects in later exercises in this course.

Objective 3—Use SSL to Secure a Service

SSL (Secure Sockets Layer) and its successor, TLS (Transport Layer Security), can be used to provide encryption for cleartext protocols. Most frequently, SSL is used to secure HTTP traffic as HTTPS. But any other protocol that uses a single communication channel, like POP3, SMTP, or IMAP, can be protected as well.

While many server daemons support encryption natively (like Postfix or OpenLDAP), others can be secured using stunnel.

 Do not use stunnel to secure SMTP. Use the STARTTLS functionality available within Postfix itself instead.

The example used here is the protocol POP3 and the POP server from the package qpopper. But the same procedure can be applied when securing IMAP or other services that use a single connection for their communication.

POP3 uses cleartext passwords for authentication. The SSL tunnel protects the password as well as the data traffic from being read by eavesdroppers. There is no need to change the POP3 server. The package stunnel provides all that is needed to secure POP3 with SSL.

SSL needs a certificate for the server that contains the public key and the name of the server. It is used by the client to authenticate the server. While it is possible to also authenticate the client with a certificate, it is usually not done. But you could, as an example, limit HTTPS access to a Web server to clients that have a certificate and corresponding private key issued by your CA.

The creation of a RootCA and of certificates is covered in "Create a Certification Authority (CA) and Issue Certificates with CLI Tools" on page 87 and "Create a Certification Authority (CA) and Issue Certificates with YaST" on page 96, respectively.

On the server side you need the private key and the certificate containing the public key. Depending on the application, the private key can be encrypted (for instance, when using it with Apache) or it can be unencrypted (for instance, when using it with stunnel).

If you used the OpenSSL command line interface, you specified the files for the keys on the command line. To create an unencrypted copy of the private key, use the following command:

```
openssl rsa < private/encrypted_key.pem \
                    > private/unencrypted_key.pem
```

If you created the certificate within the YaST CA Management module, you need to export the certificate and the private key from the module to a file. YaST exports the certificate and private key in one single file. Within the export dialog, you can choose the format and whether or not the private key will be encrypted. When exporting the keys for use with stunnel, export them without encrypting the private key. Transfer them to the server using a floppy disk, USB stick, or ssh.

Because the private key is unencrypted, only root and the stunnel process may be able to read the file on the server:

```
da10:~ # cp /media/floppy/pop3servercert.pem /etc/stunnel/stunnel.pem
da10:~ # chmod 600 /etc/stunnel/stunnel.pem
```

The configuration /etc/stunnel/stunnel.conf needs the following entries (note the missing comment signs in front of line 58 and 59):

```
13  #chroot = /var/lib/stunnel/
14  #setuid = stunnel
15  #setgid = nogroup
    ...
58  [pop3s]
59  accept  = 995
60  # connect = 110
    exec = /usr/sbin/popper
    execargs = popper -s
```

In our scenario, the first three lines above need a comment sign. To run stunnel in a change root jail would require copying additional files to the jail for it to still be able to call the POP server. And stunnel needs to call the pop server as root so that the POP server can validate the passwords.

The next lines activate POP3S. A connection on port 995 is handed over to the POP server popper (package qpopper). Most of the lines are already prepared in the configuration file.

After starting stunnel, stunnel accepts encrypted connections on port 995 and hands the decrypted text over to popper.

However, when you connect to the server now with a mail client such as Kmail, there will be the error message shown in Figure 5-1.

Figure 5-1

Selecting `Details` reveals that Kmail cannot verify the validity of the certificate offered by the server. See Figure 5-2.

Figure 5-2

To verify the validity, which is needed to avoid connecting to a bogus site claiming to be your target server, the certificates of all CAs in the certification hierarchy are required. These include the certificate of the Root CA and the certificates of any SubCA.

Again, where you find these certificates depends on how you created your certification authority. When using OpenSSL command line interface, you specified the file name in the openssl command when you created the Root CA. When using the YaST CA management module, you have to export the Root CA certificate from that module.

By selecting Cryptography Configuration and then selecting the tab SSL Signers and Import, as shown in Figure 5-3, the CA certificates are then imported into Kmail.

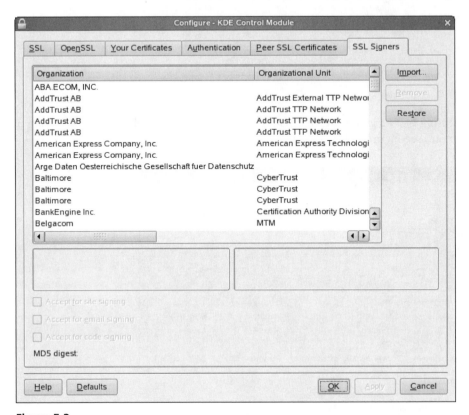

Figure 5-3

Once this has been done, the server's certificate is validated using the certificates of the CAs and, if there is no error, such as a host name mismatch, the connection to the server is established.

Exercise 5-2: Use stunnel to Secure POP3 with SSL

Time Required: 50 minutes

Objective: The purpose of this exercise is to practice securing a service with stunnel.

Description: Install the packages stunnel, qpopper and kdepim3 (the latter contains kmail). Create a root CA and create a certificate for your server, unless you have already done so as part of earlier exercises. Configure stunnel to protect POP3 traffic, using the POP3S port 995. Use Kmail to test your setup.

Detailed Steps to Complete this Exercise

1. Open a terminal window and su - to root using a password of novell.

2. Install the packages stunnel, qpopper, and kmail by entering:

   ```
   yast -i stunnel qpopper kdepim3
   ```

   Insert the appropriate media when requested.

3. Use a certificate and its corresponding private key created in Exercise 4-1, "Create a Root CA and Certificates on the Command Line" on page 93.
   You need to create a copy of the private key that is not secured with a passphrase:

   ```
   cd /root/daxx-CA
   openssl rsa < private/daxx_key.pem \
   > private/daxx_key-unenc.pem
   ```

   Copy the certificate and the private key into a single file where stunnel expects them:

   ```
   cat certs/daxx_cert.pem private/daxx_key-unenc.pem \
   > /etc/stunnel/stunnel.pem
   ```

   Also copy the RootCA certificate to the directory /tmp:

   ```
   cp /root/daxx-CA/daxx-cacert.pem /tmp/
   ```

4. (Conditional—if you completed Step 3, you don't need to do this one.)
   You can also use the certificate and private key created in Exercise 4-2, "(optional) Create a Root CA and Certificates with YaST" on page 104.
   Export them to /etc/stunnel/stunnel.pem, selecting Certificate and Key Unencrypted in PEM Format in the Export dialog.
   Also export the RootCA certificate and save it in the directory /tmp.

5. Limit access to the file /etc/stunnel/stunnel.pem by entering:

   ```
   chmod 600 /etc/stunnel/stunnel.pem
   ```

6. Using vi, modify the configuration of stunnel in the file /etc/stunnel/stunnel.conf to reflect the following entries (some lines need a comment symbol #, some need the comment symbol deleted (lines 58 and 59), and other lines need to be added—you have to look through the file to find the lines):

   ```
    13  #chroot = /var/lib/stunnel/
    14  #setuid = stunnel
    15  #setgid = nogroup
        ...
    58  [pop3s]
    59  accept  = 995
    60  # connect = 110
   (add)  exec = /usr/sbin/popper
   (add)  execargs = popper -s
   ```

7. Start stunnel by entering `rcstunnel start`.

   If there are any error messages, correct your configuration accordingly.

8. Test your POP server by configuring Kmail as geeko to pick up mail using POP3. The POP3 server is your computer da*xx*.digitalairlines.com, port 995.

   To configure Kmail, access the configuration via `Settings > Configure Kmail`.

   Select `Identities` and `Modify`, fill in appropriate values and select OK. Select `Accounts`, the `Receiving` tab, Add, `Account Type POP3`.

   Make sure that you use the `full hostname` (da*xx*.digitalairlines.com) in the host field, not just localhost, and port 995 in the Port field.

   Select the `Extras` tab and select `Use SSL for secure mail download`. Select OK twice.

   When finished with the configuration, actually try to pick up mail. You should see an error message that the server certificate failed the authenticity test.

9. Do not accept the certificate at this point by selecting Continue, but select `Details`.

10. In the dialog opening up, you should see a line stating "Certificate signing authority is unknown or invalid." Select Cryptography configuration at the bottom of the dialog.

11. Select the `SSL signers` tab; then select `Import`.

    Change directory to /tmp and choose the CA certificate suitable for the stunnel certificate, either the OpenSSL or the YaST one. Select `Open`.

12. A pop-up window opens up, asking if you want to make this certificate available in Kmail as well. Confirm by selecting `Make Available`.

    You are returned to the Cryptography configuration dialog. Scrolling through the list of Organizations you should find Digitalairlines listed amongst them.

13. Close this dialog by selecting `OK`; then close the KDE SSL Information dialog by selecting `Close`.

14. A Kleopatra window and a "Certificate Import Result - Kleopatra" dialog opens up. Select `OK` and close the Kleopatra window.

15. Leave the Server Authentication Dialog by selecting `Cancel`. Close the pop-up window informing you that you couldn't connect to da*xx*.digitalairlines.com as well as Kmail.

16. Open Kmail again and connect again to your mailbox.

    You should not get the same error message again, since the certificate can now be validated by the mail program.

    You might get a message that the certificate does not belong to the server if the common name in the certificate differs from the host name you contacted. In this case, you might want to create a new certificate with the correct name.

Objective 4—Secure Clients

Today it is not enough to secure the servers in a corporate network. The clients are no longer just a target of viruses. Despite a firewall worms can be brought into the network via notebooks that were infected while directly connecting to the Internet. Hacked Web sites can be used to install malware on the clients using vulnerabilities of Web browsers. Wireless access cards can open ways into the corporate network bypassing the firewall.

Currently most of the attacks target clients running Microsoft Windows. Such attacks are facilitated by the fact that under Windows, far too many users use an account with administrative privileges for their day-to-day work.

However, attacks that are based on vulnerabilities of browsers could work as well on clients running Linux. This is another reason to use the root account only when really needed for administrative work. The limited privileges of a normal user prevent major damage to the operating system installation on the computer.

Some actions to take are:

- Educating users not to open attachments without thinking about possible consequences.
- Updating virus scanners on the client computers.
- Patching security vulnerabilities of Web browsers as soon as possible.

5

Summary

- To effectively secure a SUSE Linux network server, you must understand the features of the various network services and protocols used on the system as well as their security weaknesses.

- DNS servers are usually susceptible to DNS spoofing attacks. As a result, DNS servers that provide public name resolution should be located in the DMZ and behind a firewall that allows communications from source port 53.

- Denial of service attacks may be used to use up the available addresses on a DHCP server. To mitigate these attacks, ensure that all DHCP servers are not exposed to the Internet and assign IP addresses to specific hosts based on the MAC address on their network card.

- If your organization uses SNMP to manage network devices, ensure that all devices support version 2 or greater of the SNMP protocol, which supports encryption and authentication.

- Many network services are time-dependant. As a result, ensure that these servers obtain their time from a reliable NTP time source using secure authentication.

- SSH encrypts network communication and allows you to copy files between remote hosts or obtain a command shell. It is a secure replacement for the Telnet and r-Tools utilities.

- NIS services transmit password hashes across the network and should be replaced by LDAP services and SSL.

- To secure NFS file sharing, ensure that the NFS servers are not exposed to external networks and that NFS-shared directories use the nosuid, noexec, root_squash or all_squash options.

- E-mail protocols are typically insecure and used to propagate spam and viruses. E-mail server authentication, TLS, GPG/PGP encryption, antivirus software and user education minimize the security risks associated with e-mail.

- Web servers are often the subject of a security attack and care should be taken to ensure that Web server content, extensions and scripts are secured.

- Web clients often run scripts such as ActiveX controls or JavaScript. These scripts may be used to steal personal information or change software and system settings. Restricting script execution and ensuring Web client software is current both minimize the chance that these attacks will occur.

- FTP can be an anonymous or authenticated protocol that typically transmits usernames and passwords without encryption. To maximize the security of FTP, you can use SSL to protect FTP transfers or use passive FTP instead of active FTP.

- Peer-to-peer networks are often used to distribute illegal files and viruses. As a result, you should block access to the ports used by peer-to-peer networking programs within your organization.

- WPA offers the best protection for wireless LAN traffic in your organization. If your wireless network must use WEP, ensure that you use an additional security mechanism such as IPSec to protect data transfer.

- TCP wrappers may be used to provide additional security for many network services by checking for restrictions specified in /etc/hosts.allow and /etc/hosts.deny before allowing a network connection. TCP wrappers may also be used to log access attempts to network services.

- SSL and TLS may be used to secure many network services using asymmetric cryptography. The OpenSSL package in SUSE Linux may be used to configure and manage SSL.

- Network security is an ongoing concern. As a result, you should continually educate users about security risks, as well as ensure that network computers contain virus scanners and the latest versions of software programs.

Key Terms

/etc/exports   The main configuration file for NFS. It lists NFS shared directories as well as access restrictions for each shared directory.

/etc/hosts.allow   A file used by the TCP wrapper that lists hosts that are allowed to connect to certain services on the Linux system.

/etc/hosts.deny   A file used by the TCP wrapper that lists hosts that are not allowed to connect to certain services on the Linux system. It is parsed only if an appropriate entry is not found in the /etc/hosts.allow file.

/etc/hosts.equiv   A file that contains computer-wide entries that are used to determine user and host access to r-Tools.

/etc/inetd.conf   The configuration file for the inetd daemon.

/etc/stunnel/stunnel.conf   The main configuration file for the **stunnel** program.

/usr/sbin/tcpd   The TCP wrapper program.

/var/log/messages   A log file that contains messages from system programs.

/var/log/xinetd.log   The log file for the xinetd daemon.

~/.rhosts   A file that contains user-specific entries that are used to determine user and host access to r-Tools.

AirSnort   A utility that may be used to capture wireless network traffic as well as crack WEP keys.

BIND (Berkeley Internet Name Domain)   The most common standard used when implementing DNS services on a network. Modern DNS services use version 9 or greater of BIND.

DHCP (Dynamic Host Configuration Protocol)   A network protocol used to provide IP configuration information to hosts that request it. It uses UDP ports 67 and 68.

DNS (Domain Name System)   A set of services and protocols used to resolve host names to IP addresses and vice versa. It uses UDP and TCP port 53.

DNS spoofing   A common attack that involves falsifying DNS name resolution information.

DNSsec   A DNS service extension that prevents DNS spoofing by ensuring that all name resolution results are digitally signed.

finger   A legacy Linux service used to obtain information about remote systems and users.

FTP (File Transfer Protocol)   The most common protocol used to transfer files across public networks such as the Internet. Active FTP uses TCP ports 20 and 21.

GPG (GNU Privacy Guard)   An Open Source implementation of PGP.

IMAP (Internet Message Access Protocol)   A protocol used to obtain e-mail messages from a mail server. IMAP typically uses TCP port 143.

inetd   The Internet Services Daemon. It is used to start other network services on legacy Linux systems.

ISC (Internet Systems Consortium)   The organization that develops and provides new standards for Internet protocols such as DNS and DHCP.

John the Ripper   A common password cracking utility that detects weak passwords that are based on dictionary words.

ldd command   Displays the libraries used by a particular program.

libwrap.so.0   The library used by xinetd and other programs to provide TCP wrapper support.

NFS (Network File System)   A file sharing protocol used on UNIX and Linux networks. NFS uses port 2049 to mount remote shared directories.

NIS (Network Information Service)   A network service and protocol used to coordinate configuration information across several UNIX and Linux computers on the network.

NTP (Network Time Protocol)   A network protocol that is used to obtain time configuration from remote computers. NTP uses TCP and UDP port 123.

OpenSSL   A Linux package that allows for the creation and management of SSL certificates.

openssl command   The configuration command for the OpenSSL package.

PGP (Pretty Good Privacy)   A widely used implementation of asymmetric cryptography developed in 1991.

POP3 (Post Office Protocol version 3)   A protocol used to obtain e-mail messages from a mail server. POP3 typically uses TCP port 110.

POP3S   An implementation of POP3 that uses SSL and TCP port 995.

portmapper   A network service that uses TCP and UDP port 111 to obtain a remote RPC connection.

qpopper   The package that provides POP3 support in modern Linux distributions.

Remote Access   The services and protocols used to connect to remote hosts and obtain a user interface or copy files. Telnet, r-Tools and SSH are common Linux remote access protocols.

RPC (Remote Procedure Calls)   A protocol that allows instructions to be executed on remote hosts.

rpcinfo command Displays RPC services running on a Linux computer.

r-Tools A set of utilities that may be used to connect to remote computers or copy files between remote computers without encryption. Some common r-Tools include rcp (remote copy), rsh (remote shell) and rlogin (remote login).

scp command Used to copy files between remote hosts using SSH.

sftp command Used to upload and download files between hosts using SSH.

SMB (Server Message Blocks) The file sharing protocol used by Windows operating systems and systems that run the Samba file sharing service.

SMTP (Simple Mail Transfer Protocol) The protocol used to send e-mail messages across computer networks. SMTP uses TCP port 25.

SNMP (Simple Network Management Protocol) A network protocol used to obtain and modify the configuration of various network devices. It typically uses UDP ports 161 and 162.

SSH (Secure Shell) A remote access protocol that may be used to connect to or copy files between remote hosts using TCP and UDP port 22. SSH protects communication using asymmetric cryptography and is a secure replacement for both Telnet and the r-Tools.

ssh command Used to obtain a remote shell interface using SSH.

SSL (Secure Sockets Layer) An asymmetric cryptography technology used by many Internet services.

stunnel command Provides SSL support for applications that do not natively support SSL.

TCP wrapper A service component that checks for restrictions listed in /etc/hosts.deny and /etc/hosts.allow before allowing access to certain network services.

tcpdchk command Detects and displays problems relating to the configuration of /etc/inetd.conf.

tcpdmatch command Tests the TCP wrapper restrictions specified in the /etc/inetd.conf file.

Telnet A remote access protocol that was traditionally used to connect to remote Linux and UNIX computers. Telnet does not encrypt the username and password during authentication.

TFTP (Trivial File Transfer Protocol) A version of the FTP protocol that uses UDP instead of TCP.

TLS (Transport Layer Security) An implementation of SSL that is used to secure Internet traffic.

Wi-Fi Protected Access (WPA) A technology used to secure the information transmitted across wireless networks. The current version is called WPA2 and provides the most security for wireless networks today.

Wired Equivalent Privacy (WEP) A legacy technology used to secure wireless LAN traffic. WEP keys may be cracked by several freely-available utilities today.

WWW (World Wide Web) The publicly available collection of Web servers on the Internet.

xinetd The Extended Internet Services Daemon. It is used to start other network services on current Linux systems.

ypcat command Used to view configuration information on remote NIS servers.

Review Questions

1. Your organization maintains a DNS server that is hosted within the DMZ. This DNS server contains name resolution records for all internal clients, internal servers and public servers within the DMZ used by Internet clients. What should you do to improve the security of your DNS service? (Choose all that apply.)

   a. Move the DNS server to the internal network

   b. Remove the name resolution records for the public servers from the DNS server in the DMZ

   c. Remove the name resolution records for the internal clients and servers from the DNS server in the DMZ

   d. Create another DNS server to host the name resolution records for the internal clients and servers

2. You have recently moved your DNS server to another subnet in your organization. Now, client computers in one of your subnets are having difficulty resolving names. You suspect that the firewall on the router is preventing DNS traffic. What port or ports should you open on the firewall to allow DNS traffic? _____

3. Which of the following technologies are considered secure in modern networks? (Choose all that apply.)

   a. SNMP Version 2

   b. WEP

   c. SMTP

   d. DHCP

   e. Telnet

   f. SNMP Version 1

   g. SSH

   h. r-Tools

   i. NIS

   j. POP3S

   k. WPA2

   l. IMAP

   m. FTP

   n. SSL

   o. TFTP

4. Which of the following services should be isolated from external networks such as the Internet? (Choose all that apply.)

   a. NTP

   b. SMTP

   c. DHCP

    d.   SNMP

    e.   SSH

    f.   NFS

    g.   FTP

5. Which command may be used to display active RPC services? _____

6. Which of the following could you do to provide security for e-mail technologies? (Choose all that apply.)

    a.   Enable SMTP authentication

    b.   Use GPG/PGP within your e-mail application

    c.   Educate users regarding e-mail attack prevention

    d.   Install antivirus software on the e-mail servers in your organization

7. What port must you configure to use POP3 with SSL in Kmail? _____

8. Which of the following may be used to provide greater security for the client computers within your organization? (Choose all that apply.)

    a.   Use firewalls to filter peer-to-peer networking protocols on your network routers

    b.   Install SNMP on each client computer

    c.   Prevent the use of ActiveX controls in client Web browsers

    d.   Download and install operating system and program updates for each client computer on a regular basis

9. What library provides support for TCP wrappers? _____

10. What program may be used to view the libraries used by the program /usr/bin/myservice? _____

11. What lines could you add to the /etc/hosts.allow and /etc/hosts.deny files to allow only the host **sparcy** the ability to successfully connect to the vsftpd service? (Choose two answers.)

    a.   /etc/hosts.allow: **vsftpd: sparcy**

    b.   /etc/hosts.allow: **vsftpd: ALL**

    c.   /etc/hosts.deny: **vsftpd: sparcy**

    d.   /etc/hosts.deny: **vsftpd: ALL**

12. What log files do the TCP wrapper daemon write failed attempts to by default? _____

13. What does the following line in the /etc/hosts.allow file do? (Choose all that apply.)
```
ALL: ALL: spawn echo "%u %a %h" > /var/log/connections
```

    a.   Allows access to all services for all hosts

    b.   Denies access to all services for all hosts

    c.   Prevents client computers from spawning shells during the session

    d.   Logs the username, IP address and hostname of every client that attempts a connection to a service that is configured to use TCP wrappers

14. You configure a network service on a Linux server in your organization that does not implement secure authentication and does not encrypt the data in transit across the network. What package could you use to provide SSL functionality with this program? _____

15. After configuring one of your network services to use SSL for security, client computers receive error messages indicating that the SSL certificate used for the communication is not trusted. How should you remedy the problem? _____

Discovery Exercises

DISCOVERY EXERCISES

Securing Wireless Networks and Clients

Portable computers are part of nearly all organizations today. Sales representatives and executives use portable computers when they travel outside the organization to give presentations, record order information, or connect remotely to a company network through the Internet. Unfortunately, this also increases the likelihood that attackers outside the organization will steal company data if the portable computer is not protected. Portable computers may also accumulate viruses, malware and spyware that could infect computers within the organization when the portable computer is connected to the organization's LAN.

Furthermore, organizations that provide wireless network access may also be allowing attackers within wireless range to use the wireless network and company resources.

Using the Internet, research the following technologies and note how they may be used to secure wireless clients and wireless networks from potential security threats:

1. Wireless DMZ
2. RADIUS
3. Encrypted File Systems
4. Faraday Cage
5. Anti-virus, anti-spyware, anti-malware software

Using TCP Wrappers

In this section, you learned how to use TCP wrappers to add additional security for network services. For each of the following, write the appropriate lines that would appear in the /etc/hosts.allow and /etc/hosts.deny files on your server:

1. Only the host sparcy is allowed to connect to the server using sshd
2. Allow access only to the vsftpd and sshd services for all hosts.
3. If the host sparcy connects to the server, it will receive the message "You are not allowed to connect to this server!"
4. Log all sshd requests from the host sparcy to the file /var/log/sparcy. Only the IP address and user name should be logged.

Identifying Service Vulnerabilities

To maximize the security of any Linux server, you should periodically analyze the security of each of your network services. Today, there are usually several Websites and newsgroups on the Internet that are dedicated to providing information regarding security vulnerabilities and fixes for specific services such as the Apache Web server or BIND DNS. For your Linux server, first identify the network services that are running using a utility such as nmap or netstat (discussed earlier in Section 2). Next, select one of these services and research the appropriate information regarding its current security issues on the Internet. Use this information to secure your service by downloading the appropriate software patches or changing its configuration.

General Firewall Design

There is no single correct way to implement a firewall. The setup differs from site to site, depending on the needs of the company. However, there are common principles that should be considered when designing and implementing firewalls. In this section, you learn about general firewall design.

Objectives

- Understand Firewall Concepts and Purpose
- Describe Components of Firewalls
- Understand Advantages and Disadvantages of Different Setups

Objective 1—Understand Firewall Concepts and Purpose

A firewall is not a single machine, but a concept of how different components are combined to achieve the desired purpose. Firewalls are supposed to monitor and control the traffic between two networks. What traffic is allowed across the firewall and what traffic is blocked is the subject of the security concept.

The difference between the two networks involved is the level of trust granted to the users in each network. Usually there is an internal network with known and trusted users and an external network where the users are not trusted and often not even known, like in the Internet. However, the same differentiation could apply between two networks within a company, if part of the network is separated from the rest of the network.

There are two basic approaches to firewalls:

- Everything that is not allowed is forbidden.
- Everything that is not forbidden is allowed.

From a security viewpoint, only the first approach is reasonable.

Objective 2—Describe Components of Firewalls

Firewalls comprise one or (usually) more of the following elements:

- Packet Filter
- Application-Level Gateway (ALG)
- Demilitarized Zone (DMZ)

Packet Filter

Packet filters decide, by means of rules based on the data in IP, ICMP, TCP, and UDP headers (source address, target address, source port, target port, and flags), what to do with IP datagrams running through them.

The data stream can be regimented on the IP protocol level and the respective transport protocols that are built upon it. Packet filters do not offer detailed filtering based on the content of the IP packets.

Figure 6-1 shows the ISO/OSI layers involved in routing. While information in layer 3 is used by a packet filter to decide on the fate of a packet, information contained in layer 4 and above is hardly, if ever, taken into consideration by a packet filter.

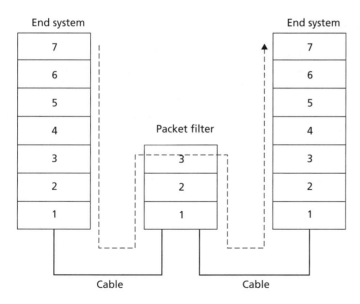

--------→ Path of a data packet

Figure 6-1

Packet filters are usually divided into two categories:

- Static packet filters
- Dynamic (also called stateful) packet filters

A static packet filter has a set of rules that do not change once they are set. This has certain disadvantages, because access to high ports usually has to be allowed, at least for certain packets, to allow answers to requests. This can be used by a potential attacker to gain information about the internal network using scanners like nmap.

If protocols that open an additional connection like FTP are allowed, access to a whole range of ports has to be allowed. Control of UDP traffic with static packet filters is not very effective, because UDP, unlike TCP, does not have connection state as part of the protocol that can be checked by rules.

Depending on the connections being made, a dynamic packet filter can change the filtering rules. If, for instance, a Web page is requested by a browser, the filter allows all return packets belonging to that one connection and no others. All ports not belonging to that connection remain closed, unless an allowed first packet initiated the connection.

With dynamic packet filters, UDP traffic can be filtered much more effectively, allowing incoming UDP packets only when they are an answer to an outgoing packet.

If a protocol is using a second connection, the ports for exactly that connection can be opened up dynamically, while the rest remain closed. In this case, data within higher ISO/OSI layers is evaluated by the packet filter (for example, the port command within the ftp communication). This kind of connection tracking requires appropriate kernel modules to be loaded.

Dynamic packet filtering makes the task of a potential attacker much more difficult.

Packet Filters are covered in detail in Section 7, Packet Filters.

Application-Level Gateway (ALG)

Application-level gateways (sometimes referred to as *application-level firewalls*) are computers on which protocol-specific or generic proxy servers run that log and check the data traffic running through them. Because proxy servers involve programs that run on the gateway, these are ideally suited for logging and access protection mechanisms.

Application-level gateways with their proxy servers have an essential advantage over packet filters: They manage traffic without IP routing between the networks they connect.

The IP datagrams are received by the proxy servers on the application level and the application data is processed. At this stage all headers of the underlying protocol levels have already been removed. The determination of the target is done on the basis of the address data inside the application data (for example, for e-mail on the basis of the e-mail address or for HTTP on the basis of the URL).

Figure 6-2 shows the relationship of the ISO/OSI layers and application-level gateways.

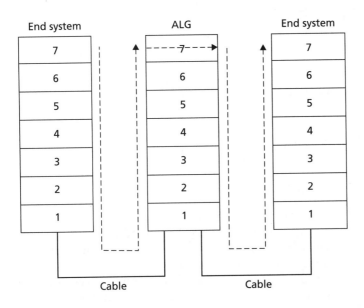

------→ Path of a data packet

Figure 6-2

Before transmitting the data to the actual target host, the application data is passed through the protocol layer downwards. Each protocol layer builds a new header of its own around the useful data, until the packet finally leaves the physical level of the ALG. This means that no header data can travel unchanged from one side of the gateway to the other beneath the application level, because they are created again by the proxy servers before being sent. Therefore, malicious headers will, in most cases, be disposed of automatically during the passage through the ALGs.

With ALGs that are aware of the protocol they relay, rules can be set that filter according to content, client software, user, and other criteria. An example for such an ALG is the HTTP-proxy `squid`.

A dedicated proxy software does not exist for every protocol. Generic proxy servers, sometimes called circuit level proxy servers, can relay protocols for which there is no dedicated proxy. They do not, however, allow the detailed control as dedicated proxy servers do. In practice they offer more or less the same functionality and level of security as packet filters. Examples of generic proxy servers are `socks` and `rinetd`.

Application-level gateways are covered in detail in Section 8, Application-Level Gateways.

Demilitarized Zone (DMZ)

Buffer zones between secure and insecure networks are referred to as demilitarized zones (DMZ). Data traffic between public networks and the DMZ is controlled and regulated through packet filters and application-level gateways exactly as data traffic is controlled between a DMZ and a secure network. See Figure 6-3.

6

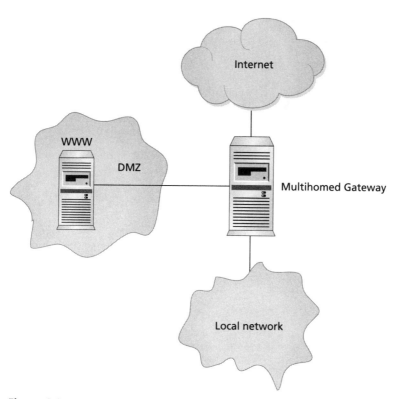

Figure 6-3

Various combinations of packet filters, application-level gateways, and servers are possible as shown in Figure 6-4. It depends on what level of security you need—and what your budget allows.

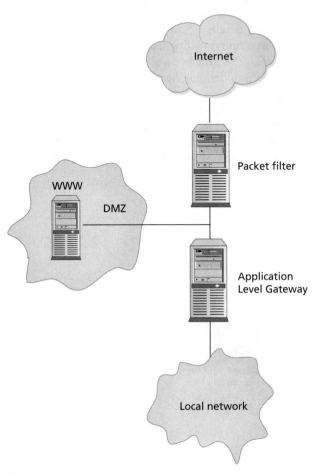

Figure 6-4

Another layout might look like Figure 6-5. Keep in mind that each additional computer increases the costs in terms of hardware, energy consumption, administrative efforts, and know-how required.

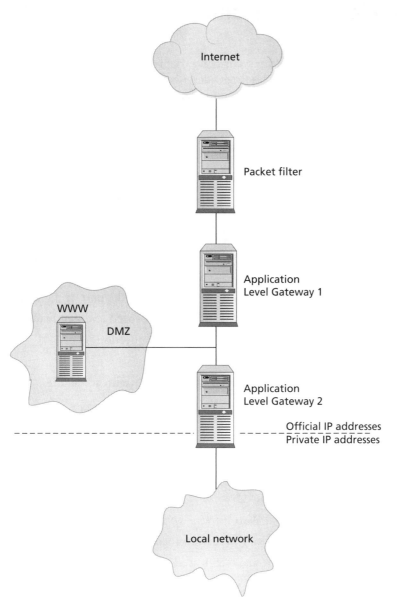

Figure 6-5

Servers operating in a DMZ typically provide services toward public (insecure) networks (WWW servers, FTP servers, etc.) and are, therefore, quite visible to potential attackers.

Servers in the DMZ require an increased administration effort compared with systems in a secure network because they are used by unknown users.

Objective 3—Understand Advantages and Disadvantages of Different Setups

The solution you deploy has to meet your security needs, provide the desired functionality, and stay within your budget. The various technologies described have advantages and disadvantages that make them more or less suitable for certain tasks.

This objective considers advantages and disadvantages of the following:

- Packet Filters
- Application-Level Gateways

And, finally, a word of caution.

Packet Filters

Packet filters:

- Allow control of the traffic based on IP address, ports, protocol, TCP flags, and state of the connection.
- Do not require modifications of clients or cooperation on the part of the user.
- Do not put a heavy burden on the network in terms of speed and bandwidth.
- Have limited ways of monitoring the content of the connection.
- Have no way to control the traffic based on the user.
- Cannot effectively control some protocols, such as UDP (with static filters), or RPC-based protocols.

Application-Level Gateways

Application-level gateways:

- Allow detailed monitoring and control of the traffic.
- Do not require routing to be enabled.
- Often need modified clients (e.g., Web browser configuration).
- Have dedicated proxy servers for only a few protocols.
- Depending on your bandwidth needs, might need powerful hardware.

Caution

It cannot be overstated that a firewall is just a component of an overall concept.

The classical concept—Internet bad and evil versus Intranet good and nice—is no longer valid (if it ever was). What used to be the rogue modems in the past are now wireless cards that allow access to notebooks while they are plugged in to the corporate LAN.

Notebooks can become infected while accessing the Internet in a hotel or at home. Infected notebooks access corporate resources via VPN, allowing someone who uses a backdoor installed on the notebook to access corporate resources.

But not only notebooks are to blame. Local workstations can get infected via e-mail or by just visiting a site that installs malware without user interaction by exploiting a browsers vulnerability.

And there are other classes of attacks that are not even covered in this course, like SQL injection. These attacks use legitimate paths through the firewall, like access to the Web server, but target other areas, for example, the database behind the Web server.

Errors in the programming of the Web frontend could lead to unauthorized database access if, for instance, the input in HTML forms is not processed correctly.

A firewall is not a panacea that cures all. You have to know its uses and its limitations.

Summary

- Firewalls are technologies that protect networks from unauthorized access by restricting the traffic that enters and leaves the network.

- Packet filters, ALGs and DMZs are commonly used to create firewalls.

- Packet filters typically exist on routers, require no client configuration, and can be used to restrict most traffic based on source and destination IP address, flags or port number. Dynamic packet filters can modify their own restrictions based on current network traffic and are more effective than static packet filters.

- Unlike packet filters, ALGs are able to control network traffic based on user account or data content using proxy server software.

- Dedicated proxy server software such as **squid** offer exceptional control, but require client configuration and cannot support all network protocols. Generic proxy servers such as **socks** and **rinetd** have support for all network protocols, but have limited control over network traffic.

- DMZs are network segments that only contain publicly accessed servers. They are isolated from the Internet and internal networks via packet filters or ALGs.

- Since firewalls do not prevent the misuse of network services, they do not offer complete protection against network attacks.

Key Terms

application-level firewall   See Application-Level Gateway.

Application-Level Gateway (ALG)   A computer that fully analyzes network traffic passing through a network using proxy server software. They are also called application-level firewalls.

circuit level proxy server   See generic proxy server.

dedicated proxy server   A proxy server that offers comprehensive protocol-specific control.

Demilitarized Zone (DMZ)   A network that contains publicly accessed information and network services. Because of their public nature, DMZs are a primary focus of network security.

dynamic packet filter   A packet filter that can change the rules it uses for restricting network traffic based on the nature of the traffic.

firewall   A technology or combination of technologies that restrict access to networks or network applications.

generic proxy server   A proxy server that offers partial control of a wide range of network protocols.

International Standard Organization's Open System Interconnect (ISO/OSI)   A model used to describe how computers use protocols to communicate on a computer network.

nmap   A powerful port scanning utility available on most Linux systems.

packet filter   A software component that drops network communication that is addressed to a particular IP address or port number.

proxy server   A software program used on application-level gateways to restrict traffic based on detailed criteria such as data content and user information.

rinetd   A common generic proxy server available on many Linux systems. It redirects TCP connections from one address and port to another.

socks   A widely-used generic proxy server that translates internal TCP requests to an external network using the SOCKS protocol standard.

SQL injection   A network attack that inserts malicious information into SQL queries that are performed on a database server.

squid   A common dedicated proxy server package found on most Linux systems.

stateful packet filter   See dynamic packet filter.

static packet filter   A packet filter that restricts network traffic based on rules that do not change.

Review Questions

1. Which of the following criteria do packet filters use when restricting network traffic? (Choose all that apply.)

   a. User account

   b. TCP source port

   c. TCP destination address

   d. UDP source port

2. What part of a packet do packet filters analyze?

   a. Data

   b. Header

   c. Payload

   d. Trailer

3. What level of the ISO/OSI model do packet filters use when analyzing network traffic?
   _____

4. What level of the ISO/OSI model do proxy servers use when restricting network traffic?
   _____

5. Which of the following describes the function of a dynamic packet filter?
   a. Inbound traffic is allowed to pass through the dynamic packet filter. Outbound traffic that originated from the inbound traffic is allowed to pass through the dynamic packet filter.
   b. Inbound traffic is not allowed to pass through the dynamic packet filter. Outbound traffic is allowed to pass through the dynamic packet filter.
   c. Outbound and inbound traffic are prevented from passing through the dynamic packet filter unless authentication has taken place.
   d. Outbound traffic is allowed to pass through the dynamic packet filter. Inbound traffic that originated from the outbound traffic is allowed to pass through the dynamic packet filter.

6. Which of the following Linux packages can be used to create a dedicated proxy server?
   a. samba
   b. socks
   c. squid
   d. rinetd

7. What is normally contained within a DMZ that is not contained within a secure network?
   _____

8. Which of the following are advantages of Application-Level Gateways when compared to packet filters? (Choose all that apply.)
   a. Require little client configuration
   b. Allow greater control over network traffic
   c. May be used to control traffic based on user
   d. Do not rely on routing services

9. You are implementing a network infrastructure in your organization and are considering the use of Application-Level Gateways and packet filters. Which technology will result in lower bandwidth usage? _____

10. What type of network traffic cannot be effectively managed using static packet filters?
    _____

Discovery Exercises

DISCOVERY EXERCISES

Selecting Firewall Technologies

While packet filters and ALGs can be used to create firewalls between networks, each technology has features that make it more appropriate in various situations. For each of the situations below, identify which technology (static packet filters, dynamic packet filters or ALGs) would be most appropriate:

1. You wish to secure the traffic that passes between two departmental networks in your organization. A great deal of information flows between these networks on a daily basis and users on one network typically use resources on the other network.

2. You wish to provide Internet access to the network in your organization via a low-cost Internet connection. Users in your organization are only allowed to use the Internet to obtain information from other office locations within your organization.

3. You wish to provide security for your current organization's high-speed Internet connection. Your organization uses the Internet to perform research on a daily basis and the internal network contains several servers that contain private content.

Analyzing Firewall Hardware Requirements

In this section, you examined the major features and usage of firewall technologies such as packet filters and ALGs. Because of the differences between these technologies, hardware requirements will differ depending on whether a packet filtering firewall or ALG firewall is being used on your network. In a brief memo, describe the hardware requirements (memory, CPU-speed, network interface speed and hard drive space) that you would require if you were to create a firewall to protect a 1000 host network using:

1. A packet filtering firewall on a Linux router

2. An ALG using Squid proxy server software on a Linux server

Researching Firewall Devices

In some environments, it is more feasible to use network-based hardware devices (also called network appliances) to provide protection for your network. Many hardware-based routers such as Cisco and Nortel typically have built-in firewall functions, and several manufacturers such as Barracuda Networks market hardware-based firewalls that may be used on your network. Use the Internet to research the features and benefits of these hardware-based firewalls and summarize your findings in a short memo.

Packet Filters

The Linux kernel allows filtering of IP packets according to various rules. Packets can be accepted, dropped, or otherwise handled depending on various criteria. This makes it possible to include Linux computers as components of firewalls.

Objectives

- Understand Packet Filters
- Understand iptables Basics
- Understand iptables Advanced Features
- Understand Network Address Translation

Objective 1—Understand Packet Filters

Packet filters control what data flows into and out of a network. To understand packet filter techniques, you need a sound basic knowledge of the TCP/IP protocol family.

This objective covers the following:

- TCP/IP Basics
- Routing
- Static Packet Filters
- Dynamic (Stateful) Packet Filters

TCP/IP Basics

A TCP/IP connection between two computers is characterized by IP addresses, ports, and the protocol used. In the case of someone connecting to a Web server, the connection could look like this:

- Client computer:
  - IP address: 217.83.16.7
  - Port: 1054
  - Protocol: TCP
- Web server:
  - IP address: 130.57.4.27
  - Port: 80
  - Protocol: TCP

To view a Web page, the browser opens a socket (the combination of IP address and port) on the client and sends a request to the IP address of the Web server and its port 80, using the TCP protocol.

As part of the TCP protocol, the connection is established first using a specific sequence of IP packets (the TCP handshake). Once that is done, the Web server sends the data to the client.

The information is not transferred between the computers on a dedicated line. It is transferred in chunks of a certain size, called *packets*. These do not necessarily all need to take the same route from source to destination. Each packet contains the IP addresses and ports of the computers involved and is independent of any other packet.

To control the flow of the packets to, from, and through (if two network cards are present) the computer, filtering rules can be set up that allow packets to continue to their destination or to be discarded, according to various criteria. Filtering can be used to prevent computer A from being contacted by other computers while still allowing computer A to contact others, or to only allow certain traffic across a gateway while denying everything else.

Such a mechanism is called a *packet filter*. In Linux the capability to filter packets, the netfilter framework, is part of the kernel. With Kernel 2.4.*x* and 2.6.*x*, this functionality is controlled by the `iptables` program.

Routing

Even if a computer has two Network Interface Cards (NIC), packets coming in on one interface cannot leave the computer on the other interface. The default configuration does not allow the routing of packets.

To turn routing on in the Linux kernel, the value in /proc/sys/net/ipv4/ip_forward has to be changed from 0 to 1.

On the command line, this can be done as follows:

```
da10:~ # echo 1 > /proc/sys/net/ipv4/ip_forward
```

This change is lost with the next reboot. To ensure routing is turned on when the computer boots, you have to change the entry IP_FORWARD to yes in the file /etc/sysconfig/sysctl:

```
...
## Type:         yesno
## Default:      no
#
# Runtime-configurable parameter: forward IP packets.
# Is this host a router? (yes/no)
#
IP_FORWARD="yes"
...
```

Static Packet Filters

A static packet filter does not use any information from previous packets or any application data within the packet to decide what to do with a packet. As far as the filter is concerned, every packet is completely independent of any other packet.

Let's have a look at an FTP connection to illustrate this.

When transferring files using FTP there are always two connections:

- One is the control connection from the client to port 21 on the server.
- The second connection is from port 20 on the server to a high port on the client (active FTP) or from a high port on the client to a high port on the server (passive FTP).

The information on the ports is exchanged within the control connection.

If you want to allow FTP transfers through your packet filter, you need to allow:

- A connection originating from a high port of the client to port 21 of the server.
- A connection originating from port 20 of the server to any port above 1024 on the client (for active FTP).
  or
  A connection originating from any port above 1024 on the client to any port above 1024 on the server (for passive FTP).

However, the filter rules do not care whether the connection from port 20 of the server is a legitimate FTP data transfer in answer to a request on port 21 or not. Therefore, with these rules anyone can open connections to the high ports of clients, as long as they originate at port 20. This leaves the high ports of the clients unprotected if you want to allow active FTP.

With passive FTP, the problem is the same on the server side. To allow passive FTP, a packet filter that should protect the server has to allow all connections from the high ports of clients to the high ports on the server.

When filtering TCP connections, static packet filters allow some control on the direction of the connection. You can allow packets with only the syn-flag in one direction (from the inside) while rejecting them when they come from the outside. (The first packet of the TCP handshake has only this flag set.)

The packets following the first one in either direction have to be allowed as well for a successful connection.

Rejecting packets with only the syn flag set from the outside prevents the TCP handshake and thus the TCP connection.

This is not possible with UDP, because there is no handshake and no flags are set. This makes it virtually impossible to effectively filter UDP connections with static packet filters, short of blocking them completely.

Dynamic (Stateful) Packet Filters

A stateful packet filter uses information about previous packets and, to some extent, application data within the packets to decide what should happen with a packet.

Let's have a look again at an FTP connection to illustrate this.

In the beginning, only a connection from the client to port 21 of the server is allowed by a filter rule. Everything else is forbidden—an answer from the server to the client as well as any connections from port 20 of the server to the client.

The first packet from the client to the server changes the filter rules to allow packets in answer to this first packet and any subsequent packets. To be allowed, they must correspond exactly to the first packet.

After the three-way handshake, the port to be used for the data transfer is transmitted within the control connection. The stateful packet engine reads this information from the data section within the packets of the control connection and configures the filter to allow exactly that data connection. But unlike static packet filtering, this rule is not port 20 of any server to any high port of the client, but only port 20 of this particular server to exactly port x on the client.

After a specific time without traffic elapses, the additional rules allowing these connections are removed from the filter. Only initial connections from the client to port 21 remain allowed.

The advantage of this is that, in general, no connections from port 20 of servers to the high ports of clients are allowed. This blocks any traffic originating from port 20 without a corresponding previous connection to port 21 on the same server. The same holds true for passive FTP. Only the single data connection corresponding to the control connection is allowed for a certain amount of time.

This mechanism can also be used to control UDP traffic. Rules can be set that allow packets from the outside only after a packet from the inside starts the connection. Therefore, stateful packet filtering allows you to control UDP connections much better than static filtering.

Objective 2—Understand iptables Basics

iptables is the program used to control the packet filtering capabilities of the netfilter framework in the Linux kernel.

You use the iptables program to set or delete the packet filter rules. Because of the many ways packets can be handled, the syntax of iptables is rather complex.

To understand iptables, you need to understand:

- Chains
- Policies
- Basic Syntax

Chains

Rules are organized in a chain. Within a chain, the rules are checked one after the other until a rule matches. If no rule matches, a default action is taken. This default action is referred to as the policy of the chain.

There are several chains. The main built-in chains are:

- INPUT
- OUTPUT
- FORWARD

Figure 7-1 and the explanation are from *http://www.netfilter.org/documentation/HOWTO/packet-filtering-HOWTO-6.html*.

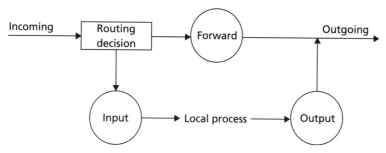

Figure 7-1

The following describes the process:

1. When a packet comes in (for example through the Ethernet card), the kernel first looks at the destination of the packet: This is called routing.

2. If the packet is destined for this computer, the packet passes downwards in the diagram, to the INPUT chain.
   If it passes this, any processes waiting for that packet will receive it.

3. Otherwise, if the kernel does not have forwarding enabled, or it doesn't know how to forward the packet, the packet is dropped.

If forwarding is enabled, and the packet is destined for another network interface (if you have another one), then the packet goes rightwards on our diagram to the FORWARD chain.

If it is ACCEPTed, it will be sent out.

4. Finally, a program running on the computer can send network packets.

These packets pass through the OUTPUT chain immediately: If it says ACCEPT, then the packet continues out to whatever interface it is destined for.

Policies

The policy decides what happens to a packet that did not match a rule in the chain. The policy could either be to accept the packet or to drop it.

Two approaches are possible:

- Everything is forbidden, except if explicitly allowed.
- Everything is allowed, except if explicitly forbidden.

From a security viewpoint, only the first approach is valid.

To set the policy, use the -P option:

```
iptables -P FORWARD DROP
```

Basic Syntax

iptables is called with various options to specify a rule. If a rule matches, the target of the rule is executed, usually accepting, rejecting, or dropping the packet.

After a match, the subsequent rules are usually not checked. Therefore, the sequence of the rules in the chain is of critical importance.

iptables options let you:

- *Add and delete rules.*

  The following commands are possible:

  - -A—Add a rule to the end of the chain.
  - -D—Delete a rule.
  - -R—Replace a rule.
  - -I—Insert a rule.

  For instance, to insert a rule at position 3 of the chain, enter:

  ```
  iptables -I INPUT 3 ...
  ```

- *Manipulate whole chains.*

  The following commands are possible:

  - -F—Delete (flush) all rules from a chain.
  - -Z—Zero the byte counter of a chain.
  - -L—List the rules of a chain (add -v for more information).
  - -N—Create a user-defined (new) chain.

- −E—Rename a user-defined chain.
- −X—Delete an empty user-defined chain.

- *Define matching rules.*

  Matches can be based, for instance, on interfaces, ports, or IP addresses.
  Not every possible option has to be specified. If an option, for example the destination port, is not specified, it is not taken into consideration.

  - Specify the interface: −i for input, −o for output: −i eth0
    -o cannot be used in the INPUT chain, -i is not possible in the OUTPUT chain.
  - Specify the protocol: −p TCP, −p UDP
    The protocol can be specified with its abbreviation or the number of the protocol from /etc/protocols. Both lower and upper case are acceptable.
  - Specify source and/or destination IP: −s 1.2.3.4, −d 192.168.0.0/24
  - Specify source and/or destination port: −−sport 1024:65535, −−dport 80
    You can specify a single port or port ranges (start:end). The port you put in the rules depends on the service you want to access. /etc/services lists the ports and the service that can usually be found on that port.
    While UDP and TCP usually have the same service on the same port, this is not necessarily so. Some of the more frequently used ports include:

    - 20—FTP data
    - 21—FTP
    - 22—SSH
    - 23—telnet
    - 25—SMTP
    - 53—domain (dns)
    - 80—WWW
    - 110—POP3
    - 111—sun-rpc
    - 113—ident
    - 137--139—NetBIOS ports
    - 143—IMAP
    - 443—HTTPS

  Additional matches can be used with the option −m. Some of the more common ones are covered in the next objective, "Understand iptables Advanced Features."

- *Set the target.*

  The target specifies what happens to a packet that matches a rule.

After a match, subsequent rules (with the exception of LOG) are not checked. The target is given after the option -j (jump). Possible targets are:

- *ACCEPT*—Depending on the chain, the packet is forwarded, delivered to a local process, or sent out via a network interface.
- *REJECT*—The packet is discarded and, depending on the type of packet, a message (default: ICMP port unreachable) is sent to the source of the packet.
- *DROP*—The packet is silently discarded.
- *LOG*—Unlike with other rules, the packet continues down the chain after it matches a logging rule. So, if you want to log packets that are rejected or dropped, put a logging rule right before the rule dropping the packet.

  Logging packets, especially rejected ones, is useful. When writing your rules, a log can be used to debug your script, and when your rules are in force, a log can give you an idea of what packets hit your packet filter.

  Packets are usually logged in /var/log/firewall. But you can configure syslog to log them into a file of their own.
- A *user-defined chain*—User-defined chains are covered in the next objective, "Understand iptables Advanced Features" on page 181.

The following are some examples of iptables rules:

- To block all incoming packets on eth1 with a source IP of 10.*x.x.x*, enter:

```
iptables -A INPUT -i eth1 -s 10.0.0.0/8 -j DROP
```

The rule is added at the end of the chain (-A).

- To reject all incoming TCP packets on eth1 with a source IP of 10.*x.x.x*, enter:

```
iptables -A INPUT -i eth1 -p tcp -s 10.0.0.0/255.0.0.0 -j REJECT
```

The default for REJECT is to send an ICMP Port Unreachable message, if applicable. (For example, no ICMP messages are sent in response to certain ICMP messages.) To specify the ICMP message (or a TCP reset) to be sent, enter:

-j REJECT --reject-with **type**

Replace *type* with the ICMP message you want sent (icmp-proto-unreachable, icmp-host-unreachable, or tcp-reset, for example).

- To accept all incoming ICMP packets on eth1, enter:

```
iptables -A INPUT -i eth1 -p icmp -j ACCEPT
```

You should not indiscriminately block all ICMP packets on your firewall. If you consider blocking them at all, you should only block certain types of packets; otherwise, network performance could suffer.

Candidates for blocking are timestamp request and reply, information request and reply, address mask request and reply, and redirect.

In any event you should allow fragmentation-needed messages. Put a rate limit on the others if you want, or just accept them.

You can get a list of types by using `iptables -p ICMP --help`.

- To accept all outgoing TCP packets to port 80, enter:

```
iptables -A OUTPUT -p tcp --dport 80 -j ACCEPT
```

Usually a second rule is needed to take care of the packets received in answer.

- To accept all incoming TCP packets from port 80 (if the syn-bit alone is not set; ! is used to negate an option), enter:

```
iptables -A INPUT -p tcp ! --syn --sport 80 -j ACCEPT
```

- To log a packet, use the LOG target. To make the log entries more informative, a string should be entered in the rule that appears in the log file:

```
iptables -A INPUT -p tcp --syn --dport 25 \
          -j LOG --log-prefix "SMTP traffic: "
```

- This produces the following entry in /var/log/firewall when a new connection is made to port 25:

```
Apr 14 12:01:02 da10 kernel: SMTP traffic: IN=eth0 OUT=
MAC=00:11:11:c2:35:f4:00:11:25:82:d7:f9:08:00 SRC=192.168.1.4
DST=10.0.0.10 LEN=60 TOS=0x10 PREC=0x00 TTL=64 ID=8108 DF PROTO=TCP
SPT=1984 DPT=25 WINDOW=5840 RES=0x00 SYN URGP=0
```

Exercise 7-1: Get Familiar with Basic iptables Syntax

Time Required: 90–120 min

Objective: In this exercise the computer that is used for testing should not have any iptables rules set. Otherwise the results also depend on the settings of this testing computer.

The purpose of this exercise is to familiarize you with the iptables syntax and to show the effect of some iptables rules.

Description: In the first part, you use iptables on the command line only. Any rules set with iptables are lost with the next reboot. Therefore they are usually included in a shell script that is executed during system startup. Part II and the subsequent parts of this exercise deal with writing such a script to set and delete rules.

Due to the length and complexity of the exercise, the instructions on what to do are given separately for each part.

There is no single right way to write such a script. Keep it as simple as possible so you don't inadvertently open security holes. Use comments within the script liberally so you can still understand it when you have to modify it later.

Work with a partner in this exercise.

You will have to coordinate with each other regarding setting and testing of rules. If you both set rules at the same time and then test them, the test might not produce the expected result, because the rules on the testing computer might interfere with the test.

This exercise consists of:

- Part I: Set iptables Rules on the Command Line
- Part II: Prepare a Structure for a Script
- Part III: Define General Variables
- Part IV: Create a Section to Delete Any Existing Rules
- Part V: Create a Section to Display the Current Rule Set
- Part VI: Add Static Rules

Part I: Set iptables Rules on the Command Line

The purpose of the first part of this exercise is to show you how iptables is used and the effect the commands have.

Create rules to block incoming and outgoing ICMP messages. View the rules, test them using ping, and then delete them.

Create a rule that prevents others from connecting to your ssh server; use one with the target DROP, test it, and then delete it; create a new rule with the target REJECT, test again, note any difference, and then delete it.

Detailed Steps to Complete this Part

1. Open a terminal window and su – to root with a password of `novell`.

2. Determine if any rules have been set already by entering:

   ```
   iptables -v -L -n
   ```

3. If there are any rules in the INPUT, OUTPUT, or FORWARD chain, delete them by entering:

   ```
   iptables -F
   ```

4. Set a rule blocking all ICMP packets *to* your computer coming from other computers by entering:

   ```
   iptables -A INPUT -i eth0 -p icmp -j DROP
   ```

   (This is only an example. Blocking all ICMP messages is generally not advisable.)

5. View the current ruleset by entering:

   ```
   iptables -v -L -n
   ```

6. Have your partner test this rule by sending an echo request (ping) to your computer.

7. Try to send an echo request to your partner's computer.

8. Delete the rule you set in Step 4 by entering:

   ```
   iptables -D INPUT -i eth0 -p icmp -j DROP
   ```

9. Set a rule blocking all ICMP packets *from* your computer to other computers by entering:

   ```
   iptables -A OUTPUT -o eth0 -p icmp -j DROP
   ```

10. Have your partner test this rule by sending an echo request (ping) to your computer.

11. Try to send an echo request to your partner's computer. (You will notice a slightly different output of the ping command compared to Step 6 above.)

12. Delete the rule you set in Step 8 by entering:

    ```
    iptables -D OUTPUT -o eth0 -p icmp -j DROP
    ```

13. Set a rule blocking all ICMP packets in the FORWARD chain by entering:

    ```
    iptables -A FORWARD -p icmp -j DROP
    ```

    If there is only one NIC in your computer, you cannot test this rule.

    However, you can test if this rule affects traffic to and from your computer (which it shouldn't) by asking your partner to ping your computer and by sending an echo request to your partner's computer.

14. Flush your ruleset by entering:

    ```
    iptables -F
    ```

15. Find out what happens when you use ssh to connect to your partner's ssh port by entering:

    ssh geeko@*partner_IP*

    When prompted, enter the password novell. After you have successfully logged in, log out again by pressing Ctrl-D.

16. Create an iptables rule that drops incoming TCP packets addressed to port 22 (SSH) by entering:

    iptables -A INPUT -i eth0 -p tcp --dport 22 -j DROP

17. After your partner sets the rule on his or her computer, try again to log in to your partner's computer using ssh and notice how the results differ from the results in Step 14.

18. Change the rule from Step 15 to use REJECT as its target instead of DROP.
    You can either delete the rule and create a new one, or replace the rule by entering:

    iptables -R INPUT 1 -i eth0 -p tcp --dport 22 -j REJECT

19. View the current ruleset by entering:

    iptables -v -L -n

20. After your partner sets the rule on his or her computer, try again to ssh to your partner's computer and find out if there is any difference to before. If yes, why is that?_____

21. Change the rule from Step 17 to REJECT with a TCP reset, instead of the ICMP message port unreachable, by entering (on one line):

    iptables -R INPUT 1 -i eth0 -p tcp --dport 22 -j REJECT --reject-with tcp-reset

22. View the current ruleset by entering:

    iptables -v -L -n

23. After your partner sets the rule on his or her computer, again connect to your partner's computer using ssh and find out if you get different results.

24. Flush your ruleset by entering:

    iptables -F

Part II: Prepare a Structure for a Script

Because any packet filter rules set with iptables are lost with the next reboot, it is common practice to write a script to set them. In addition to setting the rules (start), such a script should be able to delete the rules (stop), and to show the currently active rules (status). It should also allow integration into the runlevel concept. The file /etc/init.d/skeleton gives an outline of how such a script could be structured.

The purpose of this and the following parts of this exercise is to show you the basic elements of setting up a script to set up and delete iptables rules.

Detailed Steps to Complete this Part

1. Open a terminal window and su – to root with a password of novell.

2. Change directory to /etc/init.d/.

3. Copy the file skeleton to fw-script:

   cp /etc/init.d/skeleton /etc/init.d/fs-script

4. Change the permissions so that the script can be executed by entering

   chmod 744 /etc/init.d/fw-script

5. Open the file fw-script in a text editor.

   Modify the script, keeping the sections on init info and the case sections start, stop, status, and *. Delete any comments and sections you do not need.

   Have a look at the greybox on the following page as a guideline.

6. Create a link to this script in /sbin:

   cd /sbin
   ln -s /etc/init.d/fw-script rcfw-script

   Your result could look similar to the following:

```
#!/bin/sh
#
# /etc/init.d/fw-script and its symbolic link
# /(usr/)sbin/rcfw-script
#
### BEGIN INIT INFO
# Provides:            packetfilter
# Required-Start:      $syslog $network
# Required-Stop:       $syslog $network
# Default-Start:       3 5
# Default-Stop:        0 1 2 6
# Short-Description:   Sets packet filter rules
# Description:         Sets packet filter rules
### END INIT INFO
#
. /etc/rc.status
                                              (Continued)
```

```
# Reset status of this service
rc_reset

case "$1" in
    start|restart|reload)
        echo -n "Starting Firewall "
        # Remember status and be verbose
        rc_status -v
        ;;
    stop)
        echo -n "Shutting down Firewall "
        # Remember status and be verbose
        rc_status -v
        ;;
    status)
        echo "Current Firewall-rules "
        rc_status -v
        ;;
    *)
        echo "Usage: $0
{start|restart|reload|stop|status}"
        exit 1
        ;;
esac
rc_exit
```

(A template similar to the above can be found on the student DVD in the directory for this section.)

Part III: Define General Variables

The use of variables makes it easier to maintain the script. Define variables for the IP address used (for instance 10.0.0.10) and the available interfaces (for instance eth0).

Additionally, set certain kernel parameters as part of the start section. These include in the directory /proc/sys/net/ipv4: ip_forward, tcp_syncookies, icmp_echo_ignore_broadcasts, icmp_ignore_bogus_error_responses, conf/*/accept_redirects, and conf/*/accept_source_route.

Detailed Steps to Complete this Part

1. Above the case section, define the following variables:

```
EXT_IF=eth0
EXT_IP=<your_IP>
INT_IF=
INT_IP=
```

Because the computers in the classroom might have only one NIC, this exercise is limited to defining rules for the INPUT and OUTPUT chains. The variables INT_IF and INT_IP can, for instance, be used for a second NIC and rules for the FORWARD chain.

You can also define variables for the IP address of the nameserver and other computers. Using variables facilitates later changes, because you only have to change the variable at one point, not IP addresses within various rules.

2. In the `start` section, set kernel parameters like

```
# Remove next comment sign if this is a router:
# echo 1 > /proc/sys/net/ipv4/ip_forward
echo 1 > /proc/sys/net/ipv4/tcp_syncookies
echo 1 > /proc/sys/net/ipv4/icmp_echo_ignore_broadcasts
echo 1 >\
/proc/sys/net/ipv4/icmp_ignore_bogus_error_responses
# Protect from ICMP redirect packets:
for f in /proc/sys/net/ipv4/conf/*/accept_redirects
do
 echo 0 > $f
done

# Block source routed packets
for f in /proc/sys/net/ipv4/conf/*/accept_source_route
do
 echo 0 > $f
done
```

(If you don't want to type this, have a look at the files on the student DVD.)

To see a brief explanation of these and other parameters, start the YaST Powertweak module and select the Networking options.

The above values can also be set within the Powertweak module instead of this script.

3. Add comments to your definition of variables and kernel parameter settings.

Part IV: Create a Section to Delete Any Existing Rules

You have to be able to delete any rules you set.

Go to the `stop` section within the case statement and add iptables commands to delete any existing rules.

Detailed Steps to Complete this Part

1. Add an informative message to be displayed when the script is called with the stop parameter.

2. Flush the chains by typing:

```
iptables -F
iptables -t nat -F
```

(The NAT (Network Address Translation) table will be covered later in this section.)

3. Delete any user-defined chains by typing:

```
iptables -X
```

(User-defined chains will be covered later in this section.)

4. Set the policy of the built in chains to accept by typing:

```
iptables -P INPUT ACCEPT
iptables -P OUTPUT ACCEPT
iptables -P FORWARD ACCEPT
```

5. You can also reset the kernel parameters to previous settings in the stop section as needed.

Part V: Create a Section to Display the Current Rule Set

Viewing the current rule set helps in debugging. Go to the `status` section within the case section and add rules that allow you to view the currently set rules.

Detailed Steps to Complete this Part

1. Go to the `status` section within the case statement to add iptables commands to display the currently active rules.

2. Add the following lines to the `status` section:

```
echo "Current iptables rules in the filter table:"
echo "------------------------------- "
iptables -v -L -n
echo ""
echo "Current iptables rules in the nat table: "
echo "--------------------------- "
iptables -v -n -t nat -L
```

Part VI: Add Static Rules

Now to the main part: The actual iptables rules.

Add rules in the `start` section of the case statement that:

- Set the policy to DROP
- Flush any existing rules before setting any new ones
- Allow everything from and to the loopback interface
- Allow accessing the ssh server on your computer
- Log any packets not accepted
- Reject packets with TCP reset
- Allow the reset packet to leave your computer

Open a terminal window and run tail -f /var/log/firewall. Have your neighbor test your rules by accessing the ssh server and other services, such as HTTP, potentially available on your computer.

Add rules that allow you to connect to other ssh servers, and rules that allow ICMP messages.

Detailed Steps to Complete this Part

1. Go to the `start` section within the case statement to add your rules with iptables commands.

2. Set the default policy to DROP by typing:

```
iptables -P INPUT DROP
iptables -P FORWARD DROP
iptables -P OUTPUT DROP
```

3. Flush existing rules and delete existing user-defined chains by typing:

```
iptables -F
iptables -t nat -F
iptables -X
```

   If you do not flush the rules in the beginning, each call of the script with the parameter `start` adds the rules to the chain once more.

4. Allow all traffic to and from the loopback interface by typing:

```
iptables -A OUTPUT -o lo -j ACCEPT
iptables -A INPUT -i lo -j ACCEPT
```

5. Define rules to allow others to access the ssh server on your computer by typing:

```
iptables -A INPUT -p TCP -i $EXT_IF --dport 22 \
-j ACCEPT
iptables -A OUTPUT -p TCP -o $EXT_IF --sport 22 \
-j ACCEPT
```

6. (*Optional*) Limit the above INPUT rule to a destination IP address as well as certain source IP addresses and source ports.

7. Add a rule that logs packets that are dropped in the INPUT chain by typing:

```
iptables -A INPUT -j LOG --log-prefix "INPUT-DROP"
```

8. Add a rule that rejects packets instead of having them dropped by the default policy of the chain by typing:

```
iptables -A INPUT -p TCP -j REJECT --reject-with tcp-reset
```

9. The current ruleset of the OUTPUT chain does not allow sending tcp-reset packets. So despite the rule above, no TCP reset packets would leave your machine. Add a rule that allows them by typing above the logging rule:

```
iptables -A OUTPUT -p TCP -o $EXT_IF \
                --tcp-flags ALL ack,rst -j ACCEPT
```

10. Start your script by entering in a terminal window (as root):

```
/etc/init.d/fw-script start
```

   If there are any error messages, correct any mistakes in the syntax within your script.

11. Have your partner try to access your ssh daemon.

    If he cannot do so, it could be because there is something wrong with your rules or because rules on his or her computer do not allow him or her to contact another server (or both).

    Find out what the problem is by opening another terminal window and looking at /var/log/firewall with less or tail -f on both computers.

    It is actually a good idea to have a separate terminal window with tail -f /var/log/firewall constantly open while testing the rules.

    If it turns out his rules forbid him to contact your computer, have him call his script with the parameter stop and try again.

    Correct any errors in your own script.

12. Test if your script actually blocks traffic to other services.

    Start the Apache Web server with rcapache2 start and have your partner try to access your computer with a browser.

    You should see log entries for dropped packets in /var/log/firewall.

    ! –syn prevents other computers from establishing a TCP connection from port 22. The first packet of a TCP handshake originating at port 22 is discarded by this rule.

13. If your partner asked you if you could reach his or her ssh daemon and you tried with the current rules active, you would notice that your current rules do not allow you to do that.

    Define rules that allow you to contact the ssh daemon on other computers by entering:

    ```
    iptables -A INPUT -p TCP -i $EXT_IF ! --syn --sport 22 \
    -j ACCEPT
    iptables -A OUTPUT -p TCP -o $EXT_IF --dport 22 \
    -j ACCEPT
    ```

    (*Note*: This rule has to be set above the rules defined in step 7 and 8 of this part of the exercise.)

    Why should you add ! –syn?

    (You can find the answer to this question at the end of Section 7 in the Instructor's Manual.)

14. Add another ruleset like the one in Step 13 allowing you to contact Web servers (port 80) on other computers.

15. Add a rule that logs packets that are dropped in the OUTPUT chain by entering:

    ```
    iptables -A OUTPUT -j LOG --log-prefix \ "OUTPUT-DROP"
    ```

    This rule should be inserted right above any rule dropping or rejecting all packets; in this exercise there is no such rule for the OUTPUT chain, packets that do not match any rule hit the policy set for the OUTPUT chain (DROP) and get discarded. Therefore insert this rule after any other rules for the OUTPUT chain in the script.

16. Activate your rules by entering /etc/init.d/fw-script start (your current rules will be replaced by the new ones).

17. Try to contact the sshd on your partner's computer.

18. Try to contact a Web server.

19. Try to ping your partner's computer and watch the log file.

20. Have him turn off his rules and then have him ping you.
    Watch your log file.

21. Add rules allowing incoming and outgoing ICMP messages.

22. Restart your script.
    Ping your partner's computer and have him ping yours.

23. Add comments to describe what your rules are supposed to do.

Objective 3—Understand iptables Advanced Features

The syntax covered in Objective 2 is sufficient to define a simple static packet filter. However, the netfilter framework has many more features with further options:

- Matches and Targets
- User-Defined Chains

Matches and Targets

Matches and targets extend the functionality of iptables.
The following topics are discussed:

- State Match
- Multiport Match
- Limit Match
- Recent Match
- Mark Match and MARK Target

State Match The state match turns the Linux computer into a stateful packet filter. The match understands the following parameters:

- *NEW*—This is the first packet of a connection that doesn't exist so far. With TCP it is usually the packet with the syn flag, but this is not necessarily so. NEW just refers to the first packet seen by the connection-tracking module.

- *ESTABLISHED*—This keyword refers to the second and all subsequent packets of a connection.

- *RELATED*—Related connections covered by this parameter can be the data connection to an FTP control connection or ICMP messages that relate to an existing connection.

- *INVALID*—This is used to describe packets that are not associated with a known connection.

This module not only allows stateful filtering; it also simplifies scripts to set rules.
First, you should define a rather general rule for second and subsequent packets belonging to all connections you allow, using the parameter ESTABLISHED. Related connections should be allowed as well. Then you should define what connections are allowed by formulating rules for the first packet, using the parameter NEW.

The following example allows ssh traffic coming in on eth0 to go through the router and out on eth1:

```
# Drop everything that is invalid for some reason
iptables -A FORWARD -m state --state INVALID -j DROP
# Accept second and following packets of any connection in FORWARD
# chain
iptables -A FORWARD -m state --state ESTABLISHED,RELATED -j ACCEPT
# Accept the first ssh packet that comes in on eth0
iptables -A FORWARD -i eth0 -o eth1 -p tcp --syn --dport 22 \
                    -m state --state NEW -j ACCEPT
```

Because the state match NEW considers every first packet that does not belong to an existing connection as new, the first packet of, for instance a portscan with various flags set or no flags set would also match. To make sure that only the first packet of the TCP handshake matches NEW and is accepted, the last line combines –syn and –state NEW.

Multiport Match   Using -p tcp or -p udp, you can define rules for single ports (–dport 22) or port ranges (–dport 1024:65535). However, if you have similar rules for ports 25, 80, and 110, you have to define a separate rule for each port.

The multiport match allows you to specify up to 15 ports within one rule. The option is `--dports` or `--sports` (note the **s** at the end).

So, instead of writing three rules for 3 ports, you can write just one:

```
iptables -A FORWARD -i eth0 -o eth1 -p tcp -m multiport --dports\
25,80,110 -j ACCEPT
```

Limit Match   Another useful match is the limit match. Rules that contain that match are taken out of the chain when a certain threshold of matching packets is reached.

The limit match can be used to limit certain traffic or to reduce the number of log entries. For example, suppose you have continuous Internet traffic on ports 135 to 137 hitting your firewall that you usually reject. Logging each of those packets would just bloat your log files without providing much relevant information.

You could do the following to limit those entries:

```
iptables -A INPUT -p TCP  --dport 135:137 \
-m limit --limit 10/hour -j LOG --log-prefix "DROP -TCP "
iptables -A INPUT -p TCP  --dport 135:137 -j REJECT --reject-with tcp-
reset
```

This would limit the number of packets logged to a few every hour.

The first iptables command logs a packet. After a certain number of packets, this rule no longer matches and packets hit the next rule directly without creating a log entry. After some time with no matching packets, the rule is put back in force and packets produce log entries again.

See *http://www.faqs.org/docs/iptables/matches.html* for a detailed explanation on how the limit works.

Recent Match
The recent match can be used to dynamically create a list of IP addresses and create rules regarding those IP addresses.

There are, for instance, automated attacks that try to guess accounts and passwords via ssh. Using the recent match, you can temporarily block traffic from the machine that originates this attack.

The information is kept in /proc/net/ipt_recent/DEFAULT, unless you specify a different name with the option –name. Specifying a name is useful if you want to keep track of different IP addresses in various rules.

The following is an example for ssh:

```
# Drop if 2 hits or more within the last 60 seconds
iptables -A INPUT -p tcp --dport 22 -i eth0 -m state --state NEW -m\
recent --update --seconds 60 --hitcount 2 -j DROP
# Add the source address to the list
iptables -A INPUT -p tcp --dport 22 -i eth0 -m state --state NEW -m\
recent --set
```

For the first ssh connection, the first rule does not match. The second rule creates a new entry in the recent list DEFAULT; because there is no target defined with -j, the packet travels down the chain and gets checked by subsequent rules.

For the second ssh connection the hitcount is one, so the first rule still does not match. The second rule updates the entry in the DEFAULT list, and the hitcount is now 2.

When the third packet arrives within a minute after the second packet, the first rule matches and the packet is dropped.

A legitimate user who mistyped his password would have to wait 60 seconds to have another try after two failures.

Mark Match and MARK Target
In addition to the filter table which is used for the INPUT, OUTPUT, and FORWARD chains, there are other tables for special purposes. Unlike the filter table, which is the default, they are specified using the option -t. The table to manipulate packets in various ways is the mangle table.

The MARK target is used in the mangle table to put an internal number within the kernel space on a packet. This number can then be used to write rules matching packets with that number.

This is useful for creating rules for traffic within an IPSec tunnel. First, the IPSec packet is marked and, as the decrypted packets inherit this mark, rules can be formulated matching the traffic from within the tunnel by using this mark.

```
# Mark ESP packets
iptables -t mangle -A PREROUTING -p 50 -j MARK --set-mark 10
# Accept ESP packets
iptables -A INPUT -p 50 -j ACCEPT
# Define rule based on the mark
iptables -A FORWARD -o $INT_IF -p TCP --dport 80 -m mark --mark 10 \
-j ACCEPT
# Take care of the traffic in the other direction
iptables -A FORWARD -i $INT_IF -m state --state ESTABLISHED,RELATED \
-j ACCEPT
```

To view rules in the mangle table, enter `iptables -t mangle -n -L -v`, and to flush all rules from the mangle table enter `iptables -t mangle -F`.

The MARK target is covered in more detail in Section 9 in "Understand Packet Filtering of VPN Traffic" on page 275.

User-Defined Chains

User-defined chains can reduce the number of rules packets have to go through before they hit a match. User-defined chains can also help to make scripts to set rules easier to understand and maintain.

The sequence is as follows:

1. Create a user-defined chain.

2. Create rules within that chain.

3. Create rules within the default chains that have the user-defined chain as their target (instead of DROP, REJECT, or ACCEPT).

   The user-defined chain has to exist before it can be used as a target.

4. If no rule matches in the user-defined chain, the packet returns to the chain it came from and continues down the rules in that chain.

Figure 7-2 illustrates the path the packet takes.

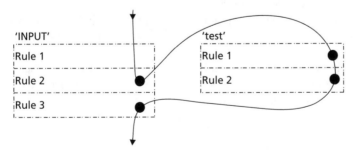

Figure 7-2

You could have a user-defined chain for each protocol or one for certain categories of traffic, such as external in, external out, internal in, and internal out.

The following example defines a chain that takes care of packets that should be logged and then dropped. The chain is first created using the option –N; then rules are added to the chain using the option –A. The new chain can only be a target in other rules after it has been created. Therefore, within a script, put these rules above those that use this chain as a target.

```
iptables -N log_drop
iptables -A log_drop  -p TCP --syn -j LOG --log-prefix "DROP-TCP-SYN "
iptables -A log_drop  -p TCP --syn -m limit --limit 5/s \
                      -j REJECT --reject-with tcp-reset
iptables -A log_drop  -p TCP --syn -j DROP
iptables -A log_drop  -p TCP     -j LOG --log-prefix "DROP-TCP "
iptables -A log_drop  -p TCP     -m limit --limit 5/s \
                      -j REJECT --reject-with tcp-reset
iptables -A log_drop  -p TCP     -j DROP
iptables -A log_drop  -p UDP     -j LOG --log-prefix "DROP-UDP "
iptables -A log_drop  -p UDP     -m limit --limit 5/s \

                      -j REJECT --reject-with icmp-port-unreachable
iptables -A log_drop  -p UDP     -j DROP
iptables -A log_drop  -p ICMP    -j LOG --log-prefix "DROP-ICMP "
iptables -A log_drop  -p ICMP    -j DROP
iptables -A log_drop  -j LOG --log-prefix "DROP-PROTO-ETC "
iptables -A log_drop  -m limit --limit 5/s \
                      -j REJECT --reject-with icmp-proto-unreachable
iptables -A log_drop  -j DROP
```

The above example rejects packets up to a certain rate; if too many packets hit the reject rules, packets are just dropped. The reasoning behind this is that rejecting is RFC-compliant but produces additional traffic. So, if the number of packets gets too high within a certain time span, packets are dropped silently.

Different kinds of packets have different log prefixes to make it easier to see in the log file what was rejected.

Because the last rule above matches any packet, no packet returns to the chain it came from. Any packet that gets to the end of the user-defined chain gets dropped.

Assuming you only want to allow ssh connections on eth0, your rules following the above might look like the following:

```
# Incoming traffic, second and subsequent packets
iptables -A INPUT  -i eth0 -m state --state ESTABLISHED,RELATED -j \
ACCEPT
# Outgoing traffic, second and subsequent packets
iptables -A OUTPUT -o eth0 -m state --state ESTABLISHED,RELATED -j \
ACCEPT
# ssh incoming on eth0, first packet
iptables -A INPUT   -i eth0 -p TCP --syn --dport 22 -m state --state NEW \
                                                      -j ACCEPT
# Everything else goes into the user-defined chain log_drop
iptables -A INPUT  -j log_drop
```

To delete a user-defined chain, you first have to delete the rules in the chain before you can delete the chain itself.

```
# Flush the user-defined chain log_drop
iptables -F log_drop
# Delete the user-defined chain log_drop
iptables -X log_drop
```

Exercise 7-2: Modify the Script to Set and Delete iptables Rules

EXERCISE

Time Required: 60–90 Minutes

Objective: The script developed in the last exercise uses static filtering rules only. In this exercise, you will modify the script to include dynamic filtering rules, and you will create and use a user-defined chain.

- Part I: Use Stateful Packet Filtering
- Part II: User-Defined Chains
- Part III: (*Optional*) View the SuSEFirewall2 Configuration and Script

Part I: Use Stateful Packet Filtering

The state match helps to simplify the script and thus makes it less error prone. And it adds the feature of stateful inspection to the computer.

Replace the rules defined for TCP connections in Exercise 7-1, "Get Familiar with Basic iptables Syntax" on page 172, Step 6, with rules using stateful packet filtering.

Detailed Steps to Complete this Part

1. Put a comment sign in front of the six TCP rules (two each for ssh in and out, and www).

2. Define rules that drop all invalid packets. Put them directly after the rules for the loopback interface:

```
# INPUT-Chain
iptables -A INPUT -m state --state INVALID -j DROP
# OUTPUT-Chain
iptables -A OUTPUT -m state --state INVALID -j DROP
```

3. Define rules for the second and all subsequent packets of a connection using the connection tracking module. Put those directly after the rules created in Step 2 above:

```
# INPUT-Chain
iptables -A INPUT -m state --state ESTABLISHED,RELATED -j \
ACCEPT
# OUTPUT-Chain
iptables -A OUTPUT -m state --state ESTABLISHED,RELATED -j \
ACCEPT
```

4. Define a rule allowing the first packet of a connection to the ssh daemon on your computer by entering:

```
iptables -A INPUT -i $EXT_IF -p TCP --syn --dport 22 -m \
state --state NEW -j ACCEPT
```

5. Set the new rules by entering:

```
/etc/init.d/fw-script start
```

Have your partner access the ssh daemon on your computer. Watch the log file.

6. View the entry tracking the connections in the /proc file system by entering:

```
cat /proc/net/ip_conntrack
```

7. Add rules that allow you to access the sshd and Web servers on other computers. Test this and the access to the Web server running on your computer to see if it is still blocked as intended.

8. Add useful comments to your script.

Part II: User-Defined Chains

User-defined chains can help reduce the number of rules packets have to run through before a hit. They can also make the script easier to understand.

The user-defined chain has to exist before any rule uses the chain as a target. Therefore, these rules should appear in the script above the rules for the built-in chains.

You may have noticed that the script so far does not allow any name resolution. Therefore, in this part of the exercise, set up a user-defined chain for UDP packets.

Create a user-defined chain that takes care of UDP packets, allowing name resolution, logging packets that are to be rejected, and rejecting them. Include rules in the INPUT and OUTPUT chain that have the new user-defined chain as a target.

Detailed Steps to Complete this Part

1. Locate an appropriate point in the script to add the user-defined chain, for instance, after the rules setting the policy and flushing the chains. Create the chain udp-rules by typing:

```
iptables -N udp-rules
```

2. Create a rule for a packet querying a nameserver by entering (on one line):

```
iptables -A udp-rules -o $EXT_IF -p UDP --dport 53 -m \
state --state NEW -j ACCEPT
```

(There is no need for a rule for the answer packets because they are covered by the rule from Part I covering second and subsequent packets.)

Under certain circumstances there is a fallback to TCP for name resolution. Therefore, a similar rule is needed for TCP port 53.

3. Packets that do not match any of the rules in the user-defined chain would continue down the built-in chain they came from.

   This is not what is intended here; therefore, insert a rule to log packets and another to reject them by entering:

   ```
   iptables -A udp-rules -j LOG --log-prefix "REJECT-udp"
   iptables -A udp-rules -j REJECT
   ```

   Because this last rule matches all packets, none return to the previous chain.

4. The rule to send all UDP packets from the output chain to the user-defined chain has to be inserted after the general rules for second and subsequent packets; otherwise, the answers to the UDP packets your computer sends out will be discarded.

   Add this rule by typing the following at an appropriate point below the general rules in the script:

   ```
   iptables -A OUTPUT -p UPD -j udp-rules
   ```

 If you want to allow incoming UDP traffic, a similar rule is needed for the INPUT chain. You can distinguish incoming and outgoing traffic by the -i and -o options within the user-defined chain.

5. Save the file; activate the rules by entering:

   ```
   /etc/init.d/fw-script start
   ```

   Find out if name resolution is now functional.

6. (*Optional*) Create another user-defined chain that takes care of the logging.

   Instead of logging packets in built-in or other user-defined chains as it is currently done, send those packets to a separate user-defined chain to be logged and then dropped or rejected.

7. (*Optional*) Watch the log file for a while.

   You will see all kinds of entries for packets being rejected.

   Write rules allowing IP traffic, such as printing via CUPS, that is needed for proper computer operation.

8. (*Optional*) Block access to the ssh daemon temporarily after two connection attempts using the recent match.

9. (*Optional*) Have your partner test your filter rules with nmap from his computer.

Part III: *(Optional)* View the SuSEFirewall2 Configuration and Script

The purpose of this exercise is to show you a sophisticated setup and its complexity. Have a look at the SUSEfirewall2 scripts. Note the use of variables and how rules are set.

Detailed Steps to Complete this Part

1. View /etc/sysconfig/SuSEfirewall2 by using less.

2. View the script /sbin/SuSEfirewall2 by using less.

3. View the scripts /etc/init.d/SuSEfirewall2_* by using less.

Objective 4—Understand Network Address Translation

Network Address Translation (NAT) is most commonly used to connect computers with private IP addresses (like 10.0.0.0/8) to the Internet. It is also used to implement transparent (also called intercepting or forced) HTTP proxy servers.

To understand NAT, you have to understand:

- PREROUTING and POSTROUTING Chains
- Types of NAT

PREROUTING and POSTROUTING Chains

In addition to the INPUT, OUTPUT, and FORWARD chain of the filter table, three other built-in chains are implemented via the `nat` table.

As the name implies, packets hit the PREROUTING chain before the routing decision is made, and the POSTROUTING chain after any routing decision, just before the packets leave the computer through the proper interface. There is also an OUTPUT chain available in the nat table.

To specify rules for these chains, the table `nat` has to be specified:

```
iptables -A PREROUTING -t nat ...
iptables -A POSTROUTING -t nat ...
```

Types of NAT

NAT is a general term that embraces the translation of the source address, the destination address, or ports.

The following is described:

- Source NAT
- Masquerading
- Destination NAT

Source NAT Source NAT means that the source address within the IP header of the packet is changed. This is used, for instance, to connect networks with private IP addresses to the Internet.

The way this is done is as follows:

```
iptables -t nat -A POSTROUTING -o eth0 -j SNAT --to-source 110.111.112.113
```

Masquerading Masquerading is a special case of Source NAT. It is used in dial-up connections, where the source IP address to be used changes with each new dial-in.

```
iptables -t nat -A POSTROUTING -o ds10 -j MASQUERADE
```

Because the packet goes through the POSTROUTING chain just before leaving the computer, it can never be used with -i for an input device.

Destination NAT Destination NAT can be used to change the destination address of packets to that of another computer or another port.

You could change the address to another computer if, for example, your Web server has as its official IP address that of the gateway, but is in fact located in the DMZ with an IP from a private network. Destination NAT could be used to change the address of any packet addressed to port 80 on the gateway to port 80 of the computer in the DMZ.

```
iptables -t nat -A PREROUTING -p tcp -i eth1 --dport 80 \
        -j DNAT --to-destination 172.16.0.1
```

Destination NAT can also be used for intercepting HTTP proxying. If your company policy requires the use of a proxy, you could redirect all traffic destined for port 80 to the Web proxy.

```
iptables -t nat -A PREROUTING -p tcp -i eth0 --dport 80 \
        -j DNAT --to-destination 10.0.0.254:3128
```

In this scenario the destination IP is that of the input interface. You could also use the target REDIRECT, which would achieve the same result:

```
iptables -t nat -A PREROUTING -p tcp -i eth0 --dport 80 \
        -j REDIRECT --to-ports 3128
```

For more information on iptables and firewalls, see the following:
  The Netfilter homepage at *http://www.netfilter.org/*
  A very good iptables tutorial at *http://iptables-tutorial.frozentux.net/iptables-tutorial.html*

Summary

- A TCP/IP connection between hosts is called a socket. Sockets use port numbers to identify services on each host, as well as packets to transmit information between hosts.

- Routers transfer packets between networks. You can enable routing in the Linux kernel and use the netfilter framework to create static and dynamic packet filters that restrict TCP/IP packets based on the information within tables.

- The default packet filter table uses chains to group common restrictions. The INPUT chain restricts traffic destined for a Linux computer, the FORWARD chain restricts passing through a Linux router, and the OUTPUT chain restricts traffic originating from a Linux computer.

- Each chain may contain several rules that match network traffic and perform target actions on that traffic such as ACCEPT, REJECT, DROP and LOG. Rules are analyzed in order, and the packet filter uses the first rule that matches the network traffic. If the traffic that enters the Linux router does not match any rules, then a default policy action will be applied.

- The **iptables** command may be used to configure packet filter rules, chains, policies and targets. A single **iptables** command may be used to specify multiple ports, limit traffic, or log packet information.

- To configure a dynamic packet filter rule, simply add the **–state NEW** option to the **iptables** command.

- Packet filter rules can also allow you to specify different restrictions for recent traffic, create user-defined chains, or use the mangle table to mark network packets for future filtering.

- The netfilter framework may also be used to connect private networks to public networks using NAT. Source NAT, Masquerading and Destination NAT are common NAT implementations.

Key Terms

/etc/services   A file that lists common port definitions. It is used by several Linux services.

/etc/sysconfig/sysctl   The file used at Linux startup to configure system configuration parameters such as routing.

/proc/net/ipt_recent/DEFAULT   A file used to store information about recently received packets.

/proc/sys/net/ipv4/ip_forward   The file used by the Linux kernel to enable routing.

/var/log/firewall   The default log file used by the netfilter framework.

chain   A packet filtering component that contains rules used to restrict traffic.

Destination NAT   An implementation of NAT that changes the destination of packets instead of the source. It may be used to redirect requests to a specific server within the internal network or DMZ.

dynamic packet filter   A packet filter that can change the rules it uses for restricting network traffic based on the nature of the traffic.

filter table   The table that contains the INPUT, FORWARD and OUTPUT chains used by the netfilter framework.

FORWARD chain   The combined set of rules in the filter table that apply to traffic that is forwarded through a Linux computer running as a packet filtering firewall router.

INPUT chain   The combined set of rules in the filter table that apply to traffic that is destined for a Linux computer running as a packet filtering firewall.

iptables command   The command used to configure the netfilter framework.

limit match   A packet filter rule that prevents future traffic after a certain number of packets have been received of a particular type.

mangle table   The table used by the netfilter framework to make changes to the headers of TCP/IP packets or mark packets for later filtering.

mark match   A packet filter rule that changes the headers of packets such that they can be easily identified later.

Masquerading   An implementation of NAT suited for routers that do not have static public IP addresses.

multiport match   A packet filter rule that applies to traffic on several different ports.

nat table   The table used by the netfilter framework to perform Network Address Translation.

netfilter framework   The software components that comprise the packet filtering firewall on most Linux systems.

Network Address Translation (NAT)   A technology that rewrites the source and destination of IP packets as they pass through a router. NAT is typically used to connect private networks to the Internet using a single IP address.

OUTPUT chain   The combined set of rules in the filter table that apply to traffic that originates from a Linux computer running as a packet filtering firewall.

packet   A single unit of transmission on a TCP/IP network.

packet filter   A software component that drops network communication that is addressed to a particular IP address or port number.

policy   The action taken that a packet filter takes on a packet when it does not match any rules within a chain.

POSTROUTING chain   The combined set of rules in the nat or mangle table that apply to traffic that is about to leave a router after being routed using the routing table.

PREROUTING chain   The combined set of rules in the nat or mangle table that apply to traffic that has entered a router and has not yet been routed using the routine table.

recent match   A packet filter rule that may be used to restrict traffic that was recently received by the Linux system.

rule   A packet filtering component that lists a specific type of network traffic and the action the packet filter will take when the traffic is detected.

socket   A connection between hosts that identifies the IP address and port number used on each host for the communication.

Source NAT   An implementation of NAT designed for routers that have static public IP address on the Internet.

state match   A packet filter rule that specifies that stateful or dynamic packet filtering should be used.

stateful packet filter   See dynamic packet filter.

static packet filter   A packet filter that restricts network traffic based on rules that do not change.

target   The part of a packet filtering rule that specifies the action that is taken when traffic matches the conditions specified in the rule.

user-defined chain   A set of packet filter rules that are parsed when a certain rule from another chain is evaluated.

Review Questions

1. You wish to restrict all traffic passing into your local network except for traffic destined for a custom application that remote users use. This application listens for traffic on port 29188 but then changes the port number it uses to a random port above 32000. What type of packet filter is best to implement and why? _____

2. You are implementing a static packet filter on one of your Linux routers. Which chain in the default filter table is used to match traffic that is passed through the router?

    a. INBOUND

    b. OUTBOUND

    c. MANGLE

    d. FORWARD

3. Why is it important to maintain the order of rules within a packet filter chain? _____

4. What command may be used to drop all packets destined for the Linux computer that do not match a packet filter rule?

    a. iptables –P FORWARD DROP

    b. iptables –P INPUT DROP

    c. iptables –D FORWARD DROP

    d. iptables –D INPUT DROP

5. What option to the **iptables** command may be used to remove all rules from a particular chain? _____

6. You wish to create a rule in your packet filter that specifies destination DNS and HTTPS traffic. Which ports would you specify and what option may be used to select them?

    a. –dports 50,80

    b. –dports 50:80

    c. –dports 53,443

    d. –dports 53:443

7. What target would you use in a packet filter rule to specify that the traffic should be dropped and an ICMP port unreachable message should be returned to the sender?

    a. DROP

    b. DESTROY

    c. LOG

    d. REJECT

8. What state match would you use when creating a rule that will apply to all traffic in a single connection other than the first packet?

    a. ESTABLISHED

    b. SUBSQT

    c. NEW

    d. RELATED

9. You are using the **iptables** command to create a packet filter rule that uses the LOG target to record connection attempts in a log file. What other option should you use in your **iptables** command to minimize excessive logging? _____

10. To label traffic that is entering your Linux router using a packet filter, you plan on using the MARK target. What table must you specify when using the MARK target?

    a. nat

    b. mangle

    c. default

    d. forward

11. You have created a new user-defined chain called MYCHAIN. How do you specify this chain in future packet filter rules?

    a. –j MYCHAIN

    b. –A MYCHAIN

    c. –m MYCHAIN

    d. –P MYCHAIN

12. Which types of NAT are commonly used to connect private networks to the Internet? (Choose all that apply.)

    a. Destination NAT

    b. Forwarding NAT

    c. Masquerading NAT

    d. Source NAT

Discovery Exercises

DISCOVERY EXERCISES

Static Packet Filters

Although dynamic packet filters have several advantages over static packet filters, static packet filters are straightforward and easy to create. As a result, many organizations use static packet filters on Linux routers and Linux hosts to restrict certain types of traffic. For each of the following questions, write the appropriate **iptables** commands that will perform the desired action in the static packet filter. In addition, assume that the Linux system you are configuring has two network interfaces: a public Internet interface on the 3.0.0.0/8 network (eth0) and a private LAN interface on the 190.14.6.0/24 network (eth1).

1. All traffic that is destined for the Linux router and that passes through the Linux router should be silently denied if it does not match a packet filtering rule. Any traffic that originates from the Linux router should be allowed if it does not match a packet filtering rule.

2. Any traffic that is received on the public Internet interface that contained a spoofed IP address (190.14.6.0/24 or 127.0.0.0/8) should be dropped.

3. Any traffic below port 1024 that passes from the private LAN interface to the public Internet interface should be allowed except for telnet traffic. The sending host should be notified if a telnet packet is dropped.

Dynamic Packet Filters

By using a state match, dynamic packet filter rules have more flexibility than the static packet filter rules discussed in the previous Discovery Exercise and are commonly configured on Linux routers that pass traffic between public and private networks. For each of the following questions, write the appropriate **iptables** commands that will perform the desired action in the dynamic packet filter. As with the previous Discovery Exercise, assume that the Linux system you are configuring has two network interfaces: a public Internet interface on the 3.0.0.0/8 network (eth0) and a private LAN interface on the 190.14.6.0/24 network (eth1).

1. Forward all new DNS, WWW and SMTP traffic that is received on the private LAN interface.

2. All packets traveling from eth1 to eth0 that are part of an existing connection should be allowed.

3. Do not forward SMTP packets if your Linux router receives more than 10 requests in 5 seconds on eth1.

Network Address Translation

In the previous two Discovery Exercises, you examined static and dynamic packet filter rules for a Linux router. Assume that you are using the same Linux router, and write the **iptables** commands that may be used to create the NAT configurations described below. As with the previous Discovery Exercises, the Linux system you are configuring has two network interfaces: a public Internet interface on the 3.0.0.0/8 network (eth0) and a private LAN interface on the 190.14.6.0/24 network (eth1).

1. Your Linux router uses Source NAT to provide Internet access for clients on the private LAN via the public interface eth0. The IP address of eth0 is 3.0.0.1.

2. Your Linux router uses Masquerading NAT to provide Internet access for clients on the private LAN. Although your public Internet interface is assigned an IP address statically, it is connected to a PPPoE connection called dsl0.

Application-Level Gateways

Application-level gateways can be used to make services available across network boundaries in a secure way. Unlike pure packet filters that do not take the content of the packets into consideration, application-level gateways offer more control over the transferred content. In this section you will learn the basics about application-level gateways. You will also learn how to configure the following packages shipped with SUSE Linux Enterprise Server 10:

- *Squid*—A very popular application-level gateway for HTTP requests.
- *Dante*—A software package implementing the generic SOCKS proxy protocol.
- *rinetd*—A port redirector.

Objectives

- Application-Level Gateway Basics
- Configure and Use Squid
- Configure and Use Dante
- Configure and Use rinetd

Objective 1—Application-Level Gateway Basics

To understand application-level gateways, you need to know the following:

- The Purpose of Application-Level Gateways
- How Application-Level Gateways Work

The Purpose of Application-Level Gateways

The term *application-level gateway* describes gateways where the connection from one side to the other is taken care of on layer 7, the application layer, of the ISO/OSI network model. This is different from a router, where the connections are taken care of in layer 3, the network layer (or layer 4 if it is a filtering router considering protocols like TCP and UDP as well).

Application-level gateways are used to connect applications over the network that cannot or should not talk to each other directly.

The following lists some possible reasons for this:

- The applications are in different networks and, for security reasons, no direct connections are allowed; for example, a browser in the internal network and a Web server outside in the Internet.

- The applications use different protocols and a gateway is needed to connect them; for example, a company uses a proprietary e-mail system and wants to integrate clients that use the IMAP protocol.

- The performance of the connection should be improved; for example, Web requests are cached by a gateway.

- The connection should only be available for authorized users; for example, access to the Internet is only allowed for certain employees of a company.

Sometimes the term *proxy server* is used instead of application-level gateway.

How Application-Level Gateways Work

As the term *application-level* indicates, application-level gateways work at the top level of the ISO/OSI reference model. Unlike routers, which only move network packets from one network to another, application-level gateways view the content within the network packets. This enables them to control and influence the data flow much more accurately than routers.

The following two diagrams (Figures 8-1 and 8-2) show the difference between a router and an application-level gateway, using the example of a Web browser accessing a Web server.

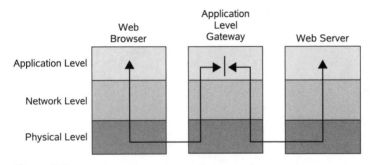

Figure 8-1

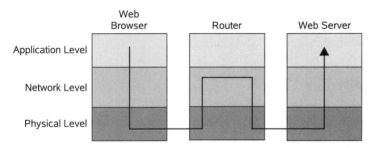

Figure 8-2

In both cases a user uses a Web browser to access an external Web site from an internal company network.

In the first example, the Web browser sends a direct HTTP request to the Web server through the router. The router might rewrite the source address of the network packets to its own (masquerading), or filter the network packets based on IP addresses or ports, but the content of the packets or the user name are not considered.

In the second example, the Web browser sends the HTTP request to the application-level gateway, in this case an HTTP (Web) proxy server. Now the application-level gateway sends its own request to the Web server and delivers the data received back to the Web browser. As you can see, there is no direct network connection between the Web browser and the Web server.

While processing requests from a Web browser and corresponding responses from a Web server, the application-level gateway can inspect the content of the transferred HTTP data. In this way certain content, like JavaScript elements, could be blocked or the content could be cached to satisfy requests from other clients.

The example in Figure 8-2 refers to an application-level gateway for the HTTP protocol (Web proxy). Application-level gateways are available for many more common internet protocols such as POP3, IMAP, SMTP, or FTP.

Objective 2—Configure and Use Squid

`Squid` is the most widely used proxy server for the HTTP protocol. Squid is open source software developed by the Squid project.

For more information on the Squid project, see
http://www.squid-cache.org/.

In this objective you will learn the following:

- Understand the Basics of HTTP
- Understand How Squid Works
- Install Squid on SUSE Linux Enterprise Server 10
- Understand the Squid Configuration File
- Control Access to Squid

- Configure Web Browsers to Use Squid
- Understand How Squid Handles SSL Connections
- Configure Proxy Authentication
- Configure URL Filtering
- Configure an Intercepting Proxy Server
- Analyze Squid Log Files

Understand the Basics of HTTP

HTTP is one of the most frequently used Internet transfer protocols. The major field of application is the transfer of Web pages and their related data (HTML, images, and JavaScript files).

The HTTP communication is based on requests and responses: The client (Web browser) sends a request and the server (Web server) answers this request with a response. Each request contains a command and several additional header fields. The most common command is GET, which requests a file from a server.

When a Web page is transferred, the client needs to make a request for each component of the page. A component could be an HTML file, a graphic file, and maybe a Flash or JavaScript file.

When clients are configured to use a proxy server, they send their requests to the proxy server instead of the actual target Web server. The proxy makes a request to the actual server on behalf of the client and forwards the data to the client.

In most cases, the proxy saves the requested data and uses this data when another client has the same request. This is called *caching*. Not all content that is transferred over HTTP is suitable for caching. Pages that are generated by a script or that are personalized for the user viewing the page are usually not cached.

Therefore, a Web server response usually contains the header fields Pragma and Cache-Control, which determine if a page can be cached. HTTP requests from clients can contain header fields that tell a proxy to not deliver data from its cache but to fetch the data from the target Web server.

With its clients, Squid speaks only HTTP. However, it is possible to encapsulate other protocols such as FTP or GOPHER into HTTP requests. Squid can handle these requests and connect to the target servers in their native protocol. Because of this feature, Squid is sometimes also called an FTP proxy. This is incorrect, because all FTP requests need to be encapsulated into HTTP by the browser. If you need a real FTP proxy, you should look at Frox (*http://frox.sourceforge.net*).

Understand How Squid Works

Squid can be used in the following ways:

- *Standard proxy server*—As a standard proxy server, Squid is used as a gateway to connect an internal network to the Internet.

  On one side Squid works as a firewall, separating the internal and the external network. On the other side, Squid caches the transferred data and reduces the load on the Internet connection. See Figure 8-3.

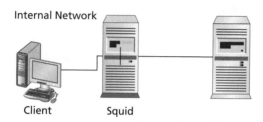

Figure 8-3

- *Intercepting proxy server*—An intercepting (or transparent) proxy server is very similar to a standard proxy server. Squid separates the involved networks and stores content in its cache. But unlike a standard proxy, no specific client (Web browser) configuration is required to use the proxy. See Figure 8-4.

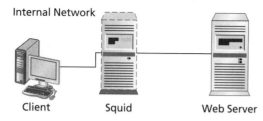

Figure 8-4

Intercepting proxying does not work for HTTPS connections.

- *HTTP accelerator*—As an HTTP accelerator, Squid works on the other side of the data flow. Instead of providing clients with access to the Internet, Squid takes the load from a Web server by caching its content. See Figure 8-5.

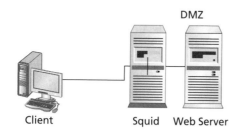

Figure 8-5

This section discusses the use of Squid as standard proxy and as intercepting proxy.

Install Squid on SUSE Linux Enterprise Server 10

Squid is shipped as an RPM package with SUSE Linux Enterprise Server 10. To install it, you need to select the package `squid` in the YaST Package Manager. You can also install the `squidGuard` package, which contains additional content and access control filters for Squid. You will learn more about SquidGuard later in this section.

After you have installed and configured Squid, you can start it by entering:

`rcsquid start`

To start Squid automatically at boot time, you can add it to the init process by entering:

`insserv squid`

Understand the Squid Configuration File

The configuration file for Squid (`/etc/squid/squid.conf`) is fully documented with extensive comments directly in the file.

Only a few entries in this file need to be adjusted to configure basic proxy server functionality; most parameters can be left with the default values. The default values will also be used if no other value is given or if the entry is prefaced with a comment sign.

A configuration option in the squid.conf file is also called a *tag*. The following is a list of the most important tags:

- Network Tags
- Cache Size Tags
- Log Files and Cache Directories Tags
- Fine-Tuning Tags
- Time-Out Tags
- Administrative Tags
- Error Tags

Network Tags You can set the following tags:

- *http_port*—The port on which Squid waits for requests is set to 3128 by default. Often another port, such as 8080, is set.

  If you run Squid on a gateway with an external and an internal network interface, you can also specify an IP address in the form `ip_address:port` on which Squid should listen. In this way you can make sure that your proxy can only be accessed from the internal network.

Cache Size Tags You can set the following tags:

- *cache_mem*—This parameter determines how much physical RAM Squid uses to cache data (most popluar replies). Besides the RAM cache, Squid also uses the hard disk for caching purposes.

  Squid's actual memory usage depends on the cache size on the disk. As a rule of thumb, Squid uses approximately 10 MB of RAM per GB of the total disk cache space, plus the amount specified in cache_mem, plus another 10-20 MB. It is recommended that the Squid server have at least twice this total amount of physical RAM available.

- *cache_swap_low, cache_swap_high*—This refers to the disk space reserved for caching files (see the cache_dir tag).

These two values define two percentage values. When the space occupied by the files on the disk surpasses the lower value (cache_swap_low), Squid starts to delete files from the disk and when the second value (cache_swap_high) is reached despite this, files are deleted more aggressively. The default values 90/95 should be suitable for most purposes.

- *maximum_object_size*—Objects (files) that are larger than this value are not cached on the hard disk. The default value is 4096 (4 MB).

- *minimum_object_size*—Objects (files) that are smaller than this value are not cached at all. The default value is 0 (0 KB).

- *maximum_object_size_in_memory*—Objects (files) that are larger than this value are not cached in the RAM cache. This value should be kept large enough so that frequently requested objects can be stored in the RAM cache.

- *ipcache_size, ipcache_low, ipcache_high*—Squid also caches the name resolution. These parameters determine how many IP addresses are cached (ipcache_size), when Squid starts to remove IP addresses from the cache (ipcache_low), and when this is done more aggressively (ipcache_high). The latter two are percentages with default values of 90 and 95, respectively.

Log Files and Cache Directories Tags   You can set the following tags:

- *cache_dir*—This tag determines where and how Squid caches data on the hard disk. This tag uses the following format:

```
cache_dir storage_format dir size L1-dirs L2-dirs options
```

- *storage_format*—Determines which method Squid uses to store data on the hard disk. The default is ufs, which is the traditional Squid storage method. Other possible methods, such as aufs, are documented directly in the Squid configuration file.

- *dir*—Determines the directory where Squid stores its cache files. In the default configuration, Squid uses /var/cache/squid.

- *size*—The size parameter sets a limit on how much disk space can be used for caching—by default this is 100 MB.

- *L1-dir*—Squid spreads the cached data over several directories and subdirectories. This has the advantage that searching for data is much quicker because directories with fewer file entries can be searched faster than directories which contain many files. L1-dir specifies the number of directories Squid can create on the first level of its caching directory.

- *L2-dir*—The number of directories that Squid can create under each of the L1 directories.

  The default values for these parameters are 16 L1 directories and 256 L2 directories.

- *options*—The options parameter can be used to pass options to Squid that are specific for the storage method used. Like the storage methods itself, these options are documented directly in the Squid configuration file.

A default configuration for cache_dir looks like:

```
cache_dir ufs /var/cache/squid 100 16 256
```

- *cache_access_log*—Determines where Squid stores the access log file. All client requests are logged in this file. The default location is /var/log/squid/access.log. Use the value none to disable logging.

- *cache_log*—Specifies where Squid stores the cache log file. This file is used to log nonclient-specific information about the Squid cache. The default location is /var/log/squid/cache.log. Use the value none to disable logging.

- *cache_store_log*—Defines the file where activity is logged. This file contains information on which files were deleted from the cache, which files were saved, and for how long they should be stored. Because there is no program available to analyze this log, it can be deactivated with the entry none.

Fine-Tuning Tags You can set the following tags:

- *request_header_max_size*—Determines the maximum HTTP header size that Squid accepts from a client. Usually HTTP headers are relatively small, so the default is set to 10 KB.

- *request_body_max_size*—Limits the amount of data that can be sent in the body of an HTTP request. This data is usually from data that comes from an HTTP file upload. If you don't want to limit this size, you can set the value to 0 (no limit). This is also the default configuration.

- *quick_abort_min, quick_abort_max, quick_abort_pct*—Squid can be configured to continue to download the requested data, even when a data transfer is aborted by a client. The limits of such a transfer being continued are set by these variables:

  - *quick_abort_min*—(in KB) If less than the given value is missing, the transfer is continued. The default value is 16 KB.

  - *quick_abort_max*—(in KB) If more than the given value is missing, the transfer is aborted. The default value is 16 KB.

  - *quick_abort_pct*—(as a percentage) If more than the specified percentage has already been transferred, the transfer is continued. The default value is 95 percent.

- *negative_ttl*—When Squid tries to fetch data for a client request, but it gets a negative response such as 404 Not Found, this fact (that there was a negative response) is cached for the amount of time specified with this option. You need to specify a value and a time unit like seconds, minutes, or hours. The default is 5 minutes.

- *positive_dns_ttl*—Squid also caches DNS responses. This tag specifies how long successful DNS requests are stored. The default value is 6 hours.

- *negative_dns_ttl*—This option specifies for how long negative (unsuccessful) DNS requests are cached. The default value is 1 minute.

Time-Out Tags You can set the following tags:

- *connect_timeout*—The time after which Squid quits an attempt to connect to a computer without success. The default value is 120 seconds.

- *request_timeout*—The amount of time Squid waits for an HTTP request after the network connection has been established by a client. The default value is 5 minutes.

- *shutdown_lifetime*—When the cache receives a SIGTERM or SIGHUP signal, it is put in Shutdown Pending mode until all connections have been terminated. Any connections remaining active after this time receive a time-out message. The default value is 30 seconds.

Administrative Tags You can set the following tags:

- *cache_mgr*—Sets the e-mail address of the cache administrator. If Squid breaks down, the administrator receives an e-mail. If the cache cannot answer a requested URL or if the access permissions are insufficient, a message containing this e-mail address is displayed in the client's browser. The default value is Webmaster.

- *cache_effective_user, cache_effective_group*—If Squid is started by root, the effective user ID and group ID are changed to these values. The default values on SUSE Linux Enterprise Server 10 are squid and nogroup. If Squid is not started by root, the user ID and group ID remain unchanged.

Error Tags You can set the following tags:

- *err_html_text*—Defines text that should be included in error messages presented to the clients. You can use HTML to format the text. To make sure that this text is displayed, you must include the variable %L in the error files in /usr/share/squid/errors where you want this text to appear.

- *error_directory*—Directory for error pages. The default value is /usr/share/squid/errors. The templates can be found in several languages in the respective directories in /usr/share/doc/packages/squid/errors.

The authoritative Squid documentation is the configuration file /etc/squid/squid.conf. Additional documentation can be found at *http://wiki.squid-cache.org/*. At *http://squid.visolve.com/* you will find documentation for the outdated version 2.4, and for the next major release, Squid 3.0, which is, at the time of this writing (2006), in an early beta stage.

The Squid version included in SLES 10 is 2.5.

Control Access to Squid

In the simplest possible setup, the Squid proxy can be used to access Web sites by anyone who can reach the network interface where the proxy is listening. However, Squid can also be used to control access to Web sites.

Squid offers very powerful access management, which lets you allow or deny access to the proxy as well as control which sites are visited when and by whom, based on parameters such as:

- IP/Network Addresses of Clients or Web Servers
- Week Day and Time
- Content Type
- Transfer Protocol

The access management of Squid is based on two different tag types in the squid.conf file:

- *acl (Access Control List)*—Defines a condition that is matched against the incoming HTTP requests.
- *http_access*—Determines whether access is allowed or denied when a given acl condition matches.

Let's assume you have the following lines in your squid.conf file:

```
acl all src 0.0.0.0/0.0.0.0
acl allowed_clients src 10.0.0.0/24

http_access allow allowed_clients
http_access deny all
```

Two acls are defined. Each acl line consists of the following components:

```
acl alc_name alc_type acl_string [acl_string ...]
```

- *acl_name*—Works as an identifier when the condition is later used in an http_access statement. You can choose any name, but it cannot use spaces or special characters.
- *acl_type*—One of the acl types that Squid supports. The type `src` in the example refers to the IP or network address of the client that makes a request to Squid.
- *acl_string*—Defines the condition that is matched against the requests. If more than one string is given, the ACL matches when one of the string matches (OR). (*Note*: Not all ACL types can have more than one string.)

  Instead of one or several strings, a filename could be given. Instead of listing the strings on one line in `/etc/squid/squid.conf`, the file would list the strings line by line:

  ```
  acl offlimits dstdomain "/etc/squid/forbidden-sites.list"
  ```

In the example, the two acl lines have the following meaning:

```
acl all src 0.0.0.0/0.0.0.0
```

This acl line matches the IP address of the requesting client. The acl string 0.0.0.0/0.0.0.0 matches any IP address.

```
acl allowed_clients src 10.0.0.0/24
```

This acl line with the name allowed_clients matches all requests coming from the network with the network address 10.0.0.0/24.

The last two lines of our example are http_access tags. They have the following basic structure:

`http_access allow/deny` **`acl_name`**

Following the http_access tag, you have either an allow or deny statement, depending on what you want to do with the line. After the allow/deny statement, the acl name which should be used to allow or deny access to the proxy is listed. If two acl names are given, the line matches when both acl_name entries match (AND).

In the example, this means the following:

1. Two acl lines are defined, one that matches every request and one that only matches requests from the 10.0.0.0/24 network.

2. The first http_access line allows access to the proxy for every request that matches the `allowed_clients` acl. This means it allows every request from the 10.0.0.0/24 network.

3. The second http_access line denies access to every request that matches the `all` acl. This means that access is denied to every request.

The http_access lines are processed from top to bottom. Once a line and its acl matches, the given access rule (allow or deny) is applied and any subsequent http_access tags are not taken into consideration.

Assume that a client from the 10.0.0.0/24 network tries to access the proxy server in the example. The first http_access line matches and access is allowed; the second http_access line is not processed at all.

When someone outside the 10.0.0.0/24 network tries to access the proxy, the first http_access line does not match and the second line is processed. This line denies access to every request with the result that this request is not allowed.

As you can see, access control management in Squid is based on two tasks:

- Define acl Tags
- Define http_access Tags

Define acl Tags The acl tags have many different acl_types that can be used to control access. Table 8-1 lists the most important acl_types.

Define http_access Tags The http_access entries in the configuration file are processed from top to bottom. As soon as one line matches the request, the allow or deny rule is applied to the request and the remaining http_access lines are skipped.

You can combine multiple acls in one http_access line. The acls are combined with a logical AND. The following example combines an src and a time acl.

```
acl dahosts src 10.0.0.0/24
acl lunch time MTWHF 12:00-13:00
http_access allow dahosts lunch
```

This setup allows access to the proxy for all hosts in the network 10.0.0.0/24 from Monday to Friday from 12:00 noon to 1:00 p.m.

ACL Type	Description
src (source)	This type will match the client's IP or network address. Usage: acl *acl_name* src *ip-address/network_mask* Example: acl internal_net src 10.0.0.0/24 For a single IP address, you have to choose network mask /32. You can also specify a range of IP addresses, such as 172.16.1.25–172.16.1.35/32
dst (destination)	This tag is similar to the src tag, but it matches the IP or network address of the destination Web server. Usage: acl *acl_name* dst *ip-address/network_mask* Example: acl novell dst 130.57.4.27/32
srcdomain (source domain)	Instead of src, you can use srcdomain to specify the matching request by a domain name. Usage: acl *acl_name* srcdomain *domain* Example: acl da srcdomain .digitalairlines.com You need to specify the leading period in the domain name, and name resolution needs to be set up for the Squid system.
dstdomain (destination domain)	This tag is like srcdomain but matches the domain of the target Web server. Usage: acl *acl_name* dstdomain *domain* Example: acl novell dstdomain .novell.com
time	This tag matches the date and time when a request happens. Usage: acl *acl_name* time *w_day start_time-end_time* Example: acl monday time M 10:00-14:00 The week days can be specified as follows: • S–Sunday • M–Monday • T–Tuesday • W–Wednesday • H–Thursday • F–Friday • A–Saturday The start time must always be less than the end time. If you want to specify a period that goes over the end of the day, you have to create two acls.
url_regex	This tag matches a given regular expression with the whole URL of a request. Usage: acl *acl_name* url_regex *pattern* Example: acl sles url_regex sles This would match any URL containing sles. By default, the expressions are case sensitive. You can change this by specifying the −i option after the url_regex acl type. Example: acl http url_regex ^http This would match any URL starting with http.
urlpath_ regex	urlpath_regex is similar to url_regex; however, it matches only the path within a URL, not the complete URL (including the protocol identifier and the host name). Example: acl gif urlpath_regex \.gif$ This would match any URL that contains a path ending in .gif.
port	This tag matches the destination server port. Usage: acl *acl_name* port *port_number* Example: acl allowed_port port 80
proto	This tag matches the used transfer protocol. Usage: acl *acl_name* proto *protocol* Example: acl allowed_proto proto HTTP
reg_mime_type	Matches the mime type of the transferred file. This can be used to block certain file types. Usage: acl *acl_name* reg_mime_type *pattern* Example: acl mp3 reg_mime_type "audio/mpeg"

Table 8-1

If you want to combine several time periods in one acl, you have to use more than one line for the acl, as in the following example:

```
acl dahosts src 10.0.0.0/24
acl breaks time MTWHF 08:00-09:00
acl breaks time MTWHF 12:00-13:00
acl breaks time MTWHF 18:00-19:00
http_access allow dahosts breaks
```

This setup allows access to the proxy for all hosts in the network 10.0.0.0/24 from Monday to Friday from 8:00 a.m. to 9:00 a.m., from 12:00 noon to 1:00 p.m., and from 6:00 p.m. to 7:00 p.m.

You can use ! before the name of an acl to negate the meaning of the http_access line:

```
acl no_internet src 10.0.2.0/24
http_access allow !no_internet
```

This allows access to the proxy for every request not coming from the network defined in the no_internet acl line.

When no http_access line matches a request, the default access rule is the opposite of the last found http_access line. An allow turns into a deny and a deny turns into an allow.

To avoid confusion, you should always have an http_access line at the end of your configuration that matches every request. This line sets the default (allow/deny) when no other acl matches.

In the default configuration shipped with Squid on SUSE Linux Enterprise Server 10, this is done with the following `acl http_access` configuration:

```
acl all src 0.0.0.0/0.0.0.0
[...]
http_access deny all
```

The default configuration also contains some reasonable default settings that can be used as a base for your own setup. Like options in the config file, the acl setup is well commented.

The configuration file is the authoritative source of documentation.

The debug level can be changed on a per-section basis; the sections are listed in /usr/share/doc/packages/squid/debug-sections.txt. For instance, Section 28: Access Control, Section 33: Client-side Routines. Debug level 1 produces little output, level 9 produces most debug messages.

If your access rules do not produce the expected result and the reason is not obvious to you, you can temporarily increase Squid's debug level. Set `debug_options ALL,1 33,2` in squid.conf and view the entries in /var/log/squid/cache.log using `tail -f /var/log/squid/cache.log`. The information in that file shows why a certain request was allowed or denied.

More information can be logged with `debug_options ALL,1 33,2 28,9`. Be sure to turn the log level back to ALL,1 later; otherwise, the log files will become very large.

Configure Web Browsers to Use Squid

When you implement Squid to give users secure access to Web pages, they need to configure their Web browsers to use the proxy server.

Later in this section you will learn how to set up Squid as an intercepting (sometimes called transparent) proxy, which does not require any configuration changes on the client side. However, this is more complex and not the best solution in all cases.

You have two different options to configure the Web browsers:

- Configure the Web Browser Manually
- Configure the Web Browsers Automatically with a PAC Script

Configure the Web Browser Manually The process for configuring a browser depends on the browser type. The following shows how to set up a proxy in Firefox, which is the default Web browser for SUSE Linux Enterprise Server 10.

If you want to configure a different Web browser, the values that you enter are the same, but the dialogs and steps are different.

Open the proxy configuration in Firefox and select `Edit > Preferences`. In the Preferences dialog, make sure the `General` tab is selected, then click on `Connection Settings`.

Figure 8-6 shows the dialog that appears.

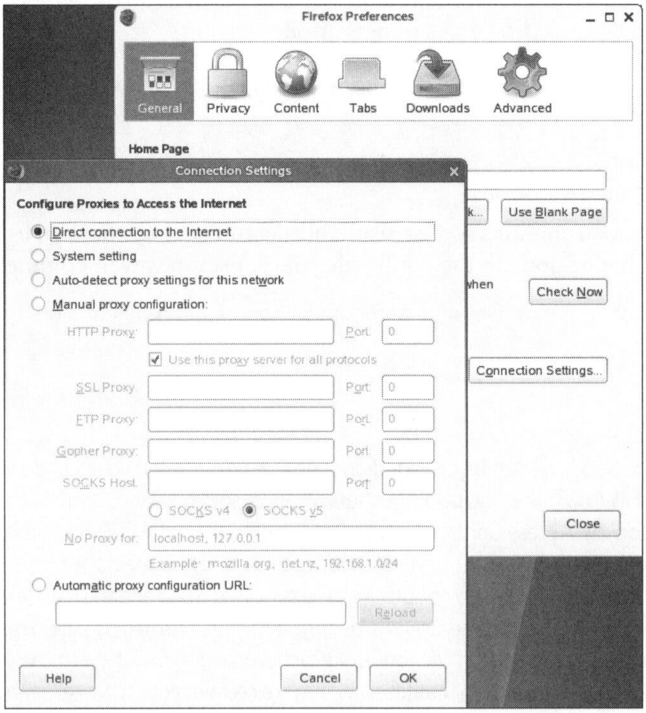

Figure 8-6

To configure the proxy manually, select Manual Proxy Configuration. You can enter the names or IP addresses of the proxy servers for HTTP, HTTPS, and FTP. The Port settings must be adjusted according to the proxy configuration.

 So far only the configuration of Squid as HTTP proxy has been covered. Other protocols will be covered later in this section.

When you leave the settings blank for one protocol, Firefox will not use a proxy for this protocol.

By selecting Use this proxy server for all protocols, Firefox will use the same proxy server for all protocols.

In the lower part of the dialog you can configure exceptions when you want Firefox to connect to a Web server directly instead of using the proxy server.

Configure the Web Browsers Automatically with a PAC Script In large environments with a lot of users, configuring the proxy settings manually can be a very time-consuming task. Therefore, it is helpful to automate this. Most of the browsers today can interpret a proxy configuration file, also called a PAC (Proxy Auto Configuration) script.

To use this feature, you have to take three steps:

- Create a PAC Script
- Publish the PAC File
- Announce the PAC Script in the Network

Create a PAC Script A PAC script is basically a plain text file that defines the JavaScript function FindProxyForURL(). A browser that is configured with PAC calls this function every time it needs to access a Web element. The URL of the element is passed to the function and the function returns one of the following strings:

- *DIRECT*—This means that the browser should not use a proxy for the given address.
- *PROXY*—Followed by the address or name of a proxy server. The browser will use the given proxy server to access the URL.
- *SOCKS*—Followed by the address or name of a SOCKS server. The browser will use the given SOCKS server. SOCKS is covered later in this section.

The following is an example of a very simple PAC file:

```
function FindProxyForURL(url,host)
{
  return "PROXY proxy.digitalairlines.com:8080";
}
```

As described on the previous page, the PAC script defines the function FindProxyForURL().
This function is called by the browser with two parameters:

- `url`—The full URL of the requested Web element.
- `host`—Just the host part of the full URL.

This example called the parameters url and host, but when you define
your own FindProxyForURL, you can choose your own names.

This example does not use these two parameters. The only thing this PAC file does is return the
proxy name proxy.digitalairlines.com and the port 8080 on which the proxy accepts connections. This means that the browser always uses a proxy server, no matter which URL it requests.
The next example uses the host parameter, which is passed to the function:

```
function FindProxyForURL(url,host)
{
  if (host == "intranet.digitalairlines.com"){
    return "DIRECT";
  }
  else{
    return "PROXY proxy.digitalairlines.com:8080";
  }
}
```

In this example the script checks whether the requested host is ***intranet.digitalairlines.com***.
In this case the string DIRECT is returned and the browser connects directly to the Intranet
server. In all other cases the name of the proxy server is returned as in the previous example.
Because a PAC script contains JavaScript code, you can use any feature JavaScript offers to
process the URL and host parameter. This way you can build very powerful PAC scripts that use
different Proxy servers for different hosts on different times of the day, etc.

A good introduction to PAC files, along with many examples, can be
found at *http://wp.netscape.com/eng/mozilla/2.0/relnotes/demo/proxy-
live.html.*

Publish the PAC File The PAC file can be placed anywhere it is reachable by the Web
browsers on the client machines. The most common way is to put the script code in a file that ends
in .pac and publish this file on an internal Web server. You can also place the file in a shared
network drive because many Web browsers can load PAC files from the file system.
When you have published the PAC script, you need to configure the Web browsers to use the
PAC file. In Firefox you have to select `Automatic proxy configuration URL` in the
Connections Settings dialog. Then you can either specify an HTTP URL or browse the file system
for a PAC file.

When you place a PAC file on a Web or file server, you have to make sure that the system is reliable. Most browsers do not have good error handling routines if a configured PAC file is not available.

Announce the PAC Script in the Network   The previously described method to configure Web browsers to use a PAC script still requires manual configuration. Although you can change the proxy configuration at a central point, this cannot be called true autoconfiguration.

The solution to this problem is the Web Proxy Auto-Discovery Protocol (WPAD). WPAD is not really a network protocol; it's more the title for the following two autodiscovery methods:

- *DNS-based*—For DNS-based autodiscovery, the browser looks for a Web server that has the hostname:

  wpad.***full_domain_name_of_client***

  For example, this means that a browser on the host da102.provo.digitalairlines.com would look for a server named wpad.provo.digitalairlines.com. If this server cannot be found, the browser would remove a subdomain and try wpad.digitalairlines.com as the next server.

  When the browser can connect to one of the hosts, it tries to download a file called wpad.dat, which contains the proxy configuration script. To use the DNS-based autoconfiguration, you have to do the following:

  - Create a DNS entry for one of the server names which a browser would look for.
  - Set up a Web server (can be a virtual host) that listens to the host name configured in DNS.
  - Make sure the Web server publishes the configuration script as wpad.dat in its document root directory.
  - Make sure the server publishes the file with the MIME type:

    application/x-ns-proxy-autoconfig

    In Apache, this can be done by adding the line:

    AddType application/x-ns-proxy-autoconfig.dat

    in the server or virtual host configuration file.

- *DHCP-based*—Another method to announce a PAC script uses a DHCP server. When using this method, the URL of the PAC script is granted as DHCP option 252 to the host. The browser then accesses the URL from the current DHCP lease.

You can find more information about proxy autoconfiguration in general and about the WPAD protocol at *http://homepages.tesco.net/~J.deBoynePollard/FGA/Web-browser-auto-proxy-configuration.html*. The section "Security considerations" is especially worth reading because it points out that the use of PAC is inherently insecure, mainly because code that is downloaded from somewhere else is automatically executed on the client.

Exercise 8-1: Install Configure Squid

Time Required: 25 Minutes

Objective: In this exercise, you practice the basic configuration of Squid and a Web browser. This exercise has four parts.

Description: In the first part, install Squid and configure it to allow access from clients in the 10.0.0.0/24 network.

In the second part, configure Firefox to use your local squid instead of directly connecting to Web sites in the Internet.

In the third part, monitor the access log of squid.

In the fourth part, work with a partner and change the configuration of Firefox to use his proxy instead of your local one.

Detailed Steps to Complete this Exercise

- Part I: Install and Configure Squid
- Part II: Configure Firefox to Use the Proxy
- Part III: Monitor Access to Squid
- Part IV: Test Your Partner's Proxy

Part I: Install and Configure Squid

1. Open a terminal window and su – to the root user; when prompted for the root password, enter novell.

2. Install squid by entering yast –i squid. Insert the appropriate media when prompted.

3. Open the file /etc/squid/squid.conf in a text editor.

4. Look for the section where the acl tags are defined.
   Insert a new line after acl all src 0.0.0.0/0.0.0.0.
   Create an acl local_net that comprises the IP addresses of the 10.0.0.0/24 network. The line should look like the following:

```
acl local_net src 10.0.0.0/24
```

5. Look for the section where the http_access tags are defined.

6. After http_access allow localhost, insert a new line and enter:

   http_access allow local_net

7. Save the file and close the text editor.

8. Start Squid by entering:

   rcsquid start

9. Monitor the output of the start script.
   The output should end with:

```
Starting WWW-proxy squid                        done
```

Part II: Configure Firefox to Use the Proxy

To configure Firefox to use the proxy, do the following:

1. Start Firefox by pressing Alt+F2, typing firefox, and selecting Run.

2. In Firefox, select Edit > Preferences.

3. In the upper part of the Firefox Preferences dialog select General.

4. Select Connection Settings.

5. Mark Manual proxy configuration; in the HTTP Proxy and the SSL Proxy line, enter the *IP_address_of_your_system* and the port number 3128.

6. Close the dialog by selecting OK.

7. Close the Firefox preferences dialog by selecting Close.

8. In the address bar, enter *http://www.novell.com/*.
   The Web site should be loaded.

Part III: Monitor Access to Squid

To monitor access to Squid, do the following:

1. Make sure Firefox is configured to use the proxy server as described in Part II.

2. Open a terminal and su - to the root user (password novell).

3. To view the content of the Squid log file, enter:

```
tail -f /var/log/squid/access.log
```

4. Press Enter a few times to insert some empty lines.

5. In the address bar of Firefox, enter *http://www.novell.com/*.
   Wait until the site is loaded.

6. Switch to the terminal window and look at the new entries that have been added to the log file.
   Every request made to the proxy server is logged in the log file.

Part IV: Test Your Partner's Proxy

Do the following:

1. Use the instructions in Part II to configure Firefox so that it uses your partner's proxy server instead of your own machine.

2. To test your partner's proxy, do the following:

   a. Wait until your partner is looking at the Squid log file as described in Part III of this exercise.

   b. In the address bar of Mozilla, enter *http://www.novell.com/*.

   c. Ask your partner if your access shows up in the log files.

3. Let your partner test your proxy.

Understand How Squid Handles SSL Connections

Secure Sockets Layer (SSL) is a technology that is used to encrypt data that is transferred over HTTP. Because of the design of SSL, encrypted HTTP requests cannot be handled like cleartext HTTP requests.

Understanding how Squid handles SSL connections includes the following:

- The CONNECT Method
- The SSL Configuration Tags
- Use Squid to Tunnel Connections

The CONNECT Method The following explains the process of SSL encryption between a browser and a Web server:

1. The browser recognizes a Web address starting with https**://**.

   This means that the connection to this server should be encrypted. The default port for SSL connections is 443 instead of port 80 (used for normal unencrypted HTTP connections).

2. The Web browser asks the server for its public RSA key.

3. The Web server sends the public key to the Web browser.

4. The Web browser verifies the key of the server with the public key of the CA that signed
the key.

5. If the key is valid, the Web browser and Web server establish a secure connection.

One important thing to understand about SSL is that it always needs a direct connection between the Web browser and the target Web server. Therefore, SSL-encrypted HTTP requests cannot be handled by proxy servers in the same way as unencrypted HTTP requests.

The CONNECT method is a way to tunnel SSL-encrypted HTTP requests through a proxy server. The term *tunneling* means that the proxy server simply passes the encrypted data from the browser to the Web server and back. Due to the encryption the transferred files can neither be inspected nor cached.

Figure 8-7 illustrates SSL tunneling.

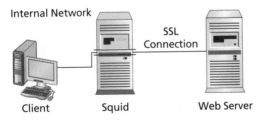

Figure 8-7

For SSL connections to go via the proxy, the SSL proxy settings of the Web browser need to be adjusted to the right proxy server and port. If there is no SSL proxy specified, the browser will try to connect directly to the target Web server without using the proxy.

Although encrypted data cannot be cached or inspected, you still have benefits when you use a proxy for SSL connections. You can limit access to the Web based on IP address and time, and you can use proxy authentication to authenticate users accessing the Web. (Proxy authentication is described later in this section.)

The CONNECT method can be used to tunnel any protocol through Squid. Someone could use SSH to connect to a system outside the internal network. If this is not acceptable, you have to disable the CONNECT method in squid.conf; however, this will also block all SSL connections to the outside.

The SSL Configuration Tags

SSL tunneling is configured with acl and http_access tags in the Squid configuration file. The following are the tags and their description as they appear in the default configuration shipped with SUSE Linux Enterprise Server 10.

```
acl SSL_ports port 443 563
```

This acl line defines an acl entry named SSL_ports which holds the port numbers 443 and 563.

```
acl CONNECT method CONNECT
```

This line defines an acl entry named CONNECT with the value CONNECT. CONNECT is the method used for SSL tunnels.

```
http_access deny CONNECT !SSL_ports
```

This http_access line denies requests for the CONNECT method on ports other than the ones defined in SSL_ports (443, 563).

When you look through the default configuration, you will see some more tags which deal with SSL (such as https_port or ssl_unclean_shutdown). These tags are used when Squid is configured as an HTTP accelerator and the requests from the clients to the accelerator will be encrypted. In this case Squid does the encryption work for the actual Web server.

Because the HTTP_accelerator role of Squid is not covered in this section, these tags are not covered in detail.

Use Squid to Tunnel Connections

While the CONNECT method is usually used to connect to Web servers using HTTPS, it can be used to tunnel other protocols through Squid as well. What is needed is a program that adds the connect request to the protocol. There are various solutions for this.

One is the package transconnect (*http://transconnect.sourceforge.net/*) that comes with the SUSE Linux distributions. An RPM package that can be installed on SUSE Linux Enterprise Server 10 can be found at *http://download.opensuse.org/distribution/SL-10.1/inst-source/suse/ i586/transconnect-1.2-274.i586.rpm.*

Another is the Perl script https-tunnel by Mark Suter, which can be found under *http:// zwitterion.org/software/ssh-https-tunnel/.*

Both are found on the *Student* DVD.

After installing transconnect with rpm, all you have to do is copy the configuration template:

```
geeko@da10:~> mkdir .tconn
geeko@da10:~> cp /usr/share/doc/packages/transconnect/tconn.conf \
~/.tconn/tconn.conf
```

Then edit it according to your network parameters. The comments in the file explain what you need to change.

When you start the application whose traffic you want to tunnel, preload the tconn library:

```
geeko@da10:~> LD_PRELOAD=/usr/lib/tconn.so ssh athome.example.com
```

This does not work in the default configuration of Squid, because port 22 is not considered safe and therefore blocked.

If you cannot or do not want to change the Squid configuration, you have to change the configuration of sshd on the computer you want to connect to. Have sshd also listen on port 443. If HTTPS is not restricted on the proxy in question, you can ssh out of the network behind the proxy.

With the Port Forwarding feature of SSH, you can connect to any Web site, or any other service that uses single connections:

```
geeko@da10:~ > LD_PRELOAD=/usr/lib/tconn.so ssh -p 443 \
   -L 8080:blocked-site.example.com:80 athome.example.com
```

As a security administrator you should be aware that closing port 22 or disabling routing does not prevent connections to the outside via SSH if Squid is running and allowing the connect method to certain ports. Users using this technique should be aware that you are most likely violating some security policy.

To prevent serious trouble, get permission before you tunnel connections that way.

Exercise 8-2: Configure SSL in Squid

Time Required: 10 Minutes

Objective: This exercise assumes that Squid has been configured as described in the previous exercise and that Firefox is using the proxy server that is installed on your system for all protocols.

Description: First, test if you can establish SSL connections via Squid by accessing with Firefox the following URL (on one line) *https://www.novell.com/ICSLogin/?%22 http://www.novell.com/%22*. Then disable SSL connections by changing /etc/squid/squid.conf to no longer allow the CONNECT method. Get Squid to reload its configuration and test to determine if you are still able to access the above URL in Firefox.

Detailed Steps to Complete this Exercise

1. Start Firefox by pressing Alt+F2, typing `firefox`, and selecting Run.

2. In the address bar, enter (on one line) *https://www.novell.com/ICSLogin/?%22http://www.novell.com/%22*.

3. Make sure that the page is loaded fully and that the address in the address bar starts with `https://` and that there is a lock icon in the lower right corner of the browser window.

4. Double-click on the lock icon and view the certificate by selecting View in the window that opens. Close both windows, but leave the browser window open.

5. When the site loads correctly, this is a sign that SSL can be used over your Squid proxy at the moment.

6. Open a terminal window and `su -` to the root user.

7. Open the file `/etc/squid/squid.conf` in a text editor.

8. Change the line:

   ```
   http_access deny CONNECT !SSL_ports
   ```

   to:

   ```
   http_access deny CONNECT
   ```

9. Save the file and close the text editor.

   The connect method is now denied in general and not only to the hosts that are not defined in SSL_ports.

10. Reload Squid by entering `rcsquid reload`.

11. In the Firefox window with the https Web page from Step 2, reload the page by clicking on the reload button.

    The access to the site should be denied now, because SSL is disabled in the proxy configuration.

12. Undo your changes in the file `/etc/squid/squid.conf` by opening it with a text editor.

   Change the line:

   `http_access deny CONNECT`

   to:

   `http_access deny CONNECT !SSL_ports`

13. Save the file and close the text editor.

14. Reload Squid by entering `rcsquid reload`.

15. Make sure SSL works again by reloading the page as in Step 2 of this exercise.

Configure Proxy Authentication

So far you have only limited the access to a Squid proxy server based on IP and network addresses, the date/time, and the access protocol. In some environments this is not sufficient and you need a better and more user-oriented access control. Squid offers the option to authenticate users before they are allowed to use the proxy. This procedure is called *proxy authentication*.

To configure Proxy Authentication with Squid, you need to do the following:

- Understand How Proxy Authentication Works
- Configure an Authentication Backend
- Configure Proxy Authentication in squid.conf

Understand How Proxy Authentication Works   Proxy authentication is a feature that is integrated into the HTTP protocol. It needs to be supported on both sides, by the Web browser and the proxy server.

When a Web browser accesses a proxy server that requires authentication, the proxy returns the HTTP message 407 (Proxy Authentication Required). Then the browser opens a dialog and prompts the user to enter a user name and password. The entered credentials are then passed to the proxy server with every subsequent request to the proxy. Some browsers offer to enter the proxy authentication credentials in their configuration dialog, so the user does not need to enter the credentials in every new browser session.

The user credentials can be passed from the Web browser to the proxy in several ways. These methods are called *authentication schemes*.

Squid supports the following schemes:

- *basic*—This is the oldest and most insecure scheme.
   User name and password are transferred in clear text and can be read by anyone who can access the transferred data. You need to be aware of this and decide if this is acceptable in your environment.

- *digest*—This is a better, more secure authentication scheme.
   Instead of passing the password in clear text, this scheme uses a hash based on the password and several other parameters.

- *NTLM*—NTLM is a protocol that is used in several Microsoft network implementations to enable single sign-on across different services.

  Squid supports NTLM for proxy authentication, although it is not an official HTTP extension.

Usually digest is the best choice, because it is a standardized and rather secure authentication scheme. However, the current Squid versions (*2.5.x*) require the passwords to be available in clear text on the system running the proxy in order to create the correct digest hash. This makes it difficult to integrate Squid into an existing authentication environment where passwords are usually only stored as a hash of the actual password. Future versions of the Squid package (starting with version 3.0) will most likely support encrypted passwords for the digest authentication scheme.

Configure an Authentication Backend

Every authentication process needs some kind of database where the user information is stored. Squid can be used with many different types of user databases, because the actual validation of the user credentials is done by an external program.

Squid feeds the user name and password into these authentication programs and the programs return whether these are valid or not. Each of these programs is designed to connect to a different type of user database. The authentication programs are located in the directory `/usr/sbin`.

Configure Proxy Authentication in squid.conf

In the following, you will configure Squid user authentication with different authentication methods and user databases.

This includes the following:

- Configure Basic User Authentication with PAM
- Configure Digest Authentication with digest_pw_auth

Configure Basic User Authentication with PAM

One option for a user database is to use PAM on the system where the proxy is running. All users that can be validated by PAM on the system where the proxy is running can be authenticated by Squid.

Three tags are used to configure user authentication in squid.conf:

- `auth_param`—This is used to determine the authentication scheme and the authentication program.
- `acl`—This is used to define an acl that holds user names.
- `http_access`—This is used last to give users access based on the defined acls.

The following is the auth_param section for PAM authentication:

```
auth_param basic program /usr/sbin/pam_auth
auth_param basic children 5
auth_param basic realm Squid proxy-caching Web server
auth_param basic credentialsttl 2 hours
```

The lines on the previous page have the following meaning:

- The first line:

```
auth_param basic program /usr/sbin/pam_auth
```

This line defines the program that should be used for user authentication. The program must be given with the full path name.

- The second line determines how many authentication processes are started in the background:

```
auth_param basic children 5
```

The value 5 should be fine in most cases. When the authentication of a user takes a longer time, you should set this to a higher value to avoid making other requests wait.

- The third line defines the realm:

```
auth_param basic realm Squid proxy-caching Web server
```

The realm can be understood as the name of the resource that requires user authentication. The default realm is Squid proxy-caching Web server.

- The fourth line determines how long a user name/password pair is considered valid after it has been successfully validated:

```
auth_param basic credentialsttl 2 hours
```

This way the authentication program does not have to be called each time a user makes a request.
The default value is 2 hours.

When the authorization program is configured, you have to create an acl line that looks like the following:

```
acl allowed_users proxy_auth fsailer blotz
```

This defines an acl of the type proxy_auth for the users fsailer and blotz. If you want an acl that matches all users and can be validated by the authentication program, you can use the keyword REQUIRED, as in the following example:

```
acl allowed_users proxy_auth REQUIRED
```

Finally you need to add an http_access line to grant access for authenticated users:

```
http_access allow allowed_users
```

When you configure user authentication, you have to keep in mind that once an http_access line matches, none of the later http_access lines are processed. The sequence of entries is therefore very important.

Let's say your goal is to grant access to the users fsailer and blotz as long as they use a machine in the internal network and no one else is to have access.

The following example does *not* produce the desired result:

```
acl all src 0.0.0.0/0.0.0.0
acl internal_network src 10.0.0.0/24
acl allowed_users proxy_auth fsailer blotz

http_access allow internal_network
http_access allow allowed_users
http_access deny all
```

Because the allow internal_network line comes before `allow allowed_users`, all requests from the internal network are allowed without authentication.

The following solution is somewhat better:

```
acl all src 0.0.0.0/0.0.0.0
acl internal_network src 10.0.0.0/24
acl allowed_users proxy_auth fsailer blotz

http_access allow allowed_users
http_access allow internal_network
http_access deny all
```

This time the first http_access line allows the authenticated users fsailer and blotz to access the proxy.

For other users, there are two scenarios:

- The user exists on the system and enters the correct password. The line http_access allow allowed_users does not match and the next line is checked. Access is granted for anyone from the internal network.

- The user does not exist on the system at all or an incorrect password is given for an existing user. In this case, the browser offers the authentication dialog again or shows the error page 407 if the user decides to abort the authentication.

This is not yet exactly what you wanted to do.

The following configuration finally produces the desired result:

```
acl all src 0.0.0.0/0.0.0.0
acl internal_network src 10.0.0.0/24
acl allowed_users proxy_auth fsailer blotz

http_access deny !internal_network
http_access allow allowed_users
http_access deny all
```

The first http_access line denies access for every request that does not come from the internal network. The second http_access line allows access only for the users fsailer and blotz. The last line finally denies access for everyone else from everywhere.

Another possible solution is the following:

```
acl all src 0.0.0.0/0.0.0.0
acl internal_network src 10.0.0.0/24
acl allowed_users proxy_auth fsailer blotz

http_access allow allowed_users internal_network
http_access deny all
```

Only users who meet the criteria for allowed_users and internal_network match the first http_access line. The next line denies all others.

Configure Digest Authentication with digest_pw_auth

To configure digest authentication, you have to adjust the auth_param lines.

The acl and http_access setup is the same as described in "Configure Basic User Authentication with PAM" on page 221.

The following is an example digest configuration:

```
auth_param digest program /usr/sbin/digest_pw_auth \
/etc/squid/proxy_passwd
auth_param digest children 5
auth_param digest realm Squid proxy-caching Web server
auth_param digest nonce_garbage_interval 5 minutes
auth_param digest nonce_max_duration 30 minutes
auth_param digest nonce_max_count 50
```

The most obvious difference to the basic authentication setup is the keyword digest that is used instead of basic in every line. The authentication program is called digest_pw_auth in / usr/sbin/ on SUSE Linux Enterprise Server 10. The program takes a password file as a parameter. The password file contains user names and clear text passwords. The user name and password are separated by a colon.

The following is an example password file:

```
pa:Eij0shae
meicks:Ci6aeyoh
blotz:Oithoh0k
mgunreben:Ahb3emae
fsailer:idooN7am
esilver:lau5aQua
jstiegemann:Daik9ilu
```

You can name the password word file in any way and place it in a directory wherever Squid has access. You just have to pass the correct full path name of the file to the authentication program.

In the current version of digest_pw_auth, the password file needs to contain the passwords in clear text. You therefore have to make sure that the password file cannot be read by anyone but the Squid user.

All other auth_param parameters starting with `nonce_` affect some details about the digest authentication. The standard settings are fine for most purposes.

Exercise 8-3: Configure Proxy Authentication

Time Required: 20 Minutes

Objective: In this exercise, you learn how to configure proxy authentication in Squid. To be able to work through this exercise, you need to have Squid and Firefox configured as described in the previous exercises of this section. The exercise has four parts.

Description: The first part has nothing directly to do with Squid: create the local user pbear, with Novell as his password.

In the second part, allow access to the user pbear using basic authentication. Create appropriate acl and http_access entries in /etc/squid/squid.conf.

The third part consists of testing the configuration by accessing a Web page in the browser.

In the fourth part, change the authentication from basic to digest. Use the password SUSE for the user pbear when he has to authenticate at the proxy. Test the configuration.

Detailed Steps to Complete this Exercise

- Part I: Add a User to the Proxy System
- Part II: Configure Basic Authentication
- Part III: Test User Authentication
- Part IV: Configure digest Authentication

Part I: Add a User to the Proxy System

Do the following:

1. Start the `YaST Control Center`; on the left side of YaST's main menu, select `Security and Users`.

2. On the right side, select User Management.

3. Make sure that Users is selected.

4. Select Add.

5. Enter the following information:

    - Full User Name: Peter Bear
    - User Login: pbear
    - Password: Novell
    - Confirm Password: Novell

6. Select Accept.

7. When YaST notifies you about a weak password, confirm the dialog by selecting Yes.

8. Select Finish.

9. Close YaST.

Part II: Configure Basic Authentication

Do the following:

1. Open a terminal window and su – to the root user.

2. Open the file /etc/squid/squid.conf with a text editor.

3. Look for the auth_param section.

4. Change the file so that only the following auth_param lines are active:

```
auth_param basic program /usr/sbin/pam_auth
auth_param basic children 5
auth_param basic realm Squid proxy-caching Web server
auth_param basic credentialsttl 2 hours
```

5. Look for the acl section in the configuration file.

6. Add the following acl line after the acl called all:

```
acl allowed_user proxy_auth pbear
```

7. Look for the http_access section in the configuration file.

8. Find the following two lines:

```
http_access allow localhost
http_access allow local_net
```

and add the new proxy_auth acl to those lines as in the following example:

```
http_access allow localhost allowed_user
http_access allow local_net allowed_user
```

The IP address and the user name must match in both lines to grant access to the proxy.

9. Save the file and close the text editor.

10. Restart Squid by entering `rcsquid restart`.

Part III: Test User Authentication

Do the following:

1. Start Firefox by pressing `Alt+F2`, typing `firefox`, and selecting `Run`.

2. Make sure your Web browser is configured to use the proxy installed on your system.

3. In the address bar, enter *http://www.novell.com*.
   When the authentication works, a password dialog should pop up.

4. Enter the following information:

   - User name: `pbear`
   - Password: `Novell`

5. Confirm the password dialog by selecting `OK`.
   The Novell Web site should be loaded.

Part IV: Configure digest Authentication

Do the following:

1. Open a terminal window and `su -` to the root user.

2. Create a file with the name `proxy_passwd` in the directory `/etc/squid/`.

3. Add the following line to the file:

   `pbear:SUSE`

4. Save the file and close the text editor.

5. Change the owner of the file by entering:

   `chown squid /etc/squid/proxy_passwd`

6. Adjust the permissions of the file by entering:

   `chmod 600 /etc/squid/proxy_passwd`

7. Open the file `/etc/squid/squid.conf` with a text editor.

8. Change the files so that only the following auth_param lines are active:

```
auth_param digest program /usr/sbin/digest_pw_auth \
        /etc/squid/proxy_passwd
auth_param digest children 5
auth_param digest realm Squid proxy-caching Web server
auth_param digest nonce_garbage_interval 5 minutes
auth_param digest nonce_max_duration 30 minutes
auth_param digest nonce_max_count 50
```

9. Save the file and close the text editor.

10. Restart Squid by entering `rcsquid restart`.

11. Close all Firefox browser windows.

12. Start Firefox by pressing `Alt+F2`, typing `firefox`, and selecting `Run`.

13. In the address bar, enter *http://www.novell.com*.
    If the authentication works, a password dialog should open up.

14. Enter the following information:

    - User name: `pbear`
    - Password: `SUSE`

15. Confirm the password dialog by selecting `OK`.
    The Novell Web site should be loaded.

Configure URL Filtering

One of the advantages of an application-level gateway is that access can be granted not only on the basis of network parameters (IP and network address) or user authentication, but also on protocol-specific parameters.

In the case of Squid this means that you can control the access to Web sites based on the URL of a site. This feature is also called *URL filtering* or *blocking*.

Basically you can configure two different types of URL filtering:

- Configure URL Filtering with url_regex
- Configure URL Filtering with squidGuard

Configure URL Filtering with url_regex A commonly used method to filter out unwanted content is to block URLs which contain certain patterns. Squid offers two acl types that can be used for this purpose:

- *url_regex*—This acl type matches the whole URL, including the protocol and the hostname.
- *urpath_regex*—This acl type matches only the path of a URL without the protocol or the hostname.

The following example defines an acl that matches all URLs containing example.com:

```
acl blocked url_regex example.com
[...]
http_access deny blocked
```

First, you create a url_regex acl with the name blocked that matches all URLs containing example.com; then you deny access to such URLs with an http_access line.

By adding the `-i` option after the url_regex statement, you can make the acl case insensitive:

```
acl blocked url_regex -i example.com
```

Now the acl matches all URLs that contain example.com, no matter if they are uppercase or lowercase.

In most cases you want to block more than just a single URL. Instead of creating an acl for every URL, you can also list all URL patterns in a file and use the path to the file as a parameter in your acl statement.

The following acl reads the patterns from the file /etc/squid/black_list:

```
acl blocked url_regex -i "/etc/squid/black_list"
```

The filename and paths are just examples and can be changed.

Such a file with patterns is usually called *blacklist*. However, the url_regex acl can also be used to allow access to URLs that match a given pattern, which is called *whitelist*.

The format of the file is very simple. You just list all patterns in the file, one pattern per line.

The following is an example listing three patterns:

```
example.com
example2.com
example3.com
```

You can also download preconfigured blacklists. This way you can block many sites that are not appropriate for being viewed in a work environment.

The following are two resources where you can download blacklists:

- *http://www.squid-cache.org/Doc/FAQ/FAQ-10.html* lists several URLs that provide blacklists.

- *http://www.squidguard.org/blacklist/*

 Please be aware that even the best blacklist will not contain all pages that might need to be blocked. Furthermore, long blacklists can decrease the performance of Squid. You should always test a blacklist before you use it in a production environment.

Configure URL Filtering with squidGuard

Besides the built-in url_regex acl type, you can also use an external filter plug-in for Squid.

One of these filter plug-ins is squidGuard. squidGuard is part of SUSE Linux Enterprise Server 10. To use it, you need to install the package squidGuard in addition to Squid.

squidGuard is implemented as a URL redirector. Squid passes every requested URL to the configured redirect program. Then the redirect program processes the URL and returns either a different URL or a blank line, which means that the URL does not need to be changed.

If the returned URL is different, Squid will fetch this URL instead of the original one. Instead of a different URL, the redirect program might also return an error code, which indicates that the URL should not be accessed.

The URL redirector is configured in the redirect_program tag of `squid.conf`:

```
redirect_program /usr/sbin/squidGuard
```

squidGuard uses the redirect method to filter out URLs which should not be accessed.

squidGuard's configuration file is located in `/etc/squidguard.conf`. At the beginning of the configuration file, two paths are configured:

```
logdir /var/log/squidGuard
dbhome /var/lib/squidGuard/db
```

The first entry configures the directory where squidGuard stores its log files. The second entry sets the directory where the pattern databases are stored.

squidGuard uses these databases to determine whether a request is allowed. The concept of the squidGuard configuration file is similar to the Squid configuration file. First, you need to define conditions which are matched against a URL. Then these conditions are used to grant or deny a request.

Besides URL matching, squidGuard can also handle conditions based on the source IP address, time of day, or the user accessing the proxy. The following is an overview of the keywords used to define conditions in squidguard.conf:

- *time*—Defines conditions which match the time of a request.
- *src*—Defines conditions which match the src of a request.
- *dest*—Defines conditions which match the destination of a request.

However, as these conditions can sufficiently be handled by Squid's internal mechanisms, we will concentrate on the URL-matching functionality of squidGuard.

The following example defines a condition that matches destination URLs:

```
dest blacklist {
domainlist blacklist/domains
urllist    blacklist/urls
}
```

- The name of the condition follows the `dest` keyword, in this example `blacklist`. The actual conditions are defined between two brackets:
  - With `domainlist` you point to a file that lists domains that are, in this example, unwanted.
  - With `urllist` you configure a file with unwanted URL components.

The definitions are combined with a logical OR. In this example, the condition blacklist matches when the requested URL matches either the domainlist or the urllist.

squidGuard looks for the domainlist or the urlist in the directory that is defined in the `dbhome` variable at the beginning of the configuration file.

You can combine multiple domain or URL lists in `dest` conditions. Another condition type works with regular expressions.

After you have defined a dest condition, you can use it to allow or deny access to URLs. This is done in an acl definition. The following is a very basic acl definition in the context of the previous examples:

```
logdir /var/log/squidGuard
dbhome /var/lib/squidGuard/db

dest blacklist {
    domainlist blacklist/domains
    urllist    blacklist/urls
}

acl {
    default {
      pass !blacklist all
      redirect
http://intranet.digitalairlines.com/access_not_allowed.html
    }
}
```

First, the path variables and the condition blacklist are defined. The acl section contains only the default entry. This entry allows (pass) access to the URLs which do not match against the blacklist condition.

When the URL matches, access is not allowed and the request is redirected to a page of the company's intranet. The default entry is used in this case because no other source conditions that could be used to match requests are defined.

NOTE This example is a very basic squidGuard setup. A more detailed description can be found at *http://www.squidguard.org/config/* or locally in /usr/share/doc/packages/squidGuard/doc/configuration.html. You can also find more information about precompiled blacklists on the squidGuard homepage (*http://www.squidguard.org/*).

Exercise 8-4: Configure URL Filtering

Time Required: 20 Minutes

EXERCISE

Objective: In this exercise, you configure URL filtering with Squid. The exercise assumes that you have already configured Squid on your system according to Exercises 8-1 to 8-3. This exercise has two parts.

Description: In the first part, create an acl and http_access entry in /etc/squid/squid.conf to block access to sites in the example.com domain.

In the second part, use squidGuard to block access to sites within the domain hotmail.com and redirect users to the site *www.novell.com*.

Detailed Steps to Complete this Exercise

- Part I: Filter URLs with url_regex
- Part II: Install and Configure squidGuard

Part I: Filter URLs with url_regex

Do the following:

1. Open a terminal window and su – to the root user.

2. Open the file `/etc/squid/squid.conf` with a text editor.

3. Scroll down to the acl section.

4. After the acl named all, insert the following line:

   `acl bad_site url_regex -i example.com`

5. Look for the line:

   `http_access allow localhost allowed_user`

   Add the following line before that line:

   `http_access deny bad_site`

6. Save the file and close the text editor.

7. Reload Squid by entering `rcsquid reload`.

8. Start Firefox by pressing `Alt+F2`, typing `firefox`, and selecting `Run`.

9. With Firefox configured to use your proxy server:

   a. In the address bar, enter *http://www.example.com/*.

   b. When the filter has been configured correctly, access to the site should be denied.

Part II: Install and Configure squidGuard

1. Open a terminal window and su – to the root user.

2. Enter `yast -i squidGuard`; when prompted, insert the requested media.

3. Open the file `/etc/squid/squid.conf` in a text editor.

4. Look for the line `TAG: redirect_program`.

5. At the end of the tag description, insert the following line:

   `redirect_program /usr/sbin/squidGuard`

6. Save the file and close the text editor.

7. Rename the squidGuard default configuration by entering:

   `mv /etc/squidguard.conf /etc/squidguard.conf.original`

8. Create a new file /etc/squidguard.conf with the following content:

```
logdir /var/log/squidGuard
dbhome /var/lib/squidGuard/db
dest blacklist {
  domainlist blacklist/domains
  urllist    blacklist/urls
}
acl {
  default {
    pass !blacklist all
    redirect 302:http://www.novell.com/index.html
  }
}
```

9. Add the domain hotmail.com to the squidGuard domain blacklist by entering (on one line):

echo "hotmail.com" >> /var/lib/squidGuard/db/blacklist/domains

10. Enter rcsquid reload.

11. Start Firefox by pressing Alt+F2, typing firefox, and selecting Run.

12. With Firefox configured to use your proxy server:

    a. In the address bar, enter *http://www.hotmail.com*.

    b. When squidGuard is configured correctly, you should be redirected to *http://www.novell.com*.

Configure an Intercepting Proxy Server

Every proxy setup discussed so far requires that the clients (Web browsers) are configured to use the proxy server. You can modify your proxy setup so that this is not necessary. In this case the proxy is also called an intercepting http proxy or a transparent http proxy.

A transparent proxy works in the following way: When a TCP packet with the destination port 80 gets to a router, the router redirects the packet to Squid. Squid checks whether the requested object is in its cache. If the object is not in the cache, Squid fetches the object from the Internet.

When configuring a transparent proxy, you have to set up a rule in your router that redirects HTTP traffic (port 80) to Squid, and you have to modify the Squid configuration.

In /etc/squid/squid.conf, the following tags have to be set:

```
httpd_accel_host virtual
httpd_accel_port 80
httpd_accel_with_proxy on
httpd_accel_uses_host_header on
```

Figure 8-8 illustrates how to set up a transparent proxy when Squid runs on the same server as the Internet gateway.

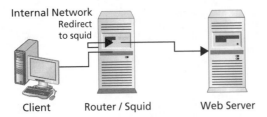

Figure 8-8

To set up the port redirection on the router, you can use the following iptables command (on one line):

```
iptables -t nat -A PREROUTING -p TCP --dport 80 -j REDIRECT --to-
port port_of_squid
```

Although a transparent proxy has a lot of advantages, it also has some drawbacks:

- A transparent proxy only works with HTTP.
- Other protocols like HTTPS, FTP, and GOPHER do not work over a transparent proxy because Web browsers need to be aware of a proxy server in order to use these protocols over a proxy.
- The connection might not be as stable compared with a direct network connection or a connection over a proxy that is configured in the clients.

Analyze Squid Log Files

Programs to analyze squid log files can provide you with information on sites visited, traffic, and other topics.

One such tool is a Perl script called `calamaris` that analyzes the Squid `/var/log/squid/access.log` log file. This script produces a statistical analysis of the requests and accesses. The analysis can be produced in ASCII or in HTML format. calamaris is available on SUSE Linux Enterprise Server 10. The package name is `calamaris`.

calamaris has a wide range of options affecting the content of the analysis. Table 8-2 shows the most important options.

Option	Meaning
-a	Performs all available analyses—corresponds to a combination of the most important options. For example, not all contacted DNS domains in the list are displayed, only the first 20.
-d *number*	Produces a list of the (*number*) most frequently requested top- and second-level domains. If all should be listed, set this to -1.
-r *number*	Produces a list of the hosts that have made the most frequent requests to Squid. Only *number* hosts are listed. The value -1 displays all hosts.
-P	Shows the number of TCP requests per minute.
-w	The output is written in HTML format. The default is plain text.

Table 8-2

The following example creates a top 10 list of the most frequently visited level 1 and level 2 domains:

```
calamaris -d 10 /var/log/squid/access.log
```

For more information on calamaris, see *http://cord.de/tools/squid/calamaris/*. Another program to analyze squid log files is Webalizer; it is primarily intended to analyze Apache log files, but works as well with squid's native log format.

Exercise 8-5: Analyze Squid Log File

Time Required: 10 Minutes

Objective: In this exercise, you learn how to analyze the Squid log file. You must have completed the previous exercises so that your access.log contains some data.

Description: Install calamaris and run it to analyze the file /var/log/squid/access.log.

Detailed Steps to Complete this Exercise

1. Open a terminal window and su – to the root user.
2. Enter yast –i calamaris; when prompted, insert the requested media.
3. Enter calamaris –d 10 /var/log/squid/access.log.
4. Scroll up in the terminal window and review the report.

Objective 3—Configure and Use Dante

Dante is an open source implementation of the SOCKS proxy protocol. To configure and use Dante, you need to do the following:

- Understand SOCKS
- Install and Configure Dante
- Configure Clients to Use a SOCKS Server

Understand SOCKS

Application-level gateways provide a secure way to allow internal clients to access Internet services. The problem is that the more services need to be accessed, the more different application-level gateways need to be installed, configured, and maintained; and an application-level gateway is not available for every protocol.

A solution for this problem is provided by the proxy protocol SOCKS. SOCKS defines how applications can request a TCP or UDP connection to an outside host from a SOCKS server. The SOCKS server then uses a set of rules to decide whether a request can be allowed.

The advantage of SOCKS is that it basically works with every application protocol, not just with a specific one. Therefore, SOCKS is not a real application-level gateway. It is more like an additional layer between the transport and application layers of the ISO/OSI reference model, which allows better access control. SOCKS version 5 also implements user authentication, which allows access rules based on user name and password.

A SOCKS server does not influence the application data. After a request has been allowed, the server passes the data back and forth between the client and the destination system. A SOCKS server cannot perform tasks like content filtering or caching.

Also, SOCKS is not transparent to the clients and requires the clients to have SOCKS support and to be configured accordingly.

Install and Configure Dante

Dante is an open source implementation of the SOCKS protocol. It consists of two parts:

- *SOCKS server (sockd)*—A server implementing the SOCKS protocol.
- *SOCKS client (socksify)*—A set of system libraries and a script that helps to implement SOCKS with clients that do not offer native SOCKS support.

These components come in separate RPM packages. You need to install the package dante-server for the server, and the package dante for the client.

After installation and configuration, start the server by entering:

```
rcsockd start
```

After changing the configuration file, restart the server by entering:

```
rcsockd restart
```

To start the server automatically at boot time, enter:

```
insserv sockd
```

The configuration for the server is located in the file:

```
/etc/sockd.conf
```

The configuration file contains two sections:

- *Server settings*—This controls the general behavior of the server.
- *Rules*—This defines the rules that are used to determine whether a request is allowed.

The server settings consist of several variables. A colon (:) is used to separate a variable from its value. You can use the # sign to write comments in the file.

Table 8-3 shows a list of the most important server settings.

Variable	Meaning and Possible Values
logoutput	This controls where the server sends the logging information. This can be <ul><li>syslog</li><li>stdout</li><li>stderr</li><li>A filename</li></ul> You can combine two or more options. Example: logoutput: syslog
internal	This option sets the IP address or interface and the port number on which the server accepts connections from clients. Example: internal: 10.0.0.1 port = 1080
external	This sets the interface that is used by the server for all outgoing connections. Usually this is the interface that is connected to the Internet. Example: external: 10.10.0.1
method	This option determines the method that is used to authenticate users for socks-rules. Possible values are <ul><li>`none`. The server does not require any user authentication.</li><li>`username`. The client needs to provide a user name and a password for authentication. In this case, Dante uses the system password file as the user database.</li><li>`pam`. The same as user name, but Dante uses pam instead of accessing the password file directly.</li><li>`rfc931`. The identity of the user is determined by an ident request as specified in RFC 931.</li></ul> You can use more than one value in order of preference. Example: method: username
clientmethod	Determines the methods of authentication for client rules. You can use the same values as for the method variable. The terms *socks-rules* and *client-rules* are described later in this section.
user.privileged	This determines which user sockd should use for privileged operations like reading the password file. Example: user.privileged: root
user.notprivileged	This determines the user ID that sockd uses for all other nonprivileged operations. Example: user.notprivileged: nobody

Table 8-3

The access rules are defined in the second part of the configuration file. There are two different kinds of rules that work at different levels.

- *Client-rules*—Determine if a client is allowed to connect to the server at all. This is done on basis of the IP address (range) or network address of the client.

   All client-rules in the configuration file are prefixed with client. The client-rules are checked before the socks-rules.

- *Socks-rules*—These rules determine what a client is allowed to do after it has connected to the server.

  Socks-rules do not have a prefix.

The following is a simple example configuration file without user authentication:

```
#Server Configuration
logoutput: /var/log/sockd.log
internal: 10.0.0.1 port = 1080
external: 137.65.81.40
method: none
clientmethod: none
user.privileged: root
user.notprivileged: nobody

#Client Rules

client pass {
   from: 10.0.0.0/24 port 1-65535 to: 0.0.0.0/0
   log: connect error
}

#Socks Rules

pass {
   from: 0.0.0.0/0 to: 0.0.0.0/0
   protocol: tcp udp
}

block {
   from: 0.0.0.0/0 to: 0.0.0.0/0
   log: connect error
}
```

The beginning of the file contains the general server configuration as described before. Then the client-rules and the socks-rules are defined.

The client-rules are processed first and then the socks-rules. A request has to pass one client-rule *and* one socks-rule to use the server.

Each rule starts either with `pass` or `block`, depending on whether the rules allow or deny access to the server. The client-rules have the additional keyword client before pass or block.

The rule itself is defined in parentheses {}. Each rule uses the keywords to and from to match the IP addresses of a request. The IP address 0.0.0.0/0 matches any address.

There are other keywords that can be used in the rules. These keywords can be either conditions that are used to match different parameters of a request or actions that are performed if the related keyword matches.

The following are valid conditions:

- `from`
- `to`
- `command`

- `method`
- `protocol`
- `proxyprotocol`
- `user`

The following are valid actions:

- bandwidth
- libwrap
- log
- redirect

Some of the keywords can be used for client-rules and socks-rules; others can only be used for one rule type.

Table 8-4 is an overview of keywords and their meaning when they are used in client-rules. (This information is taken from the sockd.conf man page.)

Keyword	Meaning and Possible Values
from	The rule applies to requests coming from the address given as the value.
to	The rule applies to the IP address of the SOCKS server that receives a request.
port	Parameter to from, to, and via. Accepts the keywords eq/=, neq/!=, ge/>=, le/<=, gt/>, lt/< followed by a number. A port range can also be given as "port <start #> - <end #>", which will match all port numbers within the range <start #> and <end #>.
libwrap	The server will pass the line to libwrap for execution.
log	Controls logging. Accepted keywords are connect, disconnect, data, error, and iooperation.
user	The server will only accept connections from users matching one of the names given as the value. If no user value is given, everyone in the password file will be matched. The rule must also allow user name-based methods.
method	Requires that the connection is authenticated using one of the given methods.
pam.servicename	Specifies which service name to use when involving PAM for user authentication. The default is sockd. This only applies when you use PAM as the authentication method.

Table 8-4

Table 8-5 is an overview of keywords and their meaning when used in socks-rules. (This information is taken from the sockd.conf man page.)

For the example in the above grey box, this means the following:

1. A request needs to pass the client-rule.

    In our example configuration, only requests from the 10.0.0.0/24 network are allowed. All other requests are blocked at this stage.

Keyword	Meaning and Possible Values
from	The rule applies to requests coming from the address given as the value.
to	The rule applies to the requested address of a destination server.
port	Parameter to from, to, and via. Accepts the keywords eq/=, neq/!=, ge/>=, le/<=, gt/>, lt/ < followed by a number. A portrange can also be given as "port <start #> - <end #>" which will match all port numbers within the range <start #> and <end #>
bandwidth	The clients matching this rule will all share this amount of bandwidth. Requires a commercial add-on. See the Dante Web site for details.
command	The rule applies to the given commands. Valid commands are • bind • bindreply • connect • udpassociate • udpreply This can be used instead of, or to complement, a protocol.
libwrap	The server will pass the line to libwrap for execution.
log	Controls logging. Accepted keywords are • connect • disconnect • data • iooperation
method	Requires that the connection is established using one of the given methods. method always refers to the source part of the rule. Valid values are the same as in the global method line.
pam.servicename	Specifies which service name to use when involving PAM. The default is sockd.
protocol	The rule applies to the given protocols. Valid values are tcp and udp. It is recommended that the command form be used since it provides more accuracy in defining rules.
proxyprotocol	The rule applies to requests using the given proxy protocol. Valid proxy protocols are socks_v4 and socks_v5.
redirect	The source or destination can be redirected using the redirect statement. This requires a commercial add-on. For more information, see the Dante Web site.
user	The server will accept connections from users matching one of the names given as the value. If no user value is given, everyone in the password file will be matched. The rule must also allow user name-based methods.

Table 8-5

2. When the client-rule has been passed, the request also needs to pass a socks-rule. The example uses the IP address 0.0.0.0/0 to allow any request.

   This is possible at this stage because unwanted connects have already been blocked by the previous client rule.

3. In the socks-rule, the log command is used to log connects and errors.

   To add user authentication to the server config, you have to use the method keyword in a client-rule or socks-rule.

The following enables PAM authentication in a socks-rule:

```
pass {
  from: 0.0.0.0/0 to: 0.0.0.0/0
  method: pam
  protocol: tcp udp
}
```

Any authentication method used in a rule must also be enabled in the general server configuration.

By default, all users that can be authenticated successfully are allowed to access the server. You can use the user keyword to limit access to a group of users:

```
pass {
  from: 0.0.0.0/0 to: 0.0.0.0/0
  method: pam
  user: fsailer blotz
  protocol: tcp udp
}
```

For a complete reference of all server options, see man `sockd.conf`.

Configure Clients to Use a SOCKS Server

Since SOCKS servers are not transparent to the clients, clients need to be configured to connect to the SOCKS server in the right way.

There are two ways to enable SOCKS support in clients:

- Configure Clients with Native SOCKS Support
- Use socksify to Enable SOCKS in Clients

Configure Clients with Native SOCKS Support Many newer network clients come with native SOCKS support. Configuring this feature is similar to setting up an HTTP proxy.

In the Firefox Web browser, shown in Figure 8-9, you can find the SOCKS setup with other proxy-related settings under `Edit > Preferences > General > Connection Settings`.

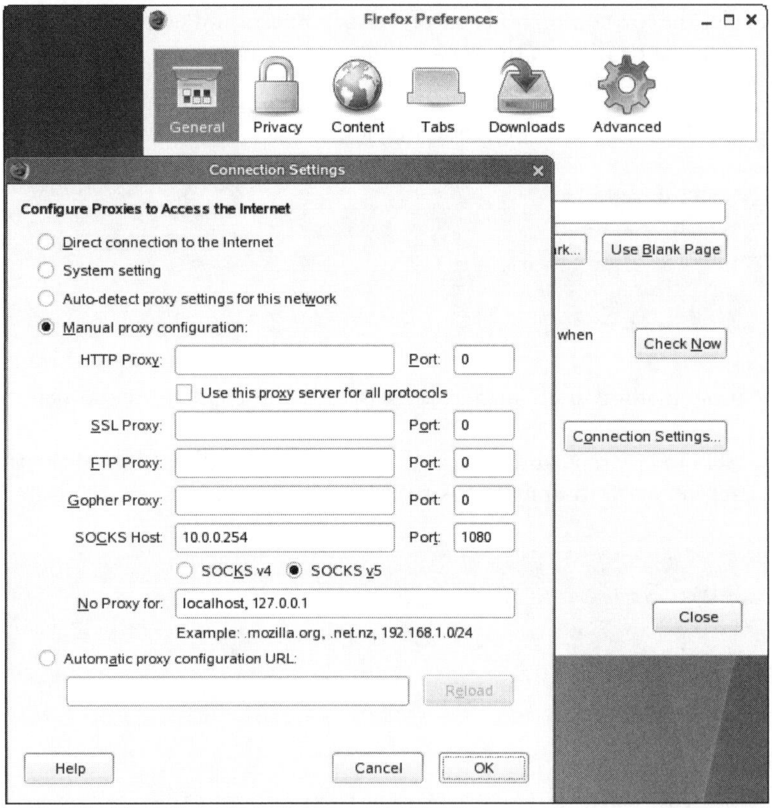

Figure 8-9

Select `Manual proxy configuration`. Enter the IP address or the DNS name of your SOCKS server in the `SOCKS Host` field and enter the port on which your SOCKS server is listening in the `Port` field. Leave all other proxy fields blank unless you want Firefox to use a proxy for one of the protocols.

You can also choose the SOCKS protocol version. Unless your SOCKS server does not support it, you should select SOCKS v5. Dante sockd supports v5.

Firefox (Version 1.5.0.4) does not support socks authentication at the time of this writing.

Instead of configuring the proxy manually, you can also use the mechanisms for Proxy-Auto-Configuration as described in "Configure the Web Browsers Automatically with a PAC Script" on page 211.

Use socksify to Enable SOCKS in Clients Socksify is a shell script that belongs to the Dante package. When client programs are invoked with the help of this script, they can access a SOCKS server although they do not provide native SOCKS support.

This is done by a mechanism called *library preloading*. This basically loads the SOCKS network code into memory before the actual client is started. When the client opens a network connection, the SOCKS network code is used and a connection to the SOCKS server is established.

The file /etc/socks.conf determines which SOCKS server should be used. The syntax of the configuration file is very similar to the syntax of the /etc/sockd.conf file.

In the configuration file you define routes, which determine if a network connection should go through a SOCKS server or not. The following example defines a basic route that sends everything to a SOCKS server:

```
route {
   from: 0.0.0.0/0 to: 0.0.0.0/0 via: 10.0.0.1 port = 1080
   protocol: tcp udp
   method: username
}
```

The from and to keywords match the requests based on the source and destination IP address. The via keyword determines to which SOCKS server and to which port requests should be sent that match the given conditions.

The keyword protocol determines which protocols can be used. The keyword method configures the authentication method.

Table 8-6 is a list of all possible configuration keywords. (This information is taken from the socks-conf man page.)

The following is an example session of using the ftp command with socksify:

```
geeko@da10:~> socksify ftp ftp.suse.com
geeko@10.0.0.1.1080 sockspassword:
Connected to ftp.suse.com.
220 "Welcome to the SUSE ftp server: Please login as user 'ftp'"
Name (ftp.suse.com:geeko):
```

As you can see, the ftp command is called with the help of the socksify script. In the example, the sockd server has been configured with user authentication; therefore, a prompt for the password is displayed.

By default, the current user ID is used to log in to the proxy. You can adjust this behavior by setting the environment variables SOCKS_USERNAME and SOCKS_PASSWORD:

```
geeko@da10:~> export SOCKS_USERNAME = "tux"
geeko@da10:~> socksify ftp ftp.suse.com
tux@149.44.174.220.1080 sockspassword:
Connected to ftp.suse.com.
220 "Welcome to the SUSE ftp server: Please login as user 'ftp'"
Name (ftp.suse.com:geeko):
```

8

Keyword	Meaning and Possible Values
debug	Setting this field to 1 turns on debugging.
logoutput	This value controls where the Socks client library sends logoutput. It can be syslog, stdout, stderr, a filename, or a combination.
resolveprotocol	The protocol used to resolve host names. Valid values are udp (default), tcp, and fake.
ROUTES	The routes are specified with a route keyword. Inside a pair of parentheses ({}), a set of keywords control the behavior of the route. Each route can contain three address specifications: from, to, and via. A route is selected for a connection based on the values within the route block. The next keywords are used in a route block.
ADDRESSES	Each address field can consist of an IP address (and where meaningful, a netmask, separated from the IP address by a /.), a hostname, or a domain name (designated by a leading period). Each address can be followed by an optional port specifier.
from	The route is used only by requests coming from the address given as the value.
to	The route is used only by requests going to the address given as the value.
via	The address of the Socks server to be used for the connection.
port	The parameter to from, to, and via. Accepts the keywords eq/=, neq/!=, ge/>=, le/<=, gt/>, lt/< followed by a number. A port range can also be given as "port <start #> - <end #>" which will match all port numbers within the range <start #> and <end #>
command	The server supports the given commands. Valid commands are • bind • bindreply • connect • udpassociate • udpreply Can be used instead of, or to complement, protocol.
method	List of authentication methods the client supports and which to offer the server. Currently supported values are none and user name.
protocol	The protocols the server supports. Supported values are tcp and udp.
proxyprotocol	The proxy protocols the server supports. Currently supported values are socks_v4, socks_v5, msproxy_v2, and http_v1.0.

Table 8-6

You can also use socksify with KDE applications by enabling SOCKS support in the Konqueror configuration dialog under `Proxy`. Although you configure it in Konqueror, SOCKS support is available for almost all KDE network applications.

On the SOCKS tab, you can enable the SOCKS support by selecting the option `Enable SOCKS Support`. This way it is not necessary to start a KDE application with the socksify script. The SOCKS network code is used automatically and can also be configured in /etc/socks.conf.

After you have adjusted the settings in Konqueror, you should restart KDE to make sure that all applications and background processes are running with the correct settings. (At the time of this writing, there was no authentication support for SOCKS in KDE (version 3.5.1).)

Exercise 8-6: Use Dante

Time Required: 40 Minutes

Objective: In this exercise, you configure a socks server and a socks client. The exercise consists of four parts.

Description: In the first part, install dante, dante-server, and wget; then configure the sockd server (/etc/sockd.conf) according to your network parameters, and allow access from the 10.0.0.0/24 network.

In the second part, configure the client via /etc/socks.conf and use wget to fetch the file index.html from *www.novell.com* to test your configuration.

The third part consists of creating the local user pbear with the password Novell; if this has been done already in a previous exercise, skip this step.

In the fourth part, change the server and client configuration to use pam to allow access for the user pbear; test this with socksify wget *www.novell.com*.

Detailed Steps to Complete this Exercise

- Part I: Install and Configure Dante
- Part II: Configure Socksify and Test Your SOCKS Server
- Part III: Create a Test User
- Part IV: Configure and Test User Authentication

Part I: Install and Configure Dante

Do the following:

1. Open a terminal window and `su -` to the root user.

2. Enter `yast -i dante dante-server wget`; when prompted, insert the media called for.

    wget is not part of dante, but you will use it in this exercise as a test application.

3. Rename the default sockd configuration file by entering:

    ```
    mv /etc/sockd.conf /etc/sockd.conf.original
    ```

4. Create a new configuration file `/etc/sockd.conf` with the following content:

```
#Server Configuration
logoutput: /var/log/sockd.log
internal: your_ip_address port = 1080
external: your_ip_address
method: none
clientmethod: none
user.privileged: root
user.notprivileged: nobody
#Client Rules
client pass {
        from: 10.0.0.0/24 port 1-65535 to: 0.0.0.0/0
        log: connect error
}
#Socks Rules
pass {
        from: 0.0.0.0/0 to: 0.0.0.0/0
        protocol: tcp udp
}
block {
        from: 0.0.0.0/0 to: 0.0.0.0/0
        log: connect error
}
```

5. Save the file and start sockd with the command `rcsockd start`.

6. Make sure that no error messages are displayed when sockd starts up. When the server starts successfully, only the following line should be displayed:

```
Starting sockd / dante server                    done
```

7. (Conditional) If there are any error messages, have a look at /var/log/sockd.log. Look at the indicated line in the configuration file and try to correct the error; then try to start sockd again.

Part II: Configure Socksify and Test Your SOCKS Server

Do the following:

1. Open a terminal window and `su -` to the root user with a password of `novell`.

2. Rename the default configuration file by entering:

   `mv /etc/socks.conf /etc/socks.conf.original`

3. Create a new configuration file /etc/socks.conf with the following content:

```
route {
    from: 0.0.0.0/0 to: 0.0.0.0/0 via: your_ip_address\
        port = 1080
    protocol: tcp udp
    method: none
}
```

4. Save the file.

5. Open the sockd log file by entering:

    `tail -f /var/log/sockd.log`

6. Enter some empty lines by pressing `Enter` a few times.

7. Open another terminal window, but do not su to the root user.

8. Enter:

    `socksify wget www.novell.com`

    The wget command should display that it was able to download the index.html file of *www.novell.com*.

9. Change to the other terminal window and check if a new line has been added to the log file.

    If sockd and socksify were configured correctly, the wget command should have created new lines in the logfile.

Part III: Create a Test User

Do the following:

1. Start the `YaST Control Center`.

2. On the left side of YaST's main menu, select `Security and Users`.

3. On the right side, select `User Management`.

4. Make sure that `Users` is selected.

5. Select `Add`.

6. Enter the following information:

    - Full User Name: `Peter Bear`
    - User Login: `pbear`
    - Password: `Novell`
    - Confirm Password: `Novell`

7. Select `Accept`.

8. When YaST notifies you about a weak password, confirm the dialog by selecting `Yes`.

9. Select `Finish`.

10. Close YaST.

Part IV: Configure and Test User Authentication

Do the following:

1. Open a terminal window and `su -` to the root user with a password of `novell`.

2. Open the file `/etc/sockd.conf` with a text editor.

3. In the general server section, change the line:

   `method: none`

   to:

   `method: pam`

4. In the SOCKS rule that starts with `pass`, insert the following two lines at the end of the rule:

   ```
   method: pam
   user: pbear
   ```

5. Save the file and close the text editor.

6. Restart sockd by entering `rcsockd restart`.

7. Open the file `/etc/socks.conf` in a text editor.

8. Change the method value in the rule to `username`.

9. The line should now look as follows:

   `method: username`

10. Save the file and close the text editor.

11. To set the SOCKS user name, enter:

    `export SOCKS_USERNAME=pbear`

12. Enter:

    `socksify wget www.novell.com`

    If everything was configured correctly, you should be prompted for the password of pbear.

13. Enter `Novell`.
    wget should now download and save the file index.html.

14. If not, check the file /var/log/messages. If there are messages like:

    Apr 28 11:17:32 (1146215852) sockd[7837]: pass(1): tcp/accept]:
    pam%pbear@ 10.0.0.10. 35446 -> 10.0.0.10.1080: pam_authenticate():
    Authentication failure

The reason could be a missing /etc/pam.d/sockd file. In this case create one with the following content and try again:

```
#%PAM-1.0
auth       include        common-auth
account    include        common-account
password   include        common-password
session    include        common-session
```

An easy way to create this file would be to use an existing file as a template, for instance:

```
cp /etc/pam.d/xdm /etc/pam.d/sockd
```

and then delete all lines except those listed above in /etc/pam.d/sockd.

Objective 4—Configure and Use rinetd

rinetd is a simple generic TCP proxy that can handle almost all protocols that work with known TCP ports (such as HTTP: port 80, HTTPS: port 443, and SMTP: port 25) and a single TCP connection. Like all generic proxies, rinetd cannot analyze and organize the contents of the data that runs through it.

The functionality offered by rinetd is ideal for use on lean application-level gateways. It can forward connections to a TCP port of the gateway on which it runs to a TCP port of any other IP address and record information in a log file. In addition, access protection on an IP address level is possible.

Unlike sockd, rinetd is generally not used to give internal clients access to external services; it is more frequently used to pass packages from an external source to an internal service.

To use rinetd on SUSE Linux Enterprise Server 10, you have to install the package rinetd. As with most services, rinetd can be started with the command:

```
rcrinetd start
```

To start rinetd automatically at boot time, you can insert it into the init process with the command:

```
insserv rinetd
```

The configuration of rinetd is located in the file /etc/rinetd.conf. You can find an example configuration file in the directory /usr/share/doc/packages/rinetd/, which you can use as a template for your setup.

The configuration file contains rules which define how rinetd forwards incoming TCP connections. Changes in the configuration file are activated either by restarting rinetd or after a hang-up signal has been sent with killall -HUP rinetd, which causes the configuration file to be reread.

With a restart, existing connections are interrupted. The hang-up signal does not interrupt existing connections.

To configure rinetd, you have to do the following:

- Configure Forwarding Rules
- Configure Allow and Deny Rules
- Configure Logging

Configure Forwarding Rules

These forwarding rules define the main functionality of rinetd—forwarding TCP connections to other addresses. The format is very simple:

local_Address local_port destination_address destination_port

For example:

```
194.46.73.3 80 192.168.1.3 80
```

This example rule will forward all connection requests to TCP port 80 on the network interface with the IP address 194.46.73.3 to the TCP port 80 of the Web server with the IP address 192.168.1.3 in the DMZ without having to activate routing on the gateway on which rinetd is running.

Instead of port numbers, service names from /etc/services can be used. The example for port 80 then appears as follows:

```
194.46.73.3 www 192.168.1.3 www
```

In addition, host names can be used instead of IP addresses, which assumes, however, that there is a working DNS or corresponding entries in /etc/hosts.

It is better at this point to work with IP addresses to avoid DNS spoofing. The IP address 0.0.0.0 stands for all available interfaces of the gateway on which rinetd is running.

Configure Allow and Deny Rules

Using allow and deny rules, you can implement effective access control on specific forwarding rules.

Allow and deny rules that are defined before the first forwarding rule are valid globally for all forwarding rules. If a deny rule matches the address of a new connection or no allow rule matches this address, the connection is refused.

Allow and deny rules that are defined after a specific forwarding rule are only valid for this one forwarding rule.

Addresses in allow and deny rules can also be written as address patterns. An address can consist of the digits 1 to 9, "." (dot), "?", and "*". The "?" stands for any character. The "*" stands for any number of any characters.

For example:

```
deny 141.73.21.*
```

This rule matches all addresses from the class C network 141.73.21.0/24 and voids any forwarding rules for computers with addresses from this network.

rinetd does not allow host names instead of IP addresses in allow and deny rules, because name resolution would cause significant drops in performance.

rinetd is a single process server—one single process has all connections under its control. Name resolution causes all other connections to be halted. The exclusive use of IP addresses is not a disadvantage at this point because, for security, only IP addresses should be used here to prevent DNS spoofing.

Configure Logging

rinetd can write log messages using syslog. The configuration option to activate this logging is `syslog`. Optional parameters are facility and priority:

```
syslog local0 info
```

If facility and priority are not specified, the defaults daemon and info are used.
Entries in /var/log/messages look like the following:

```
May 2 06:50:57 da10 rinetd[5688]: 10.0.0.43 10.0.0.34:80 10.0.0.33:80
in:0 out:0  not-allowed
May 2 06:54:15 da10 rinetd[5735]: 10.0.0.33 10.0.0.34:80 10.0.0.33:80
in:0 out:0  started
May 2 06:54:41 da10 rinetd[5735]: 10.0.0.33 10.0.0.34:80 10.0.0.33:80
in:1994 out:3088 done-local-closed
```

The manual page of rinetd describes how to configure logging to a separate file; however, this does not seem to be implemented in the version of rinetd included in SLES 10.

Exercise 8-7: Configure rinetd

Time Required: 15 Minutes

Objective: In this exercise, you learn how to configure rinetd.

Description: While rinetd is used to forward connections to other computers, for the purpose of this exercise you will forward the connection to another port on your own computer. In this way you can work with a single computer.

Install Apache2, the package apache2-example-pages, and rinetd on your computer. Start Apache and configure rinetd to connect to the locally running Apache when a connection to port 8080 of your machine is made. Test rinetd by directing your browser to http://your-ip:8080/.

Detailed Steps to Complete this Exercise

1. Open a terminal window and `su -` to root (password `novell`).

2. Install Apache by entering:

   `yast -i apache2 apache2-prefork apache2-example-pages rinetd`

   Insert the SLES 10 DVD (or CDs when using the CD set) when prompted.

3. Once the installation is finished, enter `rcapache2 start` to start the Apache Web server.

4. Start Firefox by pressing `Alt+F2`, typing `firefox`, and selecting `Run`.

5. In the address bar, enter `http://localhost`.
   The Apache test page should be displayed.

6. Create a file `/etc/rinetd.conf` with the following content:

   ```
   your_ip_address 8080 your_ip_address 80
   allow 10.0.0.*
   syslog
   ```

7. Save the file and close the text editor.

8. Start rinetd by entering `rcrinetd start`.

9. In the address bar of the Web browser, enter `http://your-ip:8080`.
   Although no Web server is listening on port 8080 of your system, the Apache test page should be loaded because rinetd redirects the request to port 80 of your computer.

Summary

- Application-Level Gateways are commonly called proxy servers and work at the Application layer of the ISO/OSI model. In addition to caching resources, they can restrict access to resources based on multiple factors including user authentication, time of day, and data content.

- Squid is the most common HTTP proxy software used on Linux systems today. It can be used to create a standard, intercepting/transparent, or HTTP accelerator proxy server. For an intercepting/transparent proxy server, a router must also be configured to forward HTTP requests to the proxy server.

- You can configure squid by editing the appropriate tags in the **/etc/squid/squid.conf** file. The **acl** and **http_access** tags may be used to restrict access to the proxy server by host, IP, network and time.

- Client Web browsers must be configured to access proxy servers. This may be done manually, using a PAC script, or automatically using WPAD. WPAD may be configured using DNS records or DHCP option 252.

- The **CONNECT** method, **transconnect** package, and **https_tunnel** script may be used to tunnel HTTP connections that use SSL through the squid proxy server.

- You can use basic, digest and NTLM authentication with squid to provide authentication security for proxy connections. PAM provides basic authentication, while the **digest_pw_auth** program provides digest authentication.

- Squid may also be configured to restrict access based on the URL in the proxy server request using the **squidGuard** program or the **url_regex** and **urpath_regex** acls.

- The **calamaris** program may be used to create custom squid access reports from the entries in the **/var/log/squid/access.log** file.

- SOCKS is an alternative to the squid proxy server that may be used to restrict access to resources. Unlike squid, SOCKS can work with several protocols in addition to HTTP, but cannot filter proxy requests based on data content.

- The SOCKS server location must be configured on each client computer. This may be done manually, by using a PAC script, or by using the **socksify** program.

- Dante is a SOCKS implementation available for most Linux systems. It may be configured using the **/etc/sockd.conf** file.

- The **rinetd** daemon is a simple TCP proxy server that is commonly used to redirect external requests to internal servers. It may be configured using the **/etc/rinetd.conf** file.

8

Key Terms

/etc/rinetd.conf   The configuration file for the rinetd TCP proxy daemon.

/etc/services   A file that lists common port numbers and their names.

/etc/sockd.conf   The main configuration file for the dante SOCKS daemon.

/etc/socks.conf   A file on a client computer that specifies the location of the SOCKS server.

/etc/squid/squid.conf   The main configuration file for the squid proxy server.

/etc/squidguard.conf   The configuration file used by squidGuard.

/usr/sbin/digest_pw_auth   A program that provides digest authentication with the squid proxy server.

/usr/share/doc/packages/rinetd   A directory that contains sample rinetd configuration files.

/usr/share/doc/packages/squid/errors   A directory that contains squid error message templates.

/usr/share/squid/errors   The directory that stores custom squid error messages.

/var/cache/squid   The directory that stores the cache used by the squid proxy server.

/var/log/messages   The Linux system information log file. It contains messages from the rinetd daemon.

/var/log/squid/access.log   A log file that stores all requests made to the squid proxy server.

/var/log/squid/cache.log   A log file that stores information about the squid cache.

Access Control List (ACL)   A list of users or computers that are granted or denied access to certain resources.

Application-Level Gateway (ALG)   A computer that fully analyzes network traffic passing through a network using proxy server software. They are also called application-level firewalls.

authentication schemes   The methods that may be used to authenticate to a proxy server.

basic   An authentication scheme used by most proxy servers that transmits the username and password in cleartext.

blacklist   A list of resources that proxy clients are not allowed to access.

blocking   See **URL** filtering.

caching   The process whereby information is stored locally for later use. Proxy servers such as Squid cache most requests to speed up future requests for the same information.

calamaris command   Produces reports based on the contents of the /var/log/squid/access.log file. client request.

CONNECT method   A process used to tunnel information through a squid HTTP proxy.

dante   A common SOCKS proxy server software package for Linux systems.

digest   An authentication scheme used by most proxy servers that transmits an encrypted hash that contains the password.

Firefox   The default Web browser on most Linux systems. It is based on the Mozilla project.

frox   A proxy server software package that uses the FTP protocol rather than the HTTP protocol.

HTTP accelerator   A proxy server that caches HTTP requests from an internal Web server to speed up access.

https-tunnel   A PERL script that may be used to tunnel HTTPS traffic through the squid proxy server.

HyperText Transfer Protocol (HTTP)   The protocol used to obtain Web pages from Web servers on the Internet.

insserv command   Changes the startup configuration files to specify the runlevels a daemon should start and stop in.

intercepting proxy server   A standard proxy server that requires no special client configuration. HTTP requests from the network router are forwarded to the intercepting proxy server for processing.

International Standard Organization's Open System Interconnect (ISO/OSI)   A model used to describe how computers use protocols to communicate on a computer network.

library preloading   The process of loading SOCKS client code into memory before network client software.

NTLM (NT LAN Manager)   An authentication scheme used by most proxy servers that transmits a random challenge that is encrypted using the password of the user.

PAC (Proxy Auto Configuration) script   A network-accessible script that may be used to configure proxy server settings on client computers.

Pluggable Authentication Modules (PAM)   A set of Linux software components that determine how users are authenticated to the system.

proxy authentication   A process whereby proxy server users are verified before their requests are handled.

proxy server   A software program used on application-level gateways to cache and restrict traffic based on detailed criteria such as data content and user information.

rinetd   A common generic proxy server available on many Linux systems. It redirects TCP connections from one address and port to another.

Secure Sockets Layer (SSL)   A technology used to provide encryption for HTTP connections.

sockd   The SOCKS daemon used by the dante package.

SOCKS   A widely-used application-independent proxy server standard that translates internal TCP and UDP requests to an external network.

socksify command   Used to create a SOCKS connection on a client computer.

squid   A common HTTP proxy server package found on most Linux systems.

squidGuard   A SUSE Linux package that contains additional tools for the squid proxy server including URL filtering.

standard proxy server   A proxy server that provides Internet access to clients on an internal network.

tag   A configuration parameter in the /etc/squid/squid.conf file.

transconnect   A package that may be used with the squid proxy server to tunnel HTTPS traffic.

transparent proxy server   See **intercepting proxy server**.

tunneling   The process of sending data formatted using a specific protocol to a remote computer by encapsulating the data within a different protocol.

URL filtering   A process used by many proxy servers that restricts access based on the URL in the source packet.

url_regex   A tag in the /etc/squid/squid.conf file that may be used to perform URL filtering.

Web Proxy Auto-Discovery Protocol (WPAD)   A configuration that uses DNS records or DHCP options to automatically configure proxy server settings on client computers.

whitelist   A list of resources that proxy clients are allowed to access.

wpad.dat   A file that stores the configuration script downloaded by WPAD clients.

Review Questions

1. Which of the following protocols is the squid proxy able to forward without encapsulation?

    a. HTTP

    b. HTTP and HTTPS

    c. HTTP and FTP

    d. HTTP and FTP and HTTPS

2. Which of the following statements best describes a transparent proxy server?

    a. A proxy server whose location and port must be configured on each client computer.

    b. A proxy server that caches all requests for resources to speed future access times.

    c. A proxy server that obtains HTTP requests forwarded to it by a router.

    d. A proxy server that separates an internal network from an external network. It provides access to external resources for internal clients.

3. Which tag in the /etc/squid/squid.conf file may be used to specify that large objects are not cached? _____

4. What is the default location of the squid cache on the file system? _____

5. You wish to modify the default text that is sent to clients when a resource request is denied. Where can you find templates to base your custom error messages on? _____

6. Which of the following acl tags should you use if you wish to restrict access to the proxy server for certain domain names requested during business hours? (Choose all that apply.)

   a. srcdomain

   b. dstdomain

   c. time

   d. url_reg

7. You have configured a proxy server address in Firefox. What port number should you normally specify alongside the proxy server address? _____

8. What do the following lines in the /etc/squid/squid.conf file perform? (Choose all that apply.)

   ```
   acl arfa1 src 192.168.1.0/24
   acl atime1 time WF 07:00-15:00
   http_access allow arfa1 atime1
   ```

   a. All clients from the 192.168.1.0 network will be allowed to obtain resources using the proxy server from 7:00am to 3:00pm on Wednesday and Friday only.

   b. No clients from the 192.168.1.0 network will be allowed to obtain resources using the proxy server from 7:00am to 3:00pm on Wednesday and Friday only.

   c. All clients from the 192.168.1.0 network will be allowed to obtain resources using the proxy server except from 7:00am to 3:00pm on Wednesday and Friday.

   d. No clients from the 192.168.1.0 network will be allowed to obtain resources using the proxy server except from 7:00am to 3:00pm on Wednesday and Friday.

9. Your PAC script contains the following line:

   ```
   if (host == "arfa.ppc.net") {
   return "DIRECT";
   }
   ```

   What does this line specify?

   a. Clients should redirect all requests to the arfa.ppc.net proxy server.

   b. Client requests for arfa.ppc.net should not be sent to the proxy server.

   c. Client requests for arfa.ppc.net should be sent to the proxy server.

   d. Clients should ignore proxy server requests for arfa.ppc.net.

10. What DHCP option may be used to configure clients with the location of a proxy server? _____

11. You are using the CONNECT method to tunnel HTTPS traffic through your squid proxy server. Assuming the default HTTPS configuration, what port should you allow the CONNECT method to use? _____

12. Which of the following statements regarding proxy authentication are true? (Choose all that apply.)

    a. PAM modules can be used to provide digest authentication

    b. Web browsers must support proxy authentication

    c. PAM modules can be used to provide basic authentication

    d. The digest_pw_auth program must be specified to provide digest authentication

13. You are configuring URL filtering with url_regex on your proxy server to prevent access to certain domain names. How can you ensure that the names you provide are not case sensitive? _____

14. What line must you add to your /etc/squid/squid.conf file in order to use squidGuard to provide URL filtering? _____

15. Which of the commands may be used to display the top 5 hosts that use your proxy server?

    a. calamaris –i 5 /var/log/squid/access.log

    b. calamaris –r 5 /var/log/squid/access.log

    c. calamaris –d 5 /var/log/squid/access.log

    d. calamaris –L 5 /var/log/squid/access.log

16. You are configuring the Dante SOCKS server on your Linux computer. What lines must you add to the /etc/sockd.conf file to create access rules? (Choose all that apply.)

    a. pass

    b. reject

    c. block

    d. accept

17. You are attempting to connect to a remote FTP server through a SOCKS proxy server using a Web browser that does not support SOCKS configuration. What alternative could you do to connect to the remote FTP server? _____

18. What line could you add to the /etc/rinetd.conf file to forward all requests on port 3389 on your external network interface (209.121.66.2) to the host 192.168.1.110 on the same port? _____

Discovery Exercises

Examining Proxy Server Internet Access

Most organizations provide some level of Internet access for client computers on internal networks. However, the method used to provide Internet access depends on the nature and needs of the organization. NAT routers examine information at Layer 3 of the ISO/OSI model, whereas proxy servers such as squid examine information at Layer 7 of the ISO/OSI model. As a result, NAT routers forward packets quicker than proxy servers, but are unable to restrict traffic by data content. To speed access, most proxy servers cache content such that future client queries may be obtained directly from the cache rather than from the Internet. Many argue that this results in faster network access than NAT routers can provide.

Set up the squid proxy server on your Linux server to provide Internet access to three or four internal client computers on your network and monitor the speed at which normal Web browsing occurs. Next, reconfigure your network such that your Linux system provides NAT routing to the same internal client computers and monitor the speed at which normal Web browsing occurs. Record your observations in a short memo. Which technology provided faster access?

Using Public Blacklists

In this section, you learned how to configure the squid proxy server to reject requests from clients based on the URL within the request itself. To block several URLs, it is more efficient to create and use a blacklist file that contains the restricted URLs. However, maintaining blacklist files can quickly become time consuming considering the large number of dangerous Web sites available on the Internet today.

Use the Internet to research popular blacklists available for use with the squid proxy server. How often are these blacklists updated? How are the blacklisted entries categorized? Does the blacklist need to be downloaded or can it be queried online?

Following this, download a blacklist from the Internet and configure squid-Guard to enforce the blacklist for client connections on your squid proxy server. Test your settings from a client computer to ensure that the blacklisted URLs are restricted.

Researching & Implementing CARP

In larger environments, it is more feasible to use several proxy servers to service Internet access requests from clients. As a result, Cache Array Routing Protocol (CARP) was introduced to load-balance HTTP requests across several different proxy servers. A hash is generated for each URL requested by clients, and each proxy server is configured to process certain ranges of hashes. Since these ranges are evenly spread across multiple proxy servers, client requests are also evenly spread to multiple servers in the CARP array.

Use the Internet to research the configuration of CARP on the squid HTTP proxy. Next, implement a two-node CARP array using your Linux server and your partner's Linux server.

Virtual Private Networks

In the past, dedicated phone lines to connect branch offices or dial-in connections for remote workers were widely used. Since they were, however, rather expensive, especially if used over a long distance, alternatives were needed. These costs were remarkably reduced using the Internet. But with the use of the Internet new problems arose, namely unauthorized access to the internal networks or unauthorized access to the data exchanged over the Internet. To solve these problems, cryptography is used, both to ensure that only authorized users access the internal network and to protect the data traveling through the Internet from being viewed by unauthorized people. Technologies that use one network infrastructure to carry the packets of another network are usually summarized under the heading VPN (Virtual Private Network).

Objectives

- VPN and IPSec Basics
- Configure and Establish an IPSec Connection
- Understand Packet Filtering of VPN Traffic

Objective 1—VPN and IPSec Basics

A VPN uses the infrastructure of another network, for instance the Internet, for its traffic. By definition, a VPN does not necessarily have to encrypt the traffic, but in practice this is done in the majority of cases. See Figure 9-1.

Various technologies are used to implement VPNs, including IPSec, OpenVPN, L2TP, HTTPS, SSH and others. In this course we cover IPSec.

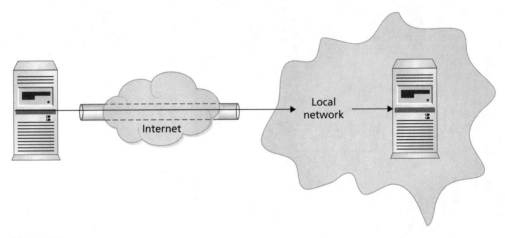

Figure 9-1

IPSec uses cryptography to authenticate users and to protect the transmitted data from eavesdropping.

IPSec consists of four different components:

- *Security protocols*—They form the basis of IPSec.
  Security protocols used are Authentication Header (AH, protocol 51) and Encapsulating Security Payload (ESP, protocol 50).

- *Security associations*—Security associations underlie connections in IPSec.
  Each security protocol needs its own security association. It has a limited validity and has to be renewed after its expiration.

- *Key management*—Different keys are used for authentication and encryption.
  Usually the exchange of keys is performed with the Internet Key Exchange (IKE) Protocol.

- *Encryption algorithms*—IPSec can use various algorithms.

When establishing an IPSec connection, the first step is the exchange of the keys and the establishment of the needed security associations. This is done using ISAKMP (Internet Security Association and Key Management Protocol) via UDP port 500.

After that the encrypted data is exchanged in a secure tunnel using protocol 50 (ESP). It is also possible to tunnel the data authenticated but unencrypted using protocol 51 (AH).

Three different methods are available to authenticate the endpoints of connections:

- Preshared keys
- Plain RSA keys
- Certificates

We do not recommend that you use preshared keys because the same key is used for all connections. It is easy to administer IPSec with plain RSA keys if there are few parties involved. If many computers require keys, certificates are probably the best choice.

In this section on IPSec we will use certificates.

Objective 2—Configure and Establish an IPSec Connection

Kernel 2.4.*x* uses the FreeSWAN kernel modules to implement IPSec. In kernel 2.6.*x* this functionality is part of the mainline kernel.

There are two different toolsets that come with SLES 10 to control IPSec connections: The packages openswan and ipsec-tools.

OpenSWAN, which is covered in this section, continues the FreeSWAN project that was discontinued a few years ago. It contains the tools that were used with kernel 2.4.*x*, ported to support the IPSec modules contained in kernel 2.6.*x*. The package ipsec-tools includes the programs setkey and racoon to control IPSec connections. These are not covered in this course.

How you configure an IPSec connection depends on what you want to do:

- Connect Two Sites with IPSec (Site-to-Site)
- Connect a Single Computer with a Site (End-to-Site)
- Connect Two Single Computers (End-to-End)

In each case, the configuration is slightly different.

Once you are done with the configuration, you need to:

- Establish the Connection
- Test the Connection

The following scenarios use certificates, which are created as described in "Create a Certification Authority (CA) and Issue Certificates with CLI Tools" and "Create a Certification Authority (CA) and Issue Certificates with YaST."

Connect Two Sites with IPSec (Site-to-Site)

To begin, it is a good idea to visualize the network in a sketch as shown in Figure 9-2. When you have a clear concept of the network, filling in the correct values in /etc/ipsec.conf is much easier and less prone to errors.

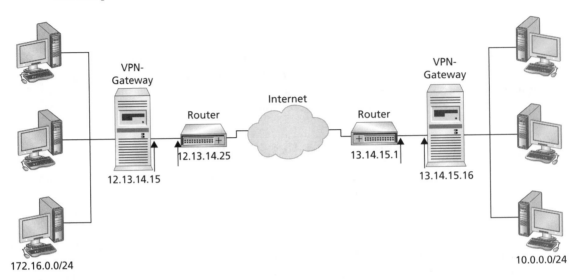

Figure 9-2

Configuring an IPSec connection consists of several parts:

- Configure /etc/ipsec.conf
- Copy Certificates and Private Keys
- Configure /etc/ipsec.secrets

Configure /etc/ipsec.conf The file /etc/ipsec.conf has several parts. The first section defines basic configuration parameters that are independent of specific connections:

```
# /etc/ipsec.conf - Openswan IPsec configuration file
# RCSID $Id: ipsec.conf.in,v 1.15.2.2 2005/11/14 20:10:27 paul Exp $
# This file:  /usr/share/doc/packages/openswan/ipsec.conf-sample
# Manual:     ipsec.conf.5
version 2.0     # conforms to second version of ipsec.conf specification
                                                            (Continued)
```

```
# basic configuration
config setup
  # plutodebug / klipsdebug = "all", "none" or a combation from below:
  # "raw crypt parsing emitting control klips pfkey natt x509 private"
  # eg:
  # plutodebug="control parsing"
  #
  # Only enable klipsdebug=all if you are a developer
  #
  # NAT-TRAVERSAL support, see README.NAT-Traversal
  # nat_traversal=yes
  # virtual_private=%v4:10.0.0.0/8,%v4:192.168.0.0/16,
%4:172.16.0.0/12
  #
  # Certificate Revocation List handling:
  #crlcheckinterval=600
  #strictcrlpolicy=yes
  #
  # Change rp_filter setting? (default is 0, disabled)
  # See also setting in the /etc/sysctl.conf file!
  #rp_filter=%unchanged
  #
  # Workaround to setup all tunnels immediately, since the new default
  # of "plutowait=no" causes "Resource temporarily unavailable" errors
  # for the first connect attempt over each tunnel, that is delayed to
  # be established later / on demand.
  #
  plutowait=yes
```

9

Table 9-1 explains the configuration parameters shown in the config section of /etc/ipsec.conf. Other parameters are explained in the man page for ipsec.conf.

Parameter	Significance
klipsdebug, plutodebug	Determine the amount of information written to the log file.
crlcheckinterval strictcrlpolicy	Determine how often the certificate revocation list is checked for changes and if an up-to-date CRL is strictly required or not.
rp_filter	Determines whether the value in /proc/sys/net/ipv4/conf/*interface*/rp_filter should be changed.
nattraversal	Activates the additional functionality to tunnel IPSec in UDP packets to traverse NAT gateways.

Table 9-1

The section conn %default covers parameters that are common to all connections. This avoids having to repeat these parameters in each connection specification.

These parameters can, however, be overwritten within specific connection specifications:

```
# default settings for connections
conn %default
        # keyingtries default to %forever
        #keyingtries=3
        # Sig keys (default: %dnsondemand)
        leftrsasigkey=%cert
        rightrsasigkey=%cert
        # Lifetimes, defaults are 1h/8hrs
        #ikelifetime=20m
        #keylife=1h
        #rekeymargin=8m
```

The next section concerns a feature called opportunistic encryption. This feature is usually turned off and is not covered in this course.

```
#Disable Opportunistic Encryption
include /etc/ipsec.d/examples/no_oe.conf
```

After that, each connection is described in a block starting with conn and an arbitrary name. All lines belonging to that block have to be indented, including comment signs within that block. A line starting in the first column ends the block.

The following sample section is included in the default configuration file and gives the relevant parameters needed for a connection:

```
# Add connections here

# sample VPN connection
#conn sample
#       # Left security gateway, subnet behind it, nexthop toward right.
#       left=10.0.0.1
#       leftsubnet=172.16.0.0/24
#       leftnexthop=10.22.33.44
#       # Right security gateway, subnet behind it, nexthop toward left.
#       right=10.12.12.1
#       rightsubnet=192.168.0.0/24
#       rightnexthop=10.101.102.103
#       # To authorize this connection, but not actually start it,
#       # at startup, uncomment this.
#       #auto=start
```

You are free in your choice of left and right. The man page for ipsec.conf suggests using *left* for the *local* and *right* for the *remote* side of the tunnel.

An example of the two connection definitions necessary for a gateway IP address of 12.13.14.15 and a network 172.16.0.0/24 behind it on one side and a gateway IP address of 13.14.15.16 and a network 10.0.0.0/24 behind it on the other side might look like this:

```
# Connection between sites
conn da10-da20
    # Left security gateway, subnet behind it, next hop toward right.
    leftsubnet=172.16.0.0/24
    left=10.0.0.10
    leftid="C=DE, ST=Bavaria, L=Munich, O=Digitalairlines,
OU=Training, CN=da10.digitalairlines.com/emailAddress=root@da10.
digitalairlines.com"
    leftcert=/etc/ipsec.d/certs/da10_cert.pem
    #leftrsasigkey=%cert  # already part of defaults
    # Right security gateway, subnet behind it,
    # next hop toward left.
    right=10.0.0.20
    rightid="C=DE, ST=Bavaria, L=Munich, O=Digitalairlines,
OU=Training, CN=da20.digitalairlines.com/emailAddress=root@da20.
digitalairlines.com"
    #rightrsasigkey=%cert # already part of defaults
    rightsubnet=192.168.0.0/24
    # To authorize this connection, but not actually start it,
    # at startup, uncomment this.
    auto=start
```

The configuration is nearly the same on the other side; the only difference is that `rightcert` is specified instead of `leftcert`:

```
# Connection between sites
conn da10-da20
    # Left security gateway, subnet behind it, next hop toward right.
    leftsubnet=172.16.0.0/24
    left=10.0.0.10
    leftid="C=DE, ST=Bavaria, L=Munich, O=Digitalairlines,
OU=Training, CN=da10.digitalairlines.com/emailAddress=root@da10.
digitalairlines.com"
    #leftrsasigkey=%cert # already part of defaults
    # Right security gateway, subnet behind it,
    # next hop toward left.
    right=10.0.0.20
    rightid="C=DE, ST=Bavaria, L=Munich, O=Digitalairlines,
OU=Training, CN=da20.digitalairlines.com/emailAddress=root@da20.
digitalairlines.com"
    rightcert=/etc/ipsec.d/certs/da20_cert.pem
    #rightrsasigkey=%cert  # already part of defaults
    rightsubnet=192.168.0.0/24
    # To authorize this connection, but not actually start it,
    # at startup, uncomment this.
    auto=start
```

Table 9-2 lists common parameters. Other parameters are explained in the man page for ipsec.conf.

Parameter	Significance
left right	The IP of the interface. If `%defaultroute` is specified, IPSec uses the current values of the interface with the default route.
leftsubnet rightsubnet	The network to be reached behind the gateway. If there is no such network, such as in the case of a notebook, it is left empty.
leftnexthop rightnexthop	If left/right is not specified as %defaultroute, this parameter is used to tell IPSec the IP of the next router. If there is no router between the two gateways, you can specify `%direct`.
leftcert rightcert	Specifies the location of the certificate.
leftrsasigkey rightrsasigkey	Specifies the public key. If set to `%cert` the key is extracted from the certificate.
leftid rightid	The identity of the host. A text string needs to be preceded by an @ sign.

auto	`add` loads the specification but does not try to establish a connection.
	  `start` loads the specification and tries to establish a connection.
	  If not specified, you can add/start connections on the command line with
	ipsec auto -add connection_name
	ipsec auto -start connection_name
	  See man ipsec_auto for more command line options.

Table 9-2

The use of certificates keeps you from having to add the public keys of the involved computers to the connection specifications. The exchange of certificates is done as part of the key exchange to establish a security association. To verify the certificates, openswan needs the root CA certificate and the certificates of any subCA. openswan expects them in /etc/ipsec.d/cacerts.

Copy Certificates and Private Keys   Certificates are used to authenticate the computers. Certificates contain information about the computer, such as its name, and the public key in a certain data structure, which is then signed by the CA.

Basically, the certificate certifies that information in the certificate belongs to the owner of the corresponding private key. Therefore, the respective computer needs to have access to the private key.

If the certificate was created with the YaST CA Management module and then exported, the certificate and the private key are in the same file. The following is an example:

```
-----BEGIN CERTIFICATE-----
MIIFezCCBGOgAwIBAgIBATANBgkqhkiG9w0BAQUFADCBoTELMAkGA1UEBhMCREUx
...
ODwHHeM24oatjco+dFhnRV0TsPDlbjKWSvPOOKqRIto7cQw2wpIK/ebZtOa8TTnr
S5BuwrmvWffnapT+rF2H
-----END CERTIFICATE-----
```
                                                              (Continued)

```
-----BEGIN RSA PRIVATE KEY-----
Proc-Type: 4,ENCRYPTED
DEK-Info: DES-EDE3-CBC,3DEAD229DBAF0516

fuNThtJ+7FmxW4uK5knnJcjOZYcNyxTPInlwKFuMt2Bma/15NJ1B/lfllLTl3CVk
...
z8v2NMpTJmfT3/MzbvS2BZ3zCysVqJcZ4JvLJ3Q5QA3RPktmbqYresr4qQSATudl
-----END RSA PRIVATE KEY-----
```

In this case, copy the private key section to a separate file in /etc/ipsec.d/private and the certificate section to a separate file in /etc/ipsec.d/certs. The file containing the private key should only be readable for the root user.

If you used openssl commands on the command line, the certificate and the private key are in separate files already. Just copy the files with the certificate and the private key to their respective directories.

Configure /etc/ipsec.secrets When no certificates are used, the file /etc/ipsec.secrets holds the private and public RSA keys. When certificates are used, the passphrase to unlock the private key is stored in this file:

```
# /etc/ipsec.secrets
: rsa /etc/ipsec.d/private/myPrivateKey.pem very_secret
```

This file may only be readable for the root user and no one else.

Only the traffic between the subnets behind the gateways is encrypted. Traffic from gateway to gateway is not!

Connect a Single Computer with a Site (End-to-Site)

This type of configuration is needed to allow users access to the corporate network when they are off site. In the openswan documentation, the single computer is usually referred to as a *road warrior*.

There are three aspects to the configuration:

- Configure /etc/ipsec.conf
- Copy Certificates and Private Keys
- Configure /etc/ipsec.secrets

Configure /etc/ipsec.conf The main difference in the configuration on the gateway side is that there is no known IP address for the road warrior. The user uses any available ISP and has its IP address dynamically assigned.

To make connections possible from behind NAT devices, you can activate the NAT traversal patch. Basically, NAT and IPSec just don't fit together: IPSec packets become invalid when the IP address in the packet is changed. However, that is exactly what NAT does—it changes the packet's IP address.

The solution is to encapsulate the IPSec packets in UDP packets and send those packets across the NAT device to the gateway on the other end of the tunnel, where they are decapsulated and handed to the ipsec stack. The port used for this purpose is usually 4500.

```
# /etc/ipsec.conf on the gateway
...
# basic configuration
config setup
      ...
      # Switch on NAT-Traversal (if patch is installed)
      nat_traversal=yes
```

When there are many road warriors, it is useful to maintain a PKI and to use certificates because it greatly simplifies /etc/ipsec.conf. Without certificates, you need a separate connection specification for each notebook.

With certificates, the entry rightrsasigkey=%cert takes care of all of them, providing they have a valid certificate. No access is granted for notebooks without certificates or with expired or revoked certificates.

Because the IP address is not known, right gets assigned the value %any:

```
# Connection gateway road warrior on the gateway
conn da10-roadwarrior
    # Left security gateway, subnet behind it, next hop toward right.
    leftsubnet=172.16.0.0/24
    left=10.0.0.10
    leftid="C=DE, ST=Bavaria, L=Munich, O=Digitalairlines,
OU=Training, CN=da10.digitalairlines.com/emailAddress=root@da10.
digitalairlines.com"
    leftcert=/etc/ipsec.d/certs/da10_cert.pem
    #leftrsasigkey=%cert # already part of defaults
    # Right security gateway, subnet behind it,
    # next hop toward left.
    # Right security gateway, subnet behind it,
    # next hop toward left.
    right=%any
    #rightrsasigkey=%cert # already part of defaults
    rightsubnet=
    # To authorize this connection, but not actually start it,
    # at startup, uncomment this.
    auto=add
```

Because the gateway just waits for connections, auto is set to add.

The road warrior mainly needs information on his gateway. The NAT traversal patch needs to be activated as needed:

```
# /etc/ipsec.conf on the gateway
...
# basic configuration
config setup
      ...
      # Switch on NAT-Traversal (if patch is installed)
      nat_traversal=yes

...

# Connection gateway road warrior on the road warrior
conn roadwarrior-da10
      # Left security gateway, subnet behind it, next hop toward right.
      leftsubnet=172.16.0.0/24
      left=10.0.0.10
      leftid="C=DE, ST=Bavaria, L=Munich, O=Digitalairlines,
OU=Training, CN=da10.digitalairlines.com/emailAddress=root@da10.
digitalairlines.com"
      #leftrsasigkey=%cert # already part of defaults
      # Right security gateway, subnet behind it,
      # next hop toward left.
      right=%defaultroute
      rightcert=/etc/ipsec.d/certs/myCert.pem
      #rightrsasigkey=%cert # already part of defaults
      rightsubnet=
      # To authorize this connection, but not actually start it,
      # at startup, uncomment this.
      auto=start
```

Since the road warrior is supposed to connect to the gateway when ipsec starts, auto is set to start.

Copy Certificates and Private Keys Each notebook needs its own certificate and corresponding private key to authenticate at the gateway.

What was said in Copy Certificates and Private Keys for site-to-site connections holds true for road warrior connections as well.

Configure /etc/ipsec.secrets This file holds the passphrase to unlock the private key and has the same syntax as described in Configure / for the site-to-site configuration.

Connect Two Single Computers (End-to-End)

Connecting two single computers with no subnet behind them is basically the same as establishing a site-to-site connection. The only difference is that in this case the parameters leftsubnet and rightsubnet remain empty.

Unlike site-to-site connections, the traffic between the two computers is now encrypted. In site-to-site connections, this traffic is cleartext; only the traffic between the subnets is encrypted in the tunnel.

Establish the Connection

To establish the connection, IPSec has to be started on both gateways.

The parameter `auto=add` in `/etc/ipsec.conf` means that the connection description is loaded, but no attempt is being made to actually establish the connection.

`auto=start` causes the connection to be established as soon as IPSec starts.

When two LANs are connected via IPSec, both sides should use auto=start to make sure that after a reboot of the computer or a restart of IPSec on either side, a connection is renegotiated immediately.

The log file /var/log/messages provides valuable information on the establishment of the connection. If the connection is established successfully, the messages will look similar to the following excerpt from /var/log/messages (time stamps have been deleted from this listing):

```
kernel: NET: Registered protocol family 15
kernel: Initializing IPsec netlink socket
ipsec_setup: KLIPS ipsec0 on eth0 10.0.0.10/255.255.255.0 broadcast
10.0.0.255
ipsec__plutorun: Starting Pluto subsystem...
ipsec_setup: ...Openswan IPsec started
ipsec_setup: Starting Openswan IPsec 2.4.4...
ipsec_setup: insmod /lib/modules/2.6.16.11-7-
default/kernel/net/key/af_key.ko
ipsec_setup: insmod /lib/modules/2.6.16.11-7-
default/kernel/net/ipv4/xfrm4_tunnel.ko
ipsec_setup: insmod /lib/modules/2.6.16.11-7-
default/kernel/net/xfrm/xfrm_user.ko
pluto[4044]: Starting Pluto (Openswan Version 2.4.4 X.509-1.5.4
PLUTO_SENDS_VENDORID PLUTO_USES_KEYRR; Vendor ID OEz}FFFfgr_e)
pluto[4044]: Setting NAT-Traversal port-4500 floating to off
pluto[4044]:     port floating activation criteria nat_t=0/port_fload=1
pluto[4044]:     including NAT-Traversal patch (Version 0.6c) [disabled]
pluto[4044]: ike_alg_register_enc(): Activating OAKLEY_AES_CBC: Ok
(ret=0)
pluto[4044]: starting up 1 cryptographic helpers
pluto[4044]: started helper pid=4054 (fd:6)
pluto[4044]: Using Linux 2.6 IPsec interface code on 2.6.16.11-7-
default
pluto[4044]: Changing to directory '/etc/ipsec.d/cacerts'
pluto[4044]:     loaded CA cert file 'da10-rootCA.pem' (1956 bytes)
pluto[4044]: Could not change to directory '/etc/ipsec.d/aacerts'
pluto[4044]: Could not change to directory '/etc/ipsec.d/ocspcerts'
pluto[4044]: Changing to directory '/etc/ipsec.d/crls'
pluto[4044]:     Warning: empty directory
pluto[4044]:     loaded host cert file '/etc/ipsec.d/certs/
da10_cert.pem'
(1960 bytes)
pluto[4044]: added connection description "da10-da20"
pluto[4044]: listening for IKE messages
pluto[4044]: adding interface eth0/eth0 10.0.0.10:500
pluto[4044]: adding interface lo/lo 127.0.0.1:500
pluto[4044]: adding interface lo/lo ::1:500
pluto[4044]: loading secrets from "/etc/ipsec.secrets"
pluto[4044]:     loaded private key file
'/etc/ipsec.d/private/da10_key.pem' (1751 bytes)
```

```
pluto[4044]: "da10-da20" #1: initiating Main Mode
pluto[4044]: "da10-da20" #1: received Vendor ID payload [Openswan
(this version) 2.4.4  X.509-1.5.4 PLUTO_SENDS_VENDORID PLUTO_
USES_KEYRR]
pluto[4044]: "da10-da20" #1: received Vendor ID payload [Dead Peer
Detection]
pluto[4044]: "da10-da20" #1: transition from state STATE_MAIN_I1
to state STATE_MAIN_I2
pluto[4044]: "da10-da20" #1: STATE_MAIN_I2: sent MI2, expecting MR2
pluto[4044]: "da10-da20" #1: I am sending my cert
pluto[4044]: "da10-da20" #1: I am sending a certificate request
pluto[4044]: "da10-da20" #1: transition from state STATE_MAIN_I2
to state STATE_MAIN_I3
pluto[4044]: "da10-da20" #1: STATE_MAIN_I3: sent MI3, expecting MR3
pluto[4044]: "da10-da20" #1: Main mode peer ID is ID_DER_ASN1_DN:
'C=DE, ST=Bavaria, L=Munich, O=Digitalairlines, OU=Training,
CN=da20.digitalairline
s.com, E=root@da20.digitalairlines.com'
pluto[4044]: "da10-da20" #1: no crl from issuer "C=DE, ST=Bavaria,
L=Munich, O=Digitalairlines, OU=Training, CN=da10 RootCA,
E=root@ da10.digitalairli
nes.com" found (strict=no)
pluto[4044]: "da10-da20" #1: transition from state STATE_MAIN_I3
to state STATE_MAIN_I4
pluto[4044]: "da10-da20" #1: STATE_MAIN_I4: ISAKMP SA established
{auth=OAKLEY_RSA_SIG cipher=oakley_3des_cbc_192 prf=oakley_md5
group=modp1536}
pluto[4044]: "da10-da20" #2: initiating Quick Mode
RSASIG+ENCRYPT+TUNNEL+PFS+UP {using isakmp#1}
pluto[4044]: "da10-da20" #2: transition from state STATE_QUICK_I1
to state STATE_QUICK_I2
pluto[4044]: "da10-da20" #2: STATE_QUICK_I2: sent QI2, IPsec SA
established {ESP=>0x780189f8 <0x8576c4ed xfrm=AES_0-HMAC_SHA1
NATD=none DPD=none}
```

9

The message IPsec SA established {{ESP=>0x780189f8 <0x8576c4ed xfrm=AES_0-HMAC_SHA1 NATD=none DPD=none} in the last line indicates that the tunnel has been successfully set up.

Test the Connection

When connecting two sites, only the connections to and from hosts in the networks behind the gateways are encrypted between the gateways.

It is possible to connect from one gateway to the other (for instance with ping), but this connection does not go through the tunnel.

Connections from one gateway to hosts behind the other gateway are not possible either. If the packet can be routed at all across the Internet, which is not the case if private address ranges are used in the local networks, the packet to the network on the other side does not go through the tunnel, while the packet back does. However, the packet in the tunnel is discarded by the IPSec stack because it doesn't belong to any IPSec connection.

To test the connection, you need to establish connections from a host behind the gateway to a host behind the other gateway. If this works, the next step is to make sure the packets between the gateways are actually encrypted.

With a 2.4.*x* kernel this is rather easy because there is an ipsec0 interface when ipsec is started. tcpdump on ipsec0 shows cleartext packets, whereas tcpdump on the network interface (eth0, eth1, etc.) shows encrypted (ESP) packets.

A 2.6.*x* kernel does not create an ipsec0 interface. tcpdump on the network interface shows encrypted as well as unencrypted packets.

To be absolutely sure that there are no unwanted cleartext packets on the wire, you have no choice but to connect another computer with a hub to that interface and run a tcpdump on that computer to see what kind of packets actually leave the network card.

Exercise 9-1: Establish a VPN Connection

Time Required: 90 Minutes

Objective: The purpose of this exercise is to familiarize you with the steps necessary to set up a VPN connection.

Description: Because the classroom computers might have only one NIC and therefore no network behind the gateway, you will set up an end-to-end connection with another student.

Decide who of you will create the needed certificates. Create a root CA and certificates as described in Exercise 4-1, "Create a Root CA and Certificates on the Command Line," or Exercise 4-2, "(Optional) Create a Root CA and Certificates with YaST". You can reuse the Root CA and certificates created earlier in this course when doing that exercise. You need a certificate for your own computer and one for the computer of the student you work with.

If you use your Root CAT, transfer the Certificate of the root CA and the certificate plus private key for your partner's machine to his machine, using ssh.

Copy the files to their proper place in the file system and have your fellow student do the same with the files you transferred to him.

Modify /etc/ipsec.conf to match your IP addresses and network setup. Add the password for the private key to /etc/ipsec.secrets.

Open another terminal window and, as root, watch /var/log/messages using tail -f.

Start ipsec with rcipsec start.

Correct any errors until you are able to establish an encrypted connection between your two computers.

Detailed Steps to Complete this Exercise

1. Open a terminal window and `su -` to root (password `novell`).

2. Install the openswan packages by entering:

   `yast -i openswan`.

3. Create two certificates with corresponding private keys, one for your own and one for your partner's computer, as described in the exercises referenced on the previous page.

   You can use any certificates you created in that exercise, providing they fit the host names of the computers you will use in this exercise.

   Discuss with your partner whose CA and certificates will be used.

4. Only for the student who created the certificates:

   Using scp, copy the certificate for your partner's computer, the corresponding private key, and the root CA certificate to your partner's computer.

   He or she will have to copy them to their correct place as described in Step 5.

5. Copy the certificate of your computer to `/etc/ipsec.d/certs/` and the corresponding private key to `/etc/ipsec.d/private/`.

   If the public and private keys are in one file, copy the private key section to a separate file in /etc/ipsec.d/private/. Copy the certificate section to a separate file in /etc/ipsec.d/certs/.

   Copy the RootCA certificate to `/etc/ipsec.d/cacerts/`.

6. Edit /etc/ipsec.secrets to include a line with the passphrase for your private key:

   ` : rsa /etc/ipsec.d/private/`***myPrivateKey***`.pem `***passphrase***

   Replace ***myPrivateKey*** and ***passphrase*** with the applicable values. You can simply add this in a new line at the end of the file. The existing content of the file can remain as it is.

7. Edit /etc/ipsec.conf to fit your and your partner's computers.

   Use section "Configure /etc/ipsec.conf" in the manual as a guideline.

   The parameters `leftsubnet` and `rightsubnet` remain empty.

   Your IP address as well as your partner's are added to `left` and `right`. Because you are in the same network as your partner, you can add `leftnexthop=%direct` and `rightnexthop=%direct`.

   `leftid`/`rightid` are taken from the respective certificates.

   The command to display the certificate in human readable form is `openssl x509 - in /path/certfile.pem -text` and the information is listed as `subject:....` Use `auto=start` within the connection specification.

9

Your connection specification should look similar to the following (areas you need to change to fit your setup are shown in italics; no changes are needed in the other sections of /etc/ipsec.conf):

```
# Connection between two computers
conn da10-da20
    # Left security gateway, subnet behind it, next hop toward right.
    leftsubnet=
    left=10.0.0.10
    leftnexthop=%direct
    # ID is the DN from the certificate, in one line
    leftid="C=DE, ST=Bavaria, L=Munich, O=Digitalairlines, OU=Training,
CN=da10.digitalairlines.com/emailAddress=root@da10.digitalairlines.
com"
    # Only on the computer 10.0.0.10
    leftcert=/etc/ipsec.d/certs/da10_cert.pem
    #leftrsasigkey=%cert # already part of defaults
    # Right security gateway, subnet behind it, next hop toward left.
    rightnexthop=%direct
    right=10.0.0.20
    # ID is the DN from the certificate, in one line
    rightid="C=DE, ST=Bavaria, L=Munich, O=Digitalairlines, OU=Training,
CN=da20.digitalairlines.com/emailAddress=root@da20.digitalairlines.
com"
    # We have leftcert; this is needed on the other side:
    # rightcert=/etc/ipsec.d/certs/da20_cert.pem
    #rightrsasigkey=%cert # already part of defaults
    rightsubnet=
    # To authorize this connection, but not actually start it,
    # at startup, uncomment this.
    auto=start
```

Save the file.

8. Open another terminal window and su – to root with a password of `novell`.

9. View the log file by entering `tail -f /var/log/messages`.

10. Back in the first terminal window, start ipsec by entering `rcipsec start`.

11. View the log entries in the other terminal window.

    If there are any error messages, stop IPSec by entering:

    `rcipsec stop`

    Correct your configuration and try again.

    Note: The computer that starts IPSec first will show error messages about a refused connection in /var/log/messages. This does not indicate an error in the configuration.

12. Once IPSec starts correctly, you will see an entry in /var/log/messages that the security association has been successfully established (IPsec SA established {ESP=>0x...).

13. Open yet another terminal window and su – to root with a password of `novell`.

14. Start `tcpdump -i eth`x `-n` (or use `ethereal`) to see the packets hitting your interface.

15. Ping your partner's computer from the first terminal window.

 You should see ICMP and ESP packets in the output of tcpdump. (tcpdump will not show all ICMP packets, despite the fact that echo requests and echo replies are being sent.)

16. (*Optional*) Modify your configuration so that one of your computers acts as a road warrior and the other as a gateway accepting connections from road warriors.

 This is done by replacing `right=`*ipaddress* by `right=%any` and deleting the line with rightid on the computer that acts as the gateway (=left).

 No changes are needed on the road warrior side.

Objective 3—Understand Packet Filtering of VPN Traffic

Kernel 2.4.*x* creates an additional interface (ipsec0, ipsec1, etc.) when IPSec is started. All traffic to and from the tunnel is going through that interface. It can be addressed within iptables commands with the options -o and -i, just as any other interface.

The interface eth0 (eth1, etc.) is used in iptables commands to control the traffic on the physical interface. To control the traffic within the tunnel, you use the interface ipsec0 (ipsec1, etc.).

Kernel 2.6.*x* does not create an interface ipsec0. This means that it is not possible to distinguish traffic to and from the tunnel simply based on the interface it is coming from or destined to. A different approach is needed to specifically address the traffic within the tunnel with iptables commands.

To filter traffic within the IPSec tunnel, you have to consider the following:

- Filter the IPSec Packets
- Connections Initiated from Road Warriors to Hosts Behind the Gateway
- Connections Initiated from Hosts Behind the Gateway to Road Warriors

Filter the IPSec Packets

An IPSec connection consists of the following types of packets:

- UDP port 500 for key management
- Protocol 50 (ESP) for encryption
- UDP port 4500 if NAT traversal is used

The packet filter has to allow these packets; otherwise, no IPSec connection can be established.

```
# Protocol 50, ESP
iptables -A INPUT  -i $EXT_IF -p 50 -m state --state NEW -j ACCEPT
# Key management, UDP port 500
iptables -A INPUT  -i $EXT_IF -p UDP -m state --state NEW \
                   --dport 500 --sport 500 -j ACCEPT
# plus in case of NAT-Traversal:
iptables -A INPUT  -i $EXT_IF -p UDP -m state --state NEW
                   --dport 4500 --sport 4500 -j ACCEPT
```

The above rules allow new incoming connections.

If the computer initiates IPSec connections to other computers, as in the case of a road warrior, these rules need to appear in the OUTPUT chain:

```
# Protocol 50, ESP
iptables -A OUTPUT  -o $EXT_IF -p 50 -m state --state NEW -j ACCEPT
# Key management, UDP port 500
iptables -A OUTPUT  -o $EXT_IF -p UDP -m state --state NEW \
--dport 500 --sport 500 -j ACCEPT
# plus in case of NAT-Traversal:
iptables -A OUTPUT  -o $EXT_IF -p UDP -m state --state NEW
--dport 4500 --sport 4500 -j ACCEPT
```

If the computer initiates, as well as receives new connections, you need rules for both the INPUT and for the OUTPUT chain.

Subsequent packets and answer packets have to be allowed, too:

```
iptables -A OUTPUT -m state --state ESTABLISHED,RELATED -j ACCEPT
iptables -A INPUT  -m state --state ESTABLISHED,RELATED -j ACCEPT
```

Because these packets are destined for the computer itself, these rules are defined in the INPUT and OUTPUT chains, not in the FORWARD chain.

Connections Initiated from Road Warriors to Hosts Behind the Gateway

It is simple to control this kind of traffic on the gateway using the connection-tracking capabilities of the netfilter framework and the mangle table.

ESP packets arriving at the gateway are part of the traffic from road warriors. Traffic control within the tunnel can be achieved as follows:

1. ESP packets from the outside are marked with an arbitrary number using the mangle table. This number does not change the packet; it exists only within the kernel space.

2. When the ESP packet is decrypted and the original packet restored, it inherits the mark that was put on the ESP packet.

3. Using this mark, cleartext packets from within the tunnel can be distinguished from other cleartext packets that came in from other computers outside the tunnel.

4. Rules can be set up for the marked packets independently from rules for packets without this mark.

5. Packets coming from the other direction that are part of connections from road warriors through the tunnel are handled by the connection-tracking module.

The iptables rules that achieve these goals could look like the following:

```
# Mark ESP packets
iptables -t mangle -A PREROUTING -p 50 -j MARK --set-mark 10
# Accept ESP packets
iptables -A INPUT -p 50 -j ACCEPT
# Define rule based on the mark
iptables -A FORWARD -o $INT_IF -p TCP --dport 80 -m mark --mark 10 \
-j ACCEPT
# Take care of the traffic in the other direction
iptables -A FORWARD -i $INT_IF -m state --state ESTABLISHED,RELATED \
-j ACCEPT
```

The rules for the traffic within the tunnel will usually be specified in the FORWARD chain.

An exception is packets that are destined to the gateway itself—for instance, when two computers are connected without a network behind them on either side.

Connections Initiated from Hosts Behind the Gateway to Road Warriors

If the road warrior had a static IP address, connections would not pose any problem. Rules could be defined based on the IP address of the road warrior.

Road warriors, like any host in the Internet, however, can have any IP address.

It is therefore not possible to implement rules on the gateway that refer to traffic destined for the tunnel based on the destination IP address of the packet.

The output interface is not suitable as distinguishing criterion either, because encrypted as well as unencrypted packets leave the computer via eth0 (or eth1, etc.).

The policy match allows you to filter traffic according to certain markers set by the ipsec stack of the kernel. This works as well for connections started by the road warrior as for connections addressed to the road warrior.

The following rules achieve the same as the rules above using a mark: The road warrior is allowed to connect to Web servers within the network behind the gateway.

```
# Accept ESP packets
iptables -A INPUT -p 50 -j ACCEPT
# Define a rule using the policy match
iptables -A FORWARD -i $EXT_IF -m policy --dir in --pol ipsec \
--mode tunnel --proto esp -p tcp --dport 80 -j ACCEPT
```

The advantage of the approach using the policy match becomes apparent when you want to regulate traffic from the internal network or the gateway to the road warriors.

The following rule allows you to use ssh from the network behind the gateway to the road warriors. This rule does not affect the traffic from the network behind the gateway to hosts that are not part of the VPN.

9

```
# Accept ESP packets
iptables -A OUTPUT -p 50 -j ACCEPT
Define a rule using the policy match
iptables -A FORWARD -o $EXT_IF -m policy --dir out --pol ipsec \
--mode tunnel --proto esp -p tcp --dport 22 -j ACCEPT
```

Documentation on the policy match is rather scarce. You can get a few hints by entering:

```
iptables -m policy -h
```

```
da10:~ # iptables -m policy --help
...
policy v1.3.5 options:
  --dir in|out                 match policy applied during
decapsulation/
                               policy to be applied during encapsulation
  --pol none|ipsec             match policy
  --strict                     match entire policy instead of single
element
                               at any position
[!] --reqid reqid              match reqid
[!] --spi spi                  match SPI
[!] --proto proto              match protocol (ah/esp/ipcomp)
[!] --mode mode                match mode (transport/tunnel)
[!] --tunnel-src addr/mask     match tunnel source
[!] --tunnel-dst addr/mask     match tunnel destination
  --next                       begin next element in policy
```

Exercise 9-2: (Optional) Filter IPSec Traffic

Time Required: 30 Minutes

Objective: Modify the script /etc/init.d/fw-script from Exercise 7-2, "Modify the Script to Set and Delete iptables Rules," to allow ssh connections only if they run through the IPSec tunnel.

Description: You will have to allow protocol 50, UPD port 500, and ssh. To distinguish packets from inside and outside the tunnel, you can mark packets or use the policy match.

Detailed Steps to Complete this Exercise

1. Open a terminal window and su – to root (password `novell`)
2. Make a copy of the script you created as part of Exercise 7-2, "Modify the Script to Set and Delete iptables Rules" on page 186.

3. Modify this script to:

- Mark incoming ESP packets
- Accept incoming and outgoing ESP packets
- Accept incoming and outgoing UDP packets to and from port 500
- Accept incoming SSH packets only from within the tunnel
- Accept packets that belong to established connections
- Flush the mangle table before setting the rules (start section) and when deleting all rules (stop section)
- Show the rules in the mangle table (status section)

Details on how this can be done are part of Exercise 7-2.

4. Start the script and correct any errors.

5. Start the IPSec connection to your partner.
Have him or her connect to your computer using SSH.
Ask another student to connect to your computer using SSH as well. (Only your partner should succeed.)

6. Modify your rules, this time using the policy match to achieve the same result.

7. Start and test the script again by repeating Steps 4 and 5.

(A sample solution can be found on the Student DVD.)

9

Summary

- VPNs are logical network connections that tunnel traffic between hosts on a network. They are typically used to provide encryption between two hosts on a network, between a host and a target network or between two networks.

- Several VPN technologies are available today including OpenVPN, L2TP, HTTPS, SSH and IPSec.

- Each VPN technology may be used in one of two modes: AH mode or ESP mode. AH mode provides authentication between hosts, whereas ESP mode provides authentication and encryption between hosts.

- To create a VPN connection, each host must first authenticate to the other host using a secure ISAKMP channel. Preshared keys, RSA keys and certificates may be used for host authentication. Following this, an AH or ESP security association is created to allow the tunneling of traffic.

- The OpenSWAN and ipsec-tools packages may be used to create and manage IPSec connections in SUSE Linux.

- To configure an IPSec VPN, you must identify both networks in the **/etc/ipsec.conf** file and configure authentication parameters in the **/etc/ipsec.secrets** file. If certificates are used for IPSec authentication, they must be copied to the appropriate subdirectory of **/etc/ipsec.d**.

- IPSec VPN connections may be tested by connecting to remote VPN resources from a host or by monitoring network traffic from another computer on the network.
- Firewalls may be used to filter IPSec traffic by marking the traffic for later identification using the netfilter mangle table. To allow VPN traffic across a firewall, you need to permit UDP port 500 and 4500 as well as protocol 50 and 51.

Key Terms

/etc/ipsec.conf   The IPSec configuration file in SUSE Linux.

/etc/ipsec.d/cacerts   The directory that stores public key certificates from trusted certification authorities for use with IPSec authentication.

/etc/ipsec.d/certs/   The directory that stores the public key used by IPSec authentication.

/etc/ipsec.d/private/   The directory that stores the private key used by IPSec authentication.

/etc/ipsec.secrets   The file that stores RSA keys and certificate passphrases for use with IPSec authentication.

/var/log/messages   The Linux system information log file. It contains information regarding the creation of IPSec security associations.

Authentication Header (AH)   A VPN security protocol that provides authentication between hosts. AH uses protocol number 51.

Encapsulating Security Payload (ESP)   A VPN security protocol that provides authentication and encryption between hosts. ESP uses protocol number 50.

FreeSWAN   A set of tools and modules that provides IPSec VPN support for Linux 2.4 kernels.

Internet Key Exchange (IKE)   The process of exchanging public keys across public networks such as the Internet.

Internet Security Association and Key Management Protocol (ISAKMP)   The component of IPSec that is responsible for exchanging asymmetric encryption keys at the onset of an IPSec negotiation. ISAKMP uses UDP port 500 for key management and UDP port 4500 for NAT transversal.

IP Security (IPSec)   A common VPN standard that uses DES or 3DES encryption to secure traffic.

ipsec0   The first virtual IPSec VPN interface used by the Linux 2.4 kernel.

ipsec-tools   A package that contains IPSec VPN tools for use in SUSE Linux.

Layer 2 Tunneling Protocol (L2TP)   A common VPN standard that uses IPSec encryption to secure traffic.

NAT traversal   A feature of IPSec VPNs that allows tunneled traffic to pass through NAT routers.

OpenSWAN   A set of tools that configures IPSec VPN support for Linux 2.6 kernels.

racoon command   Used to create and manage IPSec security associations.

road warrior   A host that connects to remote networks using a VPN.

security association   An authenticated communications channel between two VPN hosts.

security protocol   A protocol that defines the features of a VPN connection. ESP and AH are common VPN security protocols.

setkey command   Creates key combinations for use with Linux commands. It is often used to create shortcuts for IPSec VPN commands.

tcpdump command   A common packet sniffing utility on most Linux systems.

Virtual Private Network (VPN)   A virtual connection between two or more hosts on a public network used to tunnel traffic. VPNs provide authentication and encryption for tunneled traffic between the hosts to provide data security.

Review Questions

1. You plan on using IPSec to provide security for communication within your LANs. However, you need to ensure that the application layer gateways used in your organization can view the data within the IPSec packets. What should you configure?

   a. AH mode

   b. ESP mode

   c. NAT Transversal

   d. Internet Key Exchange

2. You plan on using IPSec VPN connections between your LAN and a remote host using ESP mode. What ports and protocols should you open on your NAT firewall? (Choose all that apply.)

   a. Protocol 50

   b. Protocol 51

   c. UDP port 500

   d. UDP port 4500

3. Which of the following are valid authentication methods for use with IPSec VPNs? (Choose all that apply.)

   a. Certificates

   b. Kerberos user accounts

   c. RSA keys

   d. System user accounts

4. Which authentication method in Question 3 is generally recommended for use with IPSec VPNs and why? _____

5. What line must you configure in /etc/ipsec.conf in order to tunnel IPSec VPN connections through a NAT router? _____

6. Which of the following parameters in the /etc/ipsec.conf file must be configured in order to allow two hosts to tunnel traffic using an IPSec VPN? (Choose all that apply.)

   a. leftsubnet

   b. left

   c. rightsubnet

   d. right

7. Which of the following parameters in the /etc/ipsec.conf file must be configured in order to allow two networks to tunnel traffic using an IPSec VPN? (Choose all that apply.)

   a. leftsubnet

   b. left

   c. rightsubnet

   d. right

8. What does the line **auto=start** do in /etc/ipsec.conf? _____

9. You have configured an IPSec VPN that uses certificates for authentication. Although you have placed the public and private keys in the appropriate directory, VPN connections fail and /var/log/messages indicates that the certificate authenticity could not be verified. What must you do to fix the problem? _____

10. How can ESP session traffic be separated from regular traffic by netfilter? _____

Discovery Exercises

DISCOVERY EXERCISES

Configuring a Road Warrior using IPSec

In the first section exercise, you configured an IPSec VPN between two hosts on the local network. Assuming that your computer has two network interfaces, configure your computer as a network router and create an IPSec between the external interface of your router and another host on your network (road warrior).

Communicate from the road warrior to another computer connected to the internal network interface of your router. Use a packet sniffer utility to verify that traffic sent between the road warrior and the external router interface is encrypted. Next, use the same packet sniffer utility to verify that traffic sent between the internal router interface and the internal host is unencrypted.

Configuring IPSec Tunneling between Networks

In the previous Discovery Exercise, you configured a road warrior to tunnel traffic to an internal network. Assuming that your computer and your partner's computer each have two network interfaces, connect the external interface of each computer together with a crossover cable or network switch and configure them as network routers. Next, configure each computer to tunnel traffic from the internal network interface of the first router to the internal network interface of the second router using an IPSec VPN.

Communicate from a host on the first internal network to a host on the second internal network. Use a packet sniffer utility to verify that traffic sent between the routers is encrypted and that traffic sent between the internal hosts and their gateways is unencrypted.

Using Public VPNs

Using VPNs within your organization is often useful for traffic that passes across the Internet between company locations or between a road warrior and a corporate network. However, time must be spent setting up, maintaining and auditing these VPNs. There are several public VPN servers available on the Internet that can be used as an alternative to a corporate VPN when securing traffic between a road warrior and the internal corporate network.

These public VPN servers typically provide encryption only between a road warrior and the VPN server on the Internet. Although communication between the VPN server on the Internet and the corporate router will be unencrypted, it may be used to secure road warrior communication in public networks. For example, sales representatives often travel and may need to connect to the company network to upload information from a notebook computer across a wireless Internet connection within a hotel or Internet café. Unfortunately, public wireless networks often offer little or no security and this information could be obtained by anyone with a packet sniffer on the same wireless Internet connection.

By connecting to a free public VPN server on the Internet (i.e. *http://www.secureix.com*) from the notebook computer, the sales representative will be protecting the information sent to the corporate network while it is in transit across the public wireless network, which is where data theft is most likely to occur.

Use the Internet to research three different public VPN services. Summarize their advantages and disadvantages in a short memo.

9

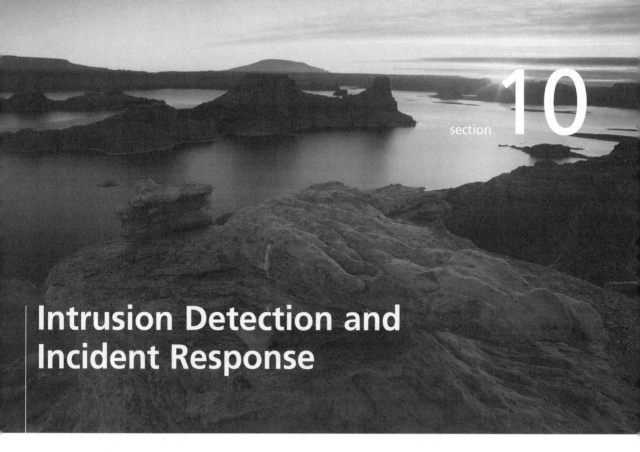

Intrusion Detection and Incident Response

There is something even worse than having your computer hacked and abused for some malicious purpose: Getting hacked and never finding out about it. There is no absolute protection against an illegal intrusion. Someone might figure out a new vulnerability and exploit it on your servers before it is publicly known that this vulnerability exists. This could happen even if you have applied all current security patches. If the vulnerability is not generally known, there is no patch to install against it. But in general, an intruder leaves some traces behind. Making it hard for the intruder to obscure his trail and interpreting any traces you find is what intrusion detection is about.

Objectives

- Log Files and Their Evaluation
- Host-Based Intrusion Detection
- Network-Based Intrusion Detection
- Incident Response

Objective 1—Log Files and Their Evaluation

Log files are a valuable tool for detecting intrusions. However, once someone has taken over a computer and become root, she can manipulate the log files to obscure any traces of her activity.

Manipulating log files can consist of deleting entries or trying to hide the relevant information by filling the log files with huge amounts of irrelevant entries.

One way to prevent the manipulation of log files by deletion of entries is to not only log on the host itself, but to send the log information across the network to another host.

The intruder could stop the sending of logging information to the log host, but the lack of entries would alert you, as would any suspicious ones.

Depending on the security needs, the log host can even write the logs onto a worm (write once, read many) medium, making it impossible to change them even if the log host is compromised.

Another approach is to have a log host without any network connection. Log messages in this case would be transferred using a serial connection. This setup would make it impossible for an intruder to access the log host via the network.

But even if the incident is logged, you still have to become aware of the relevant log entries. There are tools that help to filter relevant log entries and bring them to your attention.

This objective explains how to:

- Log to a Remote Host
- Evaluate Log Files and Run Checks

Log to a Remote Host

The syslog-ng used to log system messages on SUSE Linux Enterprise Server 10 can send messages to and receive messages from other computers. The receiving computer is sometimes referred to as loghost.

Configuration changes are necessary on both sides:

- Client Side Configuration of Syslog-ng
- Server Side Configuration of Syslog-ng

Client Side Configuration of Syslog-ng   Logging to other computers is configured in /etc/syslog-ng/syslog-ng.conf.in, as in the following example:

```
destination tologhost { udp(10.0.0.254 port(514)); };
log { source(src); destination(tologhost); };
```

The first line defines a destination *tologhost*, with protocol, IP address (you could also use the host name), and port. The second line configures logging to this destination. Because no filter is included, all messages from the source *src* get sent to the destination *tologhost*.

After editing the file /etc/syslog-ng/syslog-ng.conf.in, run SuSEconfig --module syslog-ng to transfer the changes to /etc/syslog-ng/syslog-ng.conf, which is the actual configuration file used by syslog-ng.

Server Side Configuration of Syslog-ng To receive messages, syslog-ng has to listen on a port, usually port 514. Unlike syslogd, which only supports UDP connections, syslog-ng also supports TCP.

To bind to a port, you have to add a line within a source section. You can either add it to the existing `source src` section, or create a new one, as in the following:

```
source network {
    udp(ip("10.0.0.254") port(514));
};
```

Using 0.0.0.0 as the IP address causes syslog-ng to bind to all available interfaces. Then a destination and a log entry are required:

```
destination digiair { file("/var/log/$HOST"); };
log { source(network); destination(digiair); };
```

The first line defines the destination digiair; each host's log entries get written to a file with the hostname as file name. The log entry directs messages from the source network to the destination digiair.

Exercise 10-1: Log to a Remote Host

Time Required: 10 Minutes

Objective: In this exercise you work with a partner. Decide who will send messages and who will receive them. (If both of you send and receive messages to each other, you might create an endless loop.)

Description: On the loghost configure syslog-ng to receive log messages from other hosts.

On the client configure syslog-ng to send log messages to the loghost.

Detailed Steps to Complete this Exercise

- Part I: On the Computer Receiving Messages
- Part II: On the Computer Sending Messages

Part I: On the Computer Receiving Messages

Do the following:

1. Open a terminal window and `su -` to root (password `novell`).

2. Open the file `/etc/syslog-ng/syslog-ng.conf.in` in vi.
   Add another source section after the source src section, as in the following:

```
source network {
      udp(ip("0.0.0.0") port(514));
};
```

3. At the end of the file, add a destination and a log entry to log messages that arrive via the network:

```
destination digiair { file("/var/log/$HOST"); };
log { source(network); destination(digiair); };
```

4. Save the file and quit vi.

5. Run SuSEconfig:

```
SuSEconfig --module syslog-ng
```

6. View /var/log/messages by entering:

```
tail -f /var/log/messages
```

You should see a message that syslog-ng initialized its new configuration.

7. Quit tail by pressing `ctrl+c`.

8. Once messages are sent from the client, syslog-ng will create a file `/var/log/`***daxx***, for instance, /var/log/da20. View this file by entering:

```
tail -F /var/log/daxx
```

(Replace ***daxx*** by the hostname of your neighbor's computer.)

Part II: On the Computer Sending Messages

Do the following:

1. Open a terminal window and `su -` to root (password `novell`).

2. Open the file `/etc/syslog-ng/syslog-ng.conf.in` in vi.
   At the end of the file, add a destination and a log entry to send messages to the loghost:

```
destination tologhost { udp("daxx" port(514)); };
log { source(src); destination(tologhost); };
```

Replace ***daxx*** in the above example with the host name of the loghost.

3. Save the file and quit vi.

4. Run SuSEconfig:

```
SuSEconfig --module syslog-ng
```

SuSEconfig causes syslog-ng to reread its configuration, so there is no need to do this in an extra step.

5. Create log entries by using `su -` in a terminal window or by using the program logger. The entries should appear on the loghost.

Evaluate Log Files and Run Checks

Depending on the activity on the computer, log files can grow by several MB each day. The problem you are faced with is how to find any suspicious entries within this huge amount of data.

Without specific tools, it becomes very difficult to find out about unusual activities or security violations.

There are several tools that help to extract relevant entries from log files and other sources. There are tools to:

- Extract Information from Log Files
- Run Security Checks

You can also write scripts of your own that alert you when certain entries appear in a log file.

Extract Information from Log Files

The following introduces two tools used to extract relevant information from log files:

- logcheck
- logsurfer

logcheck `logcheck` parses system logs and generates e-mail reports based on anomalies.

In the beginning, logcheck produces long reports. You have to modify the configuration of logcheck so that entries that are harmless do not turn up in the report anymore. After that initial phase, the reports mailed by logcheck should contain only relevant information on security violations and unusual activities.

logcheck should be called regularly via cron to parse log files. Because logcheck remembers the point up to which a log file was scanned previously, only the new section is scanned on the next call.

Logcheck is not included with SUSE Linux Enterprise Server 10. You can get it at *http://logcheck.org/*.

10

logsurfer The disadvantage of parsing log files line by line is that each line is independent of all other lines. However, you might want additional information when a certain entry is found in the log file.

`logsurfer` offers this functionality with contexts: Several lines matching a pattern can be stored in memory as a context. Depending on further patterns in the log file, such a context could be mailed to you for your inspection, or some other action, such as starting a program, could be triggered. The context could be deleted again if this pattern is not found within a certain time or number of lines. It is also possible to dynamically create or delete matching rules, depending on entries in the log file.

Because logsurfer can be configured in great detail, the configuration is not trivial. However, the advantage is that you can configure precisely what should happen under what circumstances.

Logsurfer is not included with SUSE Linux Enterprise Server 10. It can be found under *http://www.cert.dfn.de/eng/logsurf/*.

Run Security Checks   In addition to checking configuration files, you can run other checks to find out about system configurations that could constitute a security danger. Automated checks usually consist of scripts that are called in regular intervals and inform you, for instance, by e-mail, of what was found.

While such scripts can also detect a system compromise under certain circumstances, you should be aware that a successful intruder can modify such scripts to avoid detection.

The following are described:

- seccheck
- Custom Scripts
- Monitor Login Activity from the Command Line

seccheck   The package `seccheck` offers a series of scripts that check the computer regularly (daily, weekly, and monthly) and send reports to you. Items checked by the scripts are:

- Kernel modules loaded
- SUID files
- SGID files
- Bound sockets
- Users with accounts who never logged in
- Weak passwords

An e-mail is sent to root detailing what was found.

Custom Scripts   There is no limit to what you can check or have sent to you using shell or Perl scripts.

Some possibilities are:

- Output of last
- Output of df
- Output of netstat
- Output of ps
- /etc/passwd to check if an account other than root has UID 0

Monitor Login Activity from the Command Line   Monitoring tasks include evaluating login activity for signs of a security breach, such as multiple failed logins.

To monitor login activity, you can use the following commands:

- *who*—This command shows who is currently logged in to the system and information such as the time of the last login.

    You can use options such as -H (display column headings), -r (current runlevel), and -a (display information provided by most options).

For example, entering who -H returns information similar to the following:

```
da10: ~ # who -H
NAME       LINE       TIME             Command
root       0          Aug 23 05:41     (console)
geeko      pts/2      Aug 24 02:32     (10.0.0.50)
da10:~ #
```

- *w*—This command displays information about the users currently on the computer and the processes they are running.

  The first line includes information such as the current time, how long the system has been running, how many users are currently logged on, and the system load averages for the past 1, 5, and 15 minutes.

  Below the first line is an entry for each user that displays the login name, the tty name, the remote host, login time, idle time, JCPU, PCPU, and the command line of the user's current process.

  The JCPU time is the time used by all processes attached to the tty. It does not include past background jobs but does include currently running background jobs.

  The PCPU time, specified in the What field, is the time used by the current process.

  You can use options such as –h (don't display the header), –s (don't display the login time, JCPU, and PCPU), and –V (display version information).

  For example, entering w returns information similar to the following:

```
da10: ~ # w
USER       TTY        LOGIN@       IDLE   JCPU   PCPU   WHAT
root       0          Mon05        ?xdm?  1:48   0.02s  -0
geeko      pts/2      02:32        0.00s  0.10s  0.02s  ssh: geeko [priv]
da10:~ #
```

You could also use w within scripts.

- *finger*—This command displays information about local and remote system users. By default, the following information is displayed about each user currently logged in to the local host:

  - Login name
  - User's full name
  - Associated terminal name
  - Idle time
  - Login time and location

  You can use options such as –l (long format) and –s (short format).

  For example, entering finger -s returns information similar to the following:

```
da10: ~ # finger -s
Login      Name                    Tty      Idle   Login Time  Where
geeko      The SUSE Chameleon      pts/2    -      Tue 02:32   10.0.0.50
root       root                    0        54d    Mon 05:41   console
da10:~ #
```

- *last*—This command displays a list of the last logged-in users.

  Last searches back through the file /var/log/wtmp (or the file designated by the option -f) and displays a list of all users logged in (and out) since the file was created.

  You can specify names of users and tty's to only show information for those entries.

  You can use options such as *-num* (where *num* is the number of lines to display), -a (display the hostname in the last column), and -x (display system shutdown entries and runlevel changes).

  For example, entering last -ax returns information similar to the following:

```
da10: ~ # last -ax
root      pts/0        Thu May  4 12:00    still logged in
da10.digitalairlines.com
runlevel (to lvl 5)   Thu May  4 11:45 - 12:03  (00:17) 2.6.16.11-7-
smp
reboot    system boot  Thu May  4 11:45          (00:17) 2.6.16.11-7-
smp
shutdown system down  Thu May  4 10:26 - 12:03  (01:37) 2.6.16.11-7-
smp
runlevel (to lvl 0)   Thu May  4 10:26 - 10:26  (00:00) 2.6.16.11-7-
smp
...
wtmp begins Tue May 2 12:20:52 2006
da10:~ #
```

- *lastlog*—This command formats and prints the contents of the last login log file (/var/log/lastlog). The login name, port, and last login time are displayed.

  Entering the command without options displays the entries sorted by numerical ID.

  You can use options such as -u *login_name* (display information for designated user only) and -h (display a one-line help message).

  If a user has never logged in, the message **Never logged in** is displayed instead of the port and time.

  For example, entering lastlog returns information similar to the following:

```
da10:~ # lastlog
Username              Port     Latest
at                             **Never logged in**
bin                            **Never logged in**
...
ntp                            **Never logged in**
postfix                        **Never logged in**
root                  pts/0    Thu May  4 12:00:45 +0200 2006
sshd                           **Never logged in**
suse-ncc                       **Never logged in**
uucp                           **Never logged in**
wwwrun                         **Never logged in**
geeko                 :0       Wed May  3 09:14:55 +0200 2006
squid                          **Never logged in**
da10:~ #
```

- *faillog*—This command formats and displays the contents of the failure log (/var/log/faillog) and maintains failure counts and limits.

    You can use options such as –u *login_name* (display information for designated user only) and –p (display in UID order).

    The command faillog only lists users with no successful login since the last failure. To list a user who has had a successful login since his last failure, you must explicitly name the user with the -u option.

    Entering faillog returns information similar to the following:

```
da10:~ # faillog
Login       Failures Maximum Latest                On
geeko              1       3  03/03/06 13:33:25 +0100  /dev/tty2
da10:~ #
```

The faillog functionality has to be enabled by adding the module pam_tally.so to the respective file in /etc/pam.d/, for instance /etc/pam.d/login:

```
#%PAM-1.0
auth        required        pam_securetty.so
auth        required        pam_tally.so no_magic_root per_user
auth        include         common-auth
auth        required        pam_nologin.so
account     required        pam_tally.so    no_magic_root
...
```

The rest of the file does not need to be changed.

Reviewing files such as /var/log/messages also gives you information about login activity.

10

Objective 2—Host-Based Intrusion Detection

When someone gets access to a computer illegally, he will usually try to:

- Hide his intrusion.

- Install software to be able to come back to the computer even if the original vulnerability has been fixed.

Hiding his intrusion includes manipulating log files, but it also includes replacing system programs with modified versions. For example ps, top, and ls could be replaced by modified versions that don't show certain processes and files the intruder uses in the course of his attack.

Once the intruder manages to get root access, he can install any software he wants. This can be anything from compilers, a remote shell to allow the intruder access to the computer later, to root kits manipulating the kernel, or any other software.

After a computer has been compromised, the only reliable way to detect manipulated or added files is to boot the computer from a clean medium, such as a rescue system on CD.

Inspecting the computer while it is up and running after an attack has some value. But it does not allow you to know for sure whether files have been manipulated or not, as the tools, libraries, or the kernel involved in the check themselves might have been manipulated.

The following programs are designed to detect modified files:

- AIDE

- rpm

AIDE

AIDE (Advanced Intrusion Detection Environment) works in two stages:

- First, AIDE builds a database of checksums (MD5 and others) and other information on files in the file system.

- At a later date, the database is compared with the file system and any differences are noted.

Before building the database, you need to determine which files to monitor and you need to modify the configuration file /etc/aide.conf accordingly.

The configuration file lists which directories, files, and properties are to be monitored.

The upper part of the file defines some general variables:

```
# Configuration parameters
#
database=file:/var/lib/aide/aide.db
database_out=file:/var/lib/aide/aide.db.new
verbose=1
report_url=stdout
warn_dead_symlinks=yes
```

The custom rules define what properties are monitored.

The significances of the letters (such as p, i, and n) are explained in the man page for aide.conf.

After that, the files and directories to be monitored or to be excluded from monitoring are listed:

```
# Custom rules
#
Binlib          = p+i+n+u+g+s+b+m+c+md5+sha1
ConfFiles       = p+i+n+u+g+s+b+m+c+md5+sha1
Logs            = p+i+n+u+g+S
Devices         = p+i+n+u+g+s+b+c+md5+sha1
Databases       = p+n+u+g
StaticDir       = p+i+n+u+g
ManPages        = p+i+n+u+g+s+b+m+c+md5+sha1

                                                (Continued)
```

```
#
# Directories and files
#
# Kernel, system map, etc.
/boot                                   Binlib

# watch config files, but exclude, what changes at boot time, ...
!/etc/mtab
!/etc/lvm*
/etc                                    ConfFiles

# Binaries
/bin                                    Binlib
/sbin                                   Binlib

# Libraries
/lib                                    Binlib

# Complete /usr and /opt
/usr                                    Binlib
/opt                                    Binlib

# Log files
/var/log$                               StaticDir
#/var/log/aide/aide.log(.[0-9])?(.gz)?  Databases
#/var/log/aide/error.log(.[0-9])?(.gz)? Databases
#/var/log/setuid.changes(.[0-9])?(.gz)? Databases
/var/log                                Logs
...
```

After completing the final software installation and configuration, but before connecting to the outside network, you have the program build the initial database:

```
da10:~ # aide --init
```

To avoid manipulation of the database /var/lib/aide/aide.db.new by an intruder, you should store it elsewhere, not on the computer itself. You can burn it on a CD-ROM, together with the version of the AIDE binary from the installation media.

This database has to be updated after each software installation or software update to reflect the current state of the installation. If, at a later date, the files are checked, the program is run and the current files are compared with that database which is copied to `/var/lib/aide/aide.db`.

Any changes to programs and deleted or added files in the monitored directories are shown. The amount of information displayed depends on the value of `verbose` in the configuration file.

```
da10:~ # aide --check
AIDE found differences between database and filesystem!!
Summary:
Total number of files=161141,added files=1,removed files=0,changed
files=0
```

The previous code output shows the output with verbose=1. Increasing this value causes AIDE to give much more detailed information.

Another well known program for host-based intrusion detection is Tripwire. AIDE offers more or less the same functionality and the configuration is very similar to the Tripwire configuration.

rpm

Using rpm (RPM Package Manager), you can check the integrity of files installed from rpm packages.

Verifying the integrity is done by entering:

```
rpm -V
```

This check relies on the MD5 hash of the files, file size, permission, file type, owner, group, and modification time. These values are compared with the values in the rpm database.

RPM is no replacement for AIDE, as AIDE monitors more properties, uses several hash algorithms, and is not limited to files contained in rpm packages.

Objective 3—Network-Based Intrusion Detection

Even available patches are sometimes not applied—not necessarily due to neglect, but because of interoperability, support, or legal issues of other software.

That can put you in a tight spot: Not installing the patch might make your system vulnerable, but installing the patch might mean losing support.

One approach is to put such computers into separate subnets protected by firewalls. Another approach is to install an intrusion detection system (IDS) that ideally detects an attack and alerts you before it can cause actual harm.

Intrusion detection involves monitoring the network traffic in various ways. It ranges from detecting new network cards in the network to monitoring the traffic running across the wire.

Each method has its strengths and weaknesses and none can guarantee to detect every attack. The following topics are described:

- snort
- arpwatch
- Argus
- scanlogd
- Honeypots

snort

snort is an intrusion detection system (IDS) based on attack signatures. It is the most sophisticated open source IDS available. It scans the network traffic for any pattern of a known attack via the network.

You need to connect the computer running snort to the network in a way that it can "see" the network traffic, like to the monitor port of a switch. An advantage of snort is that you can monitor an entire network with one host.

Depending on where you place the computer (outside or inside the firewall), you will get more or fewer alerts.

Known attacks can be detected and the ability to detect unknown attacks is limited.

Similar to a virus scanner that needs up-to-date signatures, it is necessary to use up-to-date snort rule sets. Snort.org offers a paid subscription to obtain rules as soon as they are developed. Registered users can obtain these rules five days later for free.

Providing you have the necessary know-how, you can also write rules yourself.

Basic configuration is done in `/etc/sysconfig/snort` and `/etc/snort/snort.conf`. The rules are also kept in `/etc/snort/`.

Snort is started as a daemon with the start script in /etc/init.d/snort.

`snort -?` lists available options.

Depending on the configuration, snort writes to syslog, a separate log file, or sends winpopup messages to certain hosts.

For further information, visit the Snort Web site at *http://www.snort.org/*.

arpwatch

arpwatch monitors the ARP (Address Resolution Protocol) traffic and detects new MAC addresses in the network as well as IP address changes. These are reported by e-mail and in the syslog.

When started, arpwatch builds up a database of MAC addresses and the IP addresses associated with them. Later changes are detected using this database.

arpwatch is useful for detecting new hardware, such as a rogue notebook connected to the network in violation of the company's security policy.

However, if DHCP is used in the network, arpwatch produces a lot of alerts that probably have no significance.

Argus

Argus (Audit Record Generation and Utilization System) is designed to track and report on the status and performance of all network transactions seen in a data network traffic stream.

It does not monitor the content of connections, but it does monitor the connections that exist between various hosts.

While its purpose is comprehensive IP network traffic auditing in general, it can also be used to find out about connections that violate security policy.

To see all network traffic, the computer running argus has to be connected to the monitoring port of a switch or to a hub at a suitable place in the network.

Argus runs as a daemon and collects its information in a file that can become rather big, depending on the amount of network traffic. In extreme cases it could fill up the local hard disk if not rotated and copied to another location.

Therefore, we recommend that you have a dedicated host running Argus, to avoid any interference from other services running on the same computer.

Argus is started and stopped by `rcargus start` and `rcargus stop`, respectively.

The information collected by argus is written in a binary format. The tool ra is used to generate human-readable reports from this file.

```
da10:~ # ra -r /var/log/argus.log
Start_Time                      Duration Flgs Type  SrcAddr    Sport
   Dir     DstAddr     Dport  SrcPkt  Dstpkt  SrcBytes  DstBytes
State
06-04-20 16:40:42.460324         4.538683     tcp    10.0.0.10.56117
  ->        10.0.0.34.22   33     26    4200        3883          FIN
06-04-20 16:40:42.577498         0.000666     udp    10.0.0.34.32771
  <->       10.0.0.240.53   1      1      85         171
ACC
```

Filter expressions can be passed to ra, limiting the output to the connections of interest.

Let's assume your database server 10.0.0.100 is only supposed to be accessed by Web server 10.0.0.200. The following command would list all forbidden connections to and from 10.0.0.100 from other hosts:

```
da10:~ # ra -r /var/log/argus.log - -nn host 10.0.0.100 \
and not host 10.0.0.200
```

For more information on Argus, visit *http://www.qosient.com/argus/*.

scanlogd

Port scans are quite common and are basically harmless. However, they can also be the first step in an attack.

If multiple packets to different ports originating from a single source are detected within a certain time (7 privileged or 21 unprivileged ports within 3 seconds), an entry is made by scanlogd to /var/log/messages via syslog.

No other action is taken.

```
Apr 21 10:16:06 da10 scanlogd: 149.44.87.33 to 149.44.87.34 ports 80,
554, 1723, 113, 3389, 25, 443, 636, ..., fSrpauxy, TOS 00, TTL 64
@10:16:06
```

To alert you to a scan, you need to use other tools, like logsurfer, that watch the log file.

scanlogd is started and stopped by rcscanlogd start and rcscanlogd stop, respectively.

The use of scanlogd is limited, because a real attacker will avoid creating such a lot of "noise." He will stretch his port scan over several days, if not weeks, to gain the information he wants, without alerting anyone.

Honeypots

The idea of a honeypot is somewhat opposed to what has been discussed in this course so far. Instead of locking up a computer to prevent hackers from compromising it, you use a dedicated computer to detect an effort to compromise the system, to observe the hackers while they try and succeed, and to learn how they operate.

A honeypot is a computer or virtual machine whose value lies in being probed, attacked, and compromised. By analyzing what happens on such a computer, you can get an insight into the motives and tactics of actual attackers without putting your production environment at risk.

Ways to realize such a honeypot are:

- Computers specifically dedicated to this purpose
- Virtual machines or daemons on a computer

With many virtual machines or a daemon answering on IP addresses otherwise unused in your network, it is possible to create a complete virtual network of computers or, in other words, a honeynet.

A honeynet can also be used to make it more difficult for an attacker to find the machines that interest him. Even if only some computers are actually productive, the network seems to have a computer on every IP address.

An open source solution to deploy honeypots and honeynets is the Honeyd Virtual Honeypot, *http://www.honeyd.org/*.

 For more information on honeypots and honeynets, visit the honeynet homepage at *http://www.honeynet.org/* and have a look at the Know Your Enemy series at *http://www.honeynet.org/papers/kye.html*.

10

Exercise 10-2: Use Argus

Time Required: 15 Minutes

Objective: The purpose of this exercise is to give you an idea how Argus works and how reports are generated.

Description: Install Argus, produce some network traffic, and then analyze the /var/log/argus.log using ra.

Detailed Steps to Complete this Exercise

1. Open a terminal window and su - to root (password novell).
2. Install Argus by entering:

   yast -i argus argus-server argus-client

3. Make sure the interface set in /etc/sysconfig/argus is correct.
4. Start Argus by entering:

   rcargus start

5. Produce different kinds of network traffic, such as browsing the Web or using SSH to connect to your neighbor.

6. View the log file by entering:

```
ra -r /var/log/argus.log
```

7. (*Optional*) Work out filtering rules to limit the output to a certain kind of traffic of your choice.

Objective 4—Incident Response

Any system administrator would be upset to find out one of his servers has been subject to a successful attack.

There are several steps you can take in response to an attack. These steps should also be outlined in the security guidelines:

- Immediate Reaction
- Information
- Documentation and Investigation
- New Installation
- Re-Evaluate Your Security Policy

Immediate Reaction

With the wrong action you could make things even worse by inadvertently obscuring any clues the intruder left behind. The main tip here is to stay cool and to calmly consider the technical options you have:

- Do nothing but observe the activities of the intruder.

  If the intruder is still online, you could find out what she is up to. On the other hand, she might find out that she is being observed and try to obscure her trails.

- Disconnect the network connection.

  This will definitely alert the intruder if he is still online, and he might try to obscure his trail on other computers. But he cannot directly change things on the computer anymore. He might have installed a mechanism that changes things after a certain time, or upon loss of network connectivity, though.

  The advantage is that you can still find out what processes are running, you can copy the content of the RAM to another computer for later investigation, etc.

  You should be aware that any program called from the compromised system might be compromised, like a ps not showing all processes, or an ls not showing all files.

  Use statically linked programs from clean media, if possible.

- Shut down the computer.

  This might also trigger certain programs installed by the intruder to remove any available traces. Any information in the RAM is lost.

- Shut off the power supply.

   This prevents any malicious programs from doing their thing, but you will lose the information available in the RAM and it might give you an inconsistent file system.

Information

There are also nontechnical steps to take.

   Certain people need to be informed and they are listed in the security guidelines.

   With the significance IT has today, such an incident is definitely of interest for management and the appropriate corporate managers should be informed.

Documentation and Investigation

No matter what you decide to do immediately, you should document what you observe and every single step you take.

   This is also true for any further action on the computer itself, its hard disks, or on images of those hard disks.

   If you decide to do some investigation while the computer is still running, you could

- Copy the content of RAM via the network to another computer using netcat.

- Document the network configuration and connections using:

   - ifconfig

   - ip

   - route

   - netstat

- Document mounts and open files using:

   - mount

   - lsof

- Document the kernel modules loaded using lsmod.

Once again, the results might not be correct, as root kits or modified programs could hide certain things.

   Ideally any further investigation of the storage media is not done directly on the storage media themselves, but on images that were taken from the media in a read-only configuration.

   In this way, nothing is changed on the media, which might be relevant for later legal action. Then on a separate computer with a clean system, you can mount the images and investigate. Various tools are available for this purpose:

- Standard Linux tools: find, ls, file, etc.

- AIDE (if you set it up before the intrusion)

- The Coroners Toolkit (TCT)

10

For more information on TCT, visit
http://www.porcupine.org/forensics/tct.html

- The Sleuth Kit (TSK)

For more information on TSK, visit
http://www.sleuthkit.org/sleuthkit/index.php

A thorough investigation requires a large amount of resources in terms of hardware, time, and know-how.

Even if you do not go into a full-scale investigation to go to court, the very least you should find out is the vulnerability used to compromise the system and when exactly the system was compromised.

That time is necessary to decide what backup you will use to restore the system.

New Installation

If you take security seriously, there is no way around installing the system from scratch and making sure the vulnerability used for the intrusion is fixed.

The intruder might have installed a back door, a root kit, or another modification—unless you install the computer again from clean media, you cannot be sure that all modifications have been found and removed.

This applies to a certain extent to the backup as well. You have to decide which backup to use. If you use one that was made after the intrusion, you might inadvertently reinstall some of the modifications the intruder made.

Re-Evaluate Your Security Policy

If your system was compromised despite your security measures, you should look at your policies and procedures.

They might be inadequate and need some changes to prevent a similar occurrence in the future.

For more information on the recovery after a system compromise, see: "Steps for Recovering from a UNIX or NT System Compromise," *http://www.cert.org/tech_tips/win-UNIX-system_compromise.html*.

Summary

- Although you can take measures to minimize the chance of a security breach, there is no way to prevent all attacks since new security vulnerabilities arise over time. As a result, you should monitor your computers and networks for signs of intrusion on a regular basis.

- You should periodically check log files using utilities such as **logcheck** and **logsurfer** to identify abnormal patterns that may indicate a security breach. By logging to a remote loghost using **Syslog-ng**, you reduce the chance that an intruder will change log file entries to hide the security breach.

- In addition to log monitoring, you should also analyze the output of security-related scripts and commands on the system including **seccheck**, **who**, **w**, **finger**, **last**, **lastlog**, and **faillog** to determine if there are any system weaknesses or unauthorized logins.

- When a security breach occurs, the intruder typically changes system files or installs programs that provide a backdoor for future access. To detect a security breach, you can use AIDE or the **rpm** command to search for key system files that have been modified.

- To monitor intruders that attempt to connect to your computer, you may use network-based IDS such as **snort**, **arpwatch**, **Argus**, and **scanlogd**. These utilities typically identify attack patterns in network traffic, caches, and log files.

- To learn about potential network attacks or to confuse attackers, you can install a honeypot or honeynet.

- If a security breach is discovered, you should report it immediately to the appropriate people within your organization, restrict access to the computer systems, and create a copy of the system and data. This copy may be examined using Linux tools, AIDE, TCT and TSK in order to determine the damage involved and identify the intruder.

- After a security breach, it is good practice to reinstall the operating system and revise your organization's security policy to minimize the chance of future attacks.

Key Terms

/etc/aide.conf   The main configuration file used by AIDE.

/etc/init.d/snort   The file used to start snort at system initialization.

/etc/pam.d/login   Used to configure login-related modules for use by PAM.

/etc/snort/   The directory that contains snort configuration files.

/etc/snort/snort.conf   The main snort configuration file.

/etc/sysconfig/snort   A file that specifies the accounts, system parameters, and network interfaces used by snort.

/etc/syslog-ng/syslog-ng.conf   The configuration file used by Syslog-ng.

/etc/syslog-ng/syslog-ng.conf.in   A file that includes changes that should be made to the /etc/syslog-ng/syslog-ng.conf file.

/var/lib/aide/aide.db   The database used by AIDE to store checksum information for key system files.

/var/log/faillog   A data file that lists information regarding failed login attempts.

/var/log/lastlog   A data file that lists local and remote logins.

/var/log/messages   The log file used by most Linux systems to record system-related events.

/var/log/wtmp   A data file that lists successful login attempts.

AIDE (Advanced Intrusion Detection Environment)   A software package that includes utilities that may be used to determine which files have changed on a Linux system by comparing file checksums over time.

aide command   Used to generate and compare checksums for use with AIDE.

Argus (Audit Record Generation and Utilization System)   A common network-based IDS used to identify network attacks by monitoring network transactions.

ARP (Address Resolution Protocol)   A protocol used to translate IP addresses to MAC addresses for use on a LAN.

arpwatch   A common network-based IDS used to identify network attacks by monitoring the ARP cache.

faillog command   Displays information regarding users who have failed to successfully log into the system from entries in /var/log/faillog.

finger command   Displays information regarding local and remote user accounts and their current login statistics.

Honeyd Virtual Honeypot   A program that is used to create virtual hosts on a network in order to build a honeypot or honeynet.

honeynet   A network that is left insecure in order to attract attackers. Honeynets are typically used to learn about attackers and their attack patterns.

honeypot   A computer system that is left insecure in order to attract attackers. Honeypots are typically used to learn about attackers and their attack patterns.

Intrusion Detection System (IDS)   A software system designed to check for evidence of security threats and breaches.

last command   Displays the most recent users who have logged in to the system from entries in /var/log/wtmp.

lastlog command   Displays the most recent users who have logged in to the system from entries in /var/log/lastlog.

log files   Files that contain important system event information.

logcheck   A utility that may be used to locate and extract anomalies in log files.

loghost   A remote computer to which events are sent for logging.

logsurfer   A utility that may be used to check log files for patterns and perform tasks when certain patterns are found.

Pluggable Authentication Modules (PAM)   A set of Linux software components that determine how users are authenticated to the system.

rootkit   A program that provides for unauthorized access that is installed on a computer system by an attacker.

rpm command   Used to install, remove, and find information on RPM software packages. It may also be used to verify the checksum of installed packages to determine whether an attacker has replaced files.

scanlogd   A common network-based IDS used to identify network attacks by listening to traffic sent on multiple ports.

seccheck   A package that contains a series of scripts that may be used to check for security vulnerabilities on your system.

snort   A common network-based IDS used to analyze network packets and identify network traffic attacks.

SuSEconfig command   Used to update various configuration files on SUSE Linux systems from information contained in template files.

syslogd   The traditional system log daemon used on older Linux systems.

Syslog-ng   The next generation system log daemon used to record system events in log files on modern Linux systems.

The Coroners Toolkit (TCT)   A software package that may be used to examine a system after a security breach and collect information related to the nature of the attack.

The Sleuth Kit (TSK)   A software package based on TCT that may be used to examine a system after a security breach and collect information related to the nature of the attack.

Tripwire   A common network-based IDS that provides similar functionality to AIDE.

w command   Displays users who are currently logged into the system and what processes they are running.

who command   Displays users who are currently logged into the system.

worm (write once read many)   When referring to media, it describes the ability to save information a single time only.

10

Review Questions

1. Which of the following may be used to check your system for weak passwords?

    a.   snort

    b.   security –check

    c.   seccheck scripts

    d.   who -a

2. You have modified the logging entries in /etc/syslog-ng/syslog-ng.conf.in. What should you do to make the changes take effect? _____

3. Which of the following Linux Intrusion Detection Systems scans your system to detect changes to system files?

    a.   TCT

    b.   Snort

    c.   Argus

    d.   AIDE

4. Intruders typically perform several actions once they compromise a Linux system. Which of the following actions is an intruder likely to perform? (Choose all that apply.)

    a. Change system configuration files

    b. Clear or modify log files

    c. Install root kit software

    d. Replace executable files with new versions

5. What main benefit does the Syslog-ng daemon have compared to the Syslog daemon shipped with earlier versions of Linux?

    a. It supports UDP connections on port 514

    b. It support TCP connections on port 514

    c. It can be used to log to a loghost

    d. It has support for local logging

6. You wish to view a list of currently logged in users in order to determine whether unauthorized users are accessing your system. What command will allow you to view this list? (Choose all that apply.)

    a. who

    b. lastlog

    c. last

    d. finger

7. After attempting to run the **aide --check** command on your system, you receive an error message that indicates that a database has not been created. What command must you run to create the database?

    a. aide --database

    b. aide --database-create

    c. aide --init

    d. aide --init-database

8. Which of the following Linux Intrusion Detection Systems monitors network traffic on your network interface? (Choose all that apply.)

    a. Arpwatch

    b. scanlogd

    c. Snort

    d. Argus

9. You have recently discovered a security breach on one of your Linux servers. What should you do? (Choose all that apply.)

   a. Create a copy of the system and data

   b. Take the computer offline

   c. Use system tools such as AIDE, TCT, TSK to analyze the extent and nature of the damage

   d. Check other systems for signs of attack

10. You wish to create a series of custom shell scripts that will be used to detect attack patterns in log files and network traffic. What can you set up in order to learn how these attacks occur and how to recognize them? _____

Discovery Exercises

DISCOVERY EXERCISES

Using Custom Scripts to Analyze Log Files

In this section, you learned several commands that may be used to monitor log files. Create a shell script that may be used to automate the process of saving and collecting information about log files. Execute the shell script when finished and view the results. At minimum, the shell script should perform the following actions:

1. Create unique backup copies of log files for later analysis

2. Display or save a list of successful and failed login attempts

3. Display or save a list of currently logged in users

4. Display entries in /var/log/messages from the scanlogd daemon

Using logcheck, logsurfer and seccheck Scripts

Since creating custom scripts to monitor system security and log files is time consuming, several pre-made scripts exist. Ensure that you have **logcheck**, **logsurfer**, and **seccheck** installed on your system. Next, run the appropriate scripts within these packages and note their results. Compare the output of these scripts to the output of your shell script from the previous Discovery Exercise and record your observations in a short memo.

Configuring Tripwire

It is important to understand when an attack has occurred on your Linux systems so that you can take the appropriate measures to stop the attack and prevent it in the future. As a result, many administrators install an IDS that detects changes to key system files such as AIDE. An alternative to the AIDE IDS introduced in this section is Open Source Tripwire and is commonly used on Linux systems today. Download the latest version of Open Source Tripwire and Open Source Tripwire documentation from *http://sourceforge.net*. In a terminal run as the root user, extract the Tripwire file and follow the instructions in the documentation file to install and configure Tripwire on your system. When finished, perform a system

10

scan using Tripwire to create a file checksum database. Use Tripwire again to check your system against this database to see if any files have changed. Note any differences between AIDE and Open Source Tripwire in a short memo.

Analyzing Wireless Network Traffic

Although Linux servers typically do not contain wireless adapters, portable computers are common on most networks today and wireless LANs are used to connect these computers to resources on Linux servers. As a result, many attackers use wireless LANs to gain unauthorized access to Linux servers or perform network-based attacks.

In this section, you learned about the Snort network-based IDS. AirSnort is a network-based IDS for wireless LANs that offer similar functionality to Snort. Use the Internet to research the benefits that AirSnort can offer your organization and record your findings in a small report. Provided that you have a wireless adapter in your computer, configure your system with AirSnort and use it to analyze your wireless LAN.

LiveFire Exercise

In this section, you get the opportunity to apply the information covered in this course in a comprehensive scenario. It is also intended as part of your preparation for the Novell CLE 10 (Certified Linux Engineer 10) Practicum exam. You will work with other students in these scenarios to complete the following objectives.

Objectives

- Set Up the Application-Level Gateway
- Set Up the Screening Router
- Set Up a Web Server in the DMZ
- Set Up the Mail Server in the LAN
- Set Up the VPN Gateway

Remember that skills from all three Novell CLP 10 courses as well as *SUSE Linux Enterprise Server 10: Networking Services* (Course 3074) might be necessary to fulfill the required tasks.

To complete these exercises, you will need several patch cables and switches or hubs, some of the computers need two NICs.

Scenario

Digital Airlines is planning on deploying SUSE Linux Enterprise Server 10 in its central firewall environment.

This firewall environment will consist of application-level gateways, packet filters, and remote access via IPSec.

As network administrator for Digital Airlines, you worked out the network layout shown in Figure 11-1.

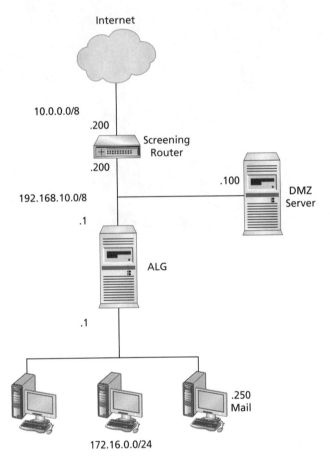

Figure 11-1

A separate computer acts as a VPN gateway to allow off-site users to connect to the LAN. See Figure 11-2.

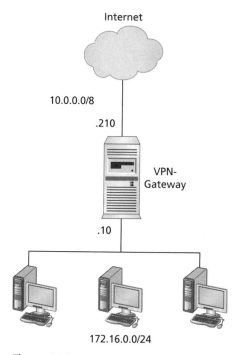

Internet

10.0.0.0/8

.210

VPN-Gateway

.10

172.16.0.0/24

Figure 11-2

You decide to start by installing a pilot installation in the test lab.

11

Objective 1—Set Up the Application-Level Gateway

The following tasks and requirements need to be performed on the application-level gateway:

- Set up the network configuration according to the network plan (this will require a switch or hub to connect to the DMZ and the screening router).
- Configure Squid to allow the clients in the local network to access the World Wide Web using HTTP and HTTPS.
- Configure a forwarding-only DNS server.
- Configure a SOCKS server, and configure the clients accordingly.
- Configure Postfix to accept mail for digitalairlines.com and to forward all mail for that domain to the internal mail server running on 172.16.0.250.
- From the internal network, mail is only accepted from the internal mail server and relayed to the mail server of the ISP.

- Write a script to set iptables rules that allow you to access only the above services (Squid, SOCKS, mail, DNS) and SSH on the application-level gateway.

- Test your configuration.

Objective 2—Set Up the Screening Router

The following tasks and requirements need to be performed on the screening router:

- Install a minimal installation of SUSE Linux Enterprise Server 10.

- Set up the network configuration according to the network plan (this will require a switch or hub to connect to the application-level gateway and the DMZ).

- Write a script that sets iptables rules to allow traffic through the router that originates from legitimate servers running on the application-level gateway or the DMZ computers.

- The only service on the screening router itself that may be accessible is sshd (from the application-level gateway only). Add this to the iptables script.

- Configure sshd to allow only public key authentication, no root login.

- Test your configuration.

Objective 3—Set Up a Web Server in the DMZ

The following tasks and requirements need to be performed on the web server:

- Set up the network configuration according to the network plan (this will require a switch or hub to connect to the application-level gateway and the screening router).

- Install a web server offering a test page visible from the Internet as well as the Intranet.

- Make this page accessible via SSL as well (coordinate with the other students on who creates the certificate).

- Test your configuration.

Objective 4—Set Up the Mail Server in the LAN

The following tasks and requirements need to be performed on the local mail server:

- Set up the network configuration according to the network plan. The mail server has IP address 172.16.0.250.

- Install Postfix as the mail server for the domain digitalairlines.com. It receives mail from the application-level gateway for the users, and the users use it as their mail server to send mail to others.

- Install qpopper or cyrus-imap for the users to pick up their mail.

- After the above works, change the configuration to secure SMTP and POP3/IMAP with SSL. This includes setting up a PKI with a RootCA and server certificates (coordinate with the other students on who creates the certificate).

- Add password authentication to Postfix.
- Modify Postfix so that it only accepts mail from users who have a valid certificate.
- Test your configuration.

Objective 5—Set Up the VPN Gateway

The following tasks and requirements need to be performed on the VPN gateway:

- Set up the network configuration according to the network plan.
- Create the necessary certificates for the gateway and a road warrior (or coordinate with the other students on who creates the certificates).
- Set up the VPN gateway so that road warrior notebooks can access the corporate LAN no matter what IP address they are assigned from their provider.
- Set up a script to set iptables rules that allow IPSec connections and traffic within the tunnel but no unencrypted traffic on the interface connected to the Internet.
- Test your configuration.

11

Glossary

~/.gnupg/pubring.gpg The location of a user's public key for use with GPG.

~/.gnupg/secring.gpg The location of a user's private key for use with GPG.

~/rhosts A file that contains user-specific entries that are used to determine user and host access to r-Tools.

/boot/grub/menu.lst The GRUB boot manager configuration file.

/etc directory Contains most configuration information for a Linux system.

/etc/aide.conf The main configuration file used by AIDE.

/etc/apparmor.d directory The location of AppArmor profiles.

/etc/apparmor.d/abstractions directory Contains files that define generic program restrictions for use within AppArmor profiles.

/etc/apparmor.d/profiles/extras directory Contains sample AppArmor profiles.

/etc/exports The main configuration file for NFS. It lists NFS shared directories as well as access restrictions for each shared directory.

/etc/fstab A file that lists mount options for file systems.

/etc/hosts.allow A file used by the TCP wrapper that lists hosts that are allowed to connect to certain services on the Linux system.

/etc/hosts.deny A file used by the TCP wrapper that lists hosts that are not allowed to connect to certain services on the Linux system. It is parsed only if an appropriate entry is not found in the /etc/hosts.allow file.

/etc/hosts.equiv A file that contains computer-wide entries that are used to determine user and host access to r-Tools.

/etc/inetd.conf The configuration file for the inetd daemon.

/etc/init.d/boot.apparmor A file used to load AppArmor kernel modules and profiles at system initialization.

/etc/init.d/snort The file used to start snort at system initialization.

/etc/ipsec.conf The IPSec configuration file in SUSE Linux.

/etc/ipsec.d/cacerts The directory that stores public key certificates from trusted certification authorities for use with IPSec authentication.

/etc/ipsec.d/certs The directory that stores the public key used by IPSec authentication.

/etc/ipsec.d/private The directory that stores the private key used by IPSec authentication.

/etc/ipsec.secrets The file that stores RSA keys and certificate passphrases for use with IPSec authentication.

/etc/openldap/slapd.conf The file that stores user passwords for the Open LDAP daemon.

/etc/pam.d/login Used to configure login-related modules for use by PAM.

/etc/permissions.* A set of files that list permission restrictions for system files and directories.

/etc/rinetd.conf The configuration file for the rinetd TCP proxy daemon.

/etc/samba/smbpasswd The file that stores Windows passwords for the Samba file sharing daemon.

/etc/services A file that lists common port definitions. It is used by several Linux services.

/etc/services A file that lists common port numbers and their names.

/etc/shadow The file that stores the passwords for local user accounts in SUSE Linux.

/etc/snort/snort.conf The main snort configuration file.

/etc/snort The directory that contains snort configuration files.

/etc/sockd.conf The main configuration file for the dante SOCKS daemon.

/etc/socks.conf A file on a client computer that specifies the location of the SOCKS server.

/etc/squid/squid.conf The main configuration file for the squid proxy server.

/etc/squidguard.conf The configuration file used by squidGuard.

/etc/ssl/openssl.cnf The main configuration file for the OpenSSL package.

/etc/stunnel/stunnel.conf The main configuration file for the stunnel program.

/etc/sysconfig/snort A file that specifies the accounts, system parameters, and network interfaces used by snort.

/etc/sysconfig/sysctl The file used at Linux startup to configure system configuration parameters such as routing.

/etc/syslog-ng/syslog-ng.conf.in A file that includes changes that should be made to the /etc/syslog-ng/syslog-ng.conf file.

/etc/syslog-ng/syslog-ng.conf The configuration file used by Syslog-ng.

/home directory The directory that stores most user home directories. It is commonly mounted to its own file system.

/opt directory The directory that typically stores optional software programs. It is commonly mounted to its own file system.

/proc/net/ipt_recent/DEFAULT A file used to store information about recently received packets.

/proc/sys/net/ipv4/ip_forward The file used by the Linux kernel to enable routing.

/root/.gnupg/suse_build_key A public key used to verify the authenticity of SUSE software packages.

/srv directory The directory that stores the content used by most network services. It is commonly mounted to its own file system.

/sys/kernel/security/apparmor/profiles A file that lists all AppArmor profiles and their current mode.

/tmp directory The directory that stores temporary files. It is commonly mounted to its own file system.

/usr directory The directory that usually stores most system software programs. It is commonly mounted to its own file system.

/usr/sbin/digest_pw_auth A program that provides digest authentication with the squid proxy server.

/usr/sbin/tcpd The TCP wrapper program.

/usr/share/doc/packages/rinetd A directory that contains sample rinetd configuration files.

/usr/share/doc/packages/squid/errors A directory that contains squid error message templates.

/usr/share/squid/errors The directory that stores custom squid error messages.

/var directory The directory that stores most log files and spool files. It is commonly mounted to its own file system.

/var/account/pacct The process accounting log file.

/var/cache/squid The directory that stores the cache used by the squid proxy server.

/var/lib/aide/aide.db The database used by AIDE to store checksum information for key system files.

/var/log/apparmor/reports-exported directory The default location for reports generated by the AppArmor module of YaST.

/var/log/audit/audit.log The file that AppArmor uses to store program-related events for later use when creating AppArmor profiles.

/var/log/faillog A data file that lists information regarding failed login attempts.

/var/log/firewall The default log file used by the netfilter framework.

/var/log/lastlog A data file that lists local and remote logins.

/var/log/messages A log file that contains messages from system programs.

/var/log/messages The Linux system information log file. It contains information regarding the creation of IPSec security associations.

/var/log/messages The Linux system information log file. It contains messages from the rinetd daemon.

/var/log/messages The log file used by most Linux systems to record system-related events.

/var/log/squid/access.log A log file that stores all requests made to the squid proxy server.

/var/log/squid/cache.log A log file that stores information about the squid cache.

/var/log/wtmp A data file that lists successful login attempts.

/var/log/wtmp A data file that lists successful login attempts.

/var/log/xinetd.log The log file for the xinetd daemon.

ac command Displays the amount of time users have been logged into the system.

Access Control List (ACL) A list of users or computers that are granted or denied access to certain resources.

access matrix A table that lists the network access needs of various users and computers within an organization as well as the technologies involved.

accton command Starts the process accounting daemons.

AES (Advanced Encryption Standard) A symmetric encryption algorithm that uses up to 256-bit keys. It was designed to be the successor to DES.

AIDE (Advanced Intrusion Detection Environment) A software package that includes utilities that may be used to determine which files have changed on a Linux system by comparing file checksums over time.

aide command Used to generate and compare checksums for use with AIDE.

AirSnort A utility that may be used to capture wireless network traffic as well as crack WEP keys.

algorithm See cryptographic algorithm.

AppArmor A technology that restricts the actions an application program can take on a Linux system.

AppArmor Control Panel A utility in the AppArmor module of YaST that may be used to start and stop AppArmor kernel modules or configure AppArmor notifications.

AppArmor Reports A utility in the AppArmor module of YaST that may be used to produce usage and incident reports about application programs that are restricted by AppArmor.

application-level firewall See Application-Level Gateway.

Application-Level Gateway (ALG) A computer that fully analyzes network traffic passing through a network using proxy server software. They are also called application-level firewalls or proxy servers.

Argus (Audit Record Generation and Utilization System) A common network-based IDS used to identify network attacks by monitoring network transactions.

ARP (Address Resolution Protocol) A protocol used to translate IP addresses to MAC addresses for use on a LAN.

arpwatch A common network-based IDS used to identify network attacks by monitoring the ARP cache.

asset A resource that requires protection within an organization. Company information and computer hardware are two examples of common assets within an organization.

asymmetric encryption An encryption method that uses a public key to encrypt data and a private key to decrypt data.

Authentication Header (AH) A VPN security protocol that provides authentication between hosts. AH uses protocol number 51.

authentication schemes The methods that may be used to authenticate to a proxy server.

autodep command Creates a default AppArmor profile for an application and sets the profile to complain mode.

availability The facet of information security that describes the ease of which information may be obtained.

backup A copy of data that may be used if the original data is lost or destroyed.

basic An authentication scheme used by most proxy servers that transmits the username and password in cleartext.

Basic Input Output System (BIOS) The program stored in the CMOS chip on a computer mainboard that is responsible for starting a computer and maintaining device access.

BIND (Berkeley Internet Name Domain) The most common standard used when implementing DNS services on a network. Modern DNS services use version 9 or greater of BIND.

blacklist A list of resources that proxy clients are not allowed to access.

blocking See URL filtering.

Blowfish A freely available symmetric encryption algorithm that uses up to 448-bit keys.

CA Management A YaST module that can implement and manage certificates and Certification Authorities.

caching The process whereby information is stored locally for later use. Proxy servers such as Squid cache most requests to speed up future requests for the same information.

calamaris command Produces reports based on the contents of the /var/log/squid/access.log file.

capabilities An AppArmor term that refers to the ability of an application program to access other processes on the system.

Certificate Revocation List (CRL) A public catalog of certificates that should not be trusted. It is located on a Certification Authority.

Certification Authority (CA) A trusted third party that verifies the identity of a public key using public key certificates.

chain A packet filtering component that contains rules used to restrict traffic.

chkconfig command Used to list and configure services that are started in each system run level.

ciphertext Data that has been encrypted using an encryption algorithm.

circuit level proxy server See generic proxy server.

cleartext Data that is not encrypted.

communication analysis A process whereby an organization's structure and technologies are analyzed to identify security weaknesses.

complain command Sets a program that has an AppArmor profile to complain mode.

complain mode For application programs that have an AppArmor profile, it refers to the state where the restrictions within the AppArmor profile are not enforced and any program actions are logged to the /var/log/audit/audit.log file.

Complimentary Metal Oxide Semiconductor (CMOS) The chip on a computer mainboard that stores configuration information and passwords for the BIOS.

confidentiality The facet of information security that describes the level to which information is kept private.

CONNECT method A process used to tunnel information through a squid HTTP proxy.

cryptographic algorithm A set of steps used with a key to scramble data.

cryptographic hash A fixed length value that is unique to a particular portion of data.

cryptography A system that encrypts sensitive information to prevent anyone who is unable to decrypt the contents from viewing it.

dante A common SOCKS proxy server software package for Linux systems.

decryption The process of unscrambling data using a cryptographic algorithm and key.

dedicated proxy server A proxy server that offers comprehensive protocol-specific control.

Demilitarized Zone (DMZ) A network that contains publicly accessed information and network services. Because of their public nature, DMZs are a primary focus of network security.

denial of service A type of threat that prevents normal access to computer resources or information.

DES (Data Encryption Standard) One of the oldest and most common symmetric encryption algorithms. DES keys are 56-bits long.

Destination NAT An implementation of NAT that changes the destination of packets instead of the source. It may be used to redirect requests to a specific server within the internal network or DMZ.

DHCP (Dynamic Host Configuration Protocol) A network protocol used to provide IP configuration information to hosts that request it. It uses UDP ports 67 and 68.

Diffie-Hellman The first widely-used asymmetric encryption algorithm.

digest An authentication scheme used by most proxy servers that transmits an encrypted hash that contains the password.

digital signature A hash that has been encrypted with a private key. Since there is typically only one copy of a private key in existence, you can obtain the associated public key, decode the hash and prove that the digital signature is authentic.

DNS (Domain Name System) A set of services and protocols used to resolve host names to IP addresses and vice versa. It uses UDP and TCP port 53.

DNS spoofing A common attack that involves falsifying DNS name resolution information.

DNSsec A DNS service extension that prevents DNS spoofing by ensuring that all name resolution results are digitally signed.

DSA (Digital Signature Algorithm) An asymmetric encryption algorithm that is endorsed by the U.S. Government for use with digital signatures.

dynamic packet filter A packet filter that can change the rules it uses for restricting network traffic based on the nature of the traffic.

Encapsulating Security Payload (ESP) A VPN security protocol that provides authentication and encryption between hosts. ESP uses protocol number 50.

encryption The process of scrambling data using a cryptographic algorithm and key.

enforce command Sets a program that has an AppArmor profile to enforce mode.

enforce mode For application programs that have an AppArmor profile, it refers to the state where the restrictions within the AppArmor profile are enforced by the AppArmor kernel modules.

ethereal A packet-sniffer utility that can be used to capture and display network traffic.

faillog command Displays information regarding users who have failed to successfully log into the system from entries in /var/log/faillog.

fdisk command Creates and lists hard drive partitions.

filter table The table that contains the INPUT, FORWARD and OUTPUT chains used by the netfilter framework.

finger A legacy Linux service used to obtain information about remote systems and users.

finger command Displays information regarding local and remote user accounts and their current login statistics.

Firefox The default Web browser on most Linux systems. It is based on the Mozilla project.

firewall A software or hardware component that restricts access to networks or network applications.

FORWARD chain The combined set of rules in the filter table that apply to traffic that is forwarded through a Linux computer running as a packet filtering firewall router.

FreeSWAN A set of tools and modules that provides IPSec VPN support for Linux 2.4 kernels.

frox A proxy server software package that uses the FTP protocol rather than the HTTP protocol.

FTP (File Transfer Protocol) The most common protocol used to transfer files across public networks such as the Internet. Active FTP uses TCP ports 20 and 21.

generic proxy server A proxy server that offers partial control of a wide range of network protocols.

genprof (generate profile) command Creates a new profile for an application and sets the application to complain mode.

glob A process whereby multiple file names may be specified using wildcard characters such as asterisk (*).

GNU Privacy Guard (GPG) An Open Source implementation of PGP.

gpg command Generates keys, digitally signs, encrypts and decrypts data using GPG.

GRand Unified Bootloader (GRUB) The default boot manager for SUSE Linux. It is responsible for loading the Linux operating system kernel during system initialization.

grub-md5-crypt command Used to generate an MD5 encrypted password for use in the GRUB configuration file.

hash See cryptographic hash.

hash algorithm An algorithm used to produce a hash. MD5, SHA1 and Ripe160 are common hash algorithms.

Honeyd Virtual Honeypot A program that is used to create virtual hosts on a network in order to build a honeypot or honeynet.

honeynet A network that is left insecure in order to attract attackers. Honeynets are typically used to learn about attackers and their attack patterns.

honeypot A computer system that is left insecure in order to attract attackers. Honeypots are typically used to learn about attackers and their attack patterns.

HTTP accelerator A proxy server that caches HTTP requests from an internal Web server to speed up access.

https-tunnel A PERL script that may be used to tunnel HTTPS traffic through the squid proxy server.

HyperText Transfer Protocol (HTTP) The protocol used to obtain Web pages from Web servers on the Internet.

IDEA (International Data Encryption Algorithm) A commonly used symmetric encryption algorithm that uses 128-bit keys.

IMAP (Internet Message Access Protocol) A protocol used to obtain e-mail messages from a mail server. IMAP typically uses TCP port 143.

inetd The Internet Services Daemon. It is used to start other network services on legacy Linux systems.

INPUT chain The combined set of rules in the filter table that apply to traffic that is destined for a Linux computer running as a packet filtering firewall.

insecure network A network that contains unknown users. Publicly accessed networks are insecure networks.

inssserv command Changes the startup configuration files to specify the runlevels a daemon should start and stop in.

intercepting proxy server A standard proxy server that requires no special client configuration. HTTP requests from the network router are forwarded to the intercepting proxy server for processing.

International Standard Organization's Open System Interconnect (ISO/OSI) A model used to describe how computers use protocols to communicate on a computer network.

Internet Key Exchange (IKE) The process of exchanging public keys across public networks such as the Internet.

Internet Security Association and Key Management Protocol (ISAKMP) The component of IPSec that is responsible for exchanging asymmetric encryption keys at the onset of an IPSec negotiation. ISAKMP uses UDP port 500 for key management and UDP port 4500 for NAT transversal.

Intrusion Detection System (IDS) A software system designed to check for evidence of security threats and breaches.

iostat (input output statistics command) Displays read and write statistics for system storage devices.

IP Security (IPSec) A common VPN standard that uses DES or 3DES encryption to secure traffic.

ipsec-tools A package that contains IPSec VPN tools for use in SUSE Linux.

ipsec0 The first virtual IPSec VPN interface used by the Linux 2.4 kernel.

iptables command The command used to configure the netfilter framework.

isag (interactive system activity grapher) command Displays a graph of the performance statistics stored in the /var/log/sa directory.

ISC (Internet System Consortium) The organization that develops and provides new standards for Internet protocols such as DNS and DHCP.

John the Ripper A common password cracking utility that detects weak passwords that are based on dictionary words.

key A random component used alongside an encryption algorithm to make the result of the encryption algorithm difficult to decode. Longer keys result in stronger encryption.

Kmail A common mail client in SUSE Linux that can use GPG keys.

last command Displays the most recent users who have logged in to the system from entries in /var/log/wtmp.

lastcomm command Displays the process accounting log file.

lastlog command Displays the most recent users who have logged in to the system from entries in /var/log/lastlog.

Layer 2 Tunneling Protocol (L2TP) A common VPN standard that uses IPSec encryption to secure traffic.

ldd command Displays the libraries used by a particular program.

learning mode See complain mode.

library preloading The process of loading SOCKS client code into memory before network client software.

libwrap.so.0 The library used by xinetd and other programs to provide TCP wrapper support.

limit match A packet filter rule that prevents future traffic after a certain number of packets have been received of a particular type.

log files Files that contain important system event information.

logcheck A utility that may be used to locate and extract anomalies in log files.

logging The process whereby system events are saved to a file for later analysis.

loghost A remote computer to which events are sent for logging.

logprof (log profile) command Analyzes the entries in the /var/log/audit/audit.log file for a particular application and allows you to create entries in an AppArmor profile based on them.

logsurfer A utility that may be used to check log files for patterns and perform tasks when certain patterns are found.

mangle table The table used by the netfilter framework to make changes to the headers of TCP/IP packets or mark packets for later filtering.

mark match A packet filter rule that changes the headers of packets such that they can be easily identified later.

Masquerading An implementation of NAT suited for routers that do not have static public IP addresses.

MD5 (Message Digest Algorithm 5) A common hash algorithm that is used to store passwords and verify file contents.

mpstat (multiple processor statistics) command Displays processor and system load statistics.

multiport match A packet filter rule that applies to traffic on several different ports.

nat table The table used by the netfilter framework to perform Network Address Translation.

NAT traversal A feature of IPSec VPNs that allows tunneled traffic to pass through NAT routers.

nessus A program that may be used to monitor security settings on network computers.

nessus-update-plugins command Downloads the latest plugins for use with nessus.

netfilter framework The software components that comprise the packet filtering firewall on most Linux systems.

netstat command Displays network statistics and open sockets.

Network Address Translation (NAT) A technology that rewrites the source and destination of IP packets as they pass through a router. NAT is typically used to connect private networks to the Internet using a single IP address.

NFS (Network File System) A file sharing protocol used on UNIX and Linux networks. NFS uses port 2049 to mount remote shared directories.

NIS (Network Information Service) A network service and protocol used to coordinate configuration information across several UNIX and Linux computers on the network.

nmap A powerful port scanning utility available on most Linux systems.

nmap command Probes for and displays open network ports on network computers.

NTLM (NT LAN Manager) An authentication scheme used by most proxy servers that transmits a random challenge that is encrypted using the password of the user.

NTP (Network Time Protocol) A network protocol that is used to obtain time configuration from remote computers. NTP uses TCP and UDP port 123.

openssl command The configuration command for the OpenSSL package. It may be used to create and issue certificates as well as manage Certification Authorities.

OpenSSL A Linux package that allows for the creation and management of SSL certificates and Certification Authorities.

OpenSWAN A set of tools that configures IPSec VPN support for Linux 2.6 kernels.

OUTPUT chain The combined set of rules in the filter table that apply to traffic that originates from a Linux computer running as a packet filtering firewall.

PAC (Proxy Auto Configuration) script A network-accessible script that may be used to configure proxy server settings on client computers.

packet A single unit of transmission on a TCP/IP network.

packet filter A software component that drops network communication that is addressed to a particular IP address or port number.

PGP (Pretty Good Privacy) A widely used implementation of asymmetric cryptography developed in 1991.

Pluggable Authentication Modules (PAM) A set of Linux software components that determine how users are authenticated to the system.

policy The action taken that a packet filter takes on a packet when it does not match any rules within a chain.

POP3 (Post Office Protocol Version 3) A protocol used to obtain e-mail messages from a mail server. POP3 typically uses TCP port 110.

POP3S An implementation of POP3 that uses SSL and TCP port 995.

portmapper A network service that uses TCP and UDP port 111 to obtain a remote RPC connection.

POSTROUTING chain The combined set of rules in the nat or mangle table that apply to traffic that is about to leave a router after being routed using the routing table.

PREROUTING chain The combined set of rules in the nat or mangle table that apply to traffic that has entered a router and has not yet been routed using the routine table.

private key An asymmetric encryption key typically used to decrypt data encrypted using the associated public key.

process accounting A system that logs information about running processes to a file for later analysis.

profile A file that lists AppArmor restrictions for an application program.

proxy authentication A process whereby proxy server users are verified before their requests are handled.

proxy server A software program used on application-level gateways to cache and restrict traffic based on detailed criteria such as data content and user information.

public key An asymmetric encryption key typically used to encrypt data.

Public Key Infrastructure (PKI) A system that uses a Certification Authority to verify the authenticity of public keys used for asymmetric encryption.

qpopper The package that provides POP3 support in modern Linux distributions.

r-Tools A set of utilities that may be used to connect to remote computers or copy files between remote computers without encryption. Some common r-Tools include rcp (remote copy), rsh (remote shell) and rlogin (remote login).

racoon command Used to create and manage IPSec security associations.

rcapparmor command Used to start and stop the AppArmor kernel modules, load and unload AppArmor profiles, and view the status of AppArmor.

recent match A packet filter rule that may be used to restrict traffic that was recently received by the Linux system.

Remote Access The services and protocols used to connect to remote hosts and obtain a user interface or copy files. Telnet, r-tools and SSH are common Linux remote access protocols.

Remote Access Service (RAS) A server service that allows remote computers the ability to connect to the local network and access resources.

resources See asset.

rinetd A common generic proxy server available on many Linux systems. It redirects TCP connections from one address and port to another.

Ripe160 A strong hash algorithm originally intended to replace MD5.

risk The likelihood that confidential information or network resources will be compromised by a security breach.

road warrior A host that connects to remote networks using a VPN.

root kit A program that provides for unauthorized access that is installed on a computer system by an attacker.

RPC (Remote Procedure Calls) A protocol that allows instructions to be executed on remote hosts.

rpcinfo command Displays RPC services running on a Linux computer.

rpm command Used to install, remove, and find information on RPM software packages. It may also be used to verify the checksum of installed packages to determine whether an attacker has replaced files.

RSA (Rivest, Shamir, Adleman) An asymmetric encryption algorithm that is widely used in many Web applications.

rule 1. A line within an AppArmor profile that lists the access an AppArmor-controlled program has to other processes and files. 2. A packet filtering component that lists a specific type of network traffic and the action the packet filter will take when the traffic is detected.

sa (summarize accounting) command Displays a process accounting report based on certain criteria.

sadc (system activity data collector) command Collects system performance information and logs it to the /var/log/sa directory.

sar (system activity report) command Monitors the performance of a Linux system.

scanlogd A common network-based IDS used to identify network attacks by listening to traffic sent on multiple ports.

scp command Used to copy files between remote hosts using SSH.

screening router A router that analyzes traffic with packet filters or firewall software before passing it to other networks.

seccheck A package that contains a series of scripts that may be used to check for security vulnerabilities on your system.

secure network A network that allows little or no public access.

Secure Sockets Layer (SSL) A technology used to provide encryption for HTTP connections.

security association An authenticated communications channel between two VPN hosts.

security concept A comprehensive security plan for an organization that lists the individual steps that an organization takes to secure computers and information from potential security breaches.

Security Event Notification A feature of AppArmor that can be configured in YaST to notify administrators when certain AppArmor-related events occur.

Security Event Report A list of AppArmor-related events that can be generated by the AppArmor module of YaST.

security policy The goals that an organization needs to achieve in order to secure its computers and information.

security protocol A protocol that defines the features of a VPN connection. ESP and AH are common VPN security protocols.

security strategy The plan that an organization takes to secure its computers and data. This plan uses the steps outlined in the organization's security concept to achieve the organization's security policy.

security zone A set of computers or networks that have similar security requirements.

Set Group ID (SGID) A special permission set on executable files and directories. When you run an executable program that has the SUID permission set, you become the group owner of the executable file for the duration of the program. On a directory, the SGID sets the group that gets attached to newly created files.

Set User ID (SUID) A special permission set on executable files. When you run an executable program that has the SUID permission set, you become the owner of the executable file for the duration of the program.

setkey command Creates key combinations for use with Linux commands. It is often used to create shortcuts for IPSec VPN commands.

sftp command Used to upload and download files between hosts using SSH.

SHA1 (Secure Hash Algorithm 1) A strong hash algorithm developed by the National Institute of Standards and Technology.

sitar command Creates a report of system configuration information.

SMB (Server Message Blocks) The file sharing protocol used by Windows operating systems and systems that run the Samba file sharing service.

SMTP (Simple Mail Transfer Protocol) The protocol used to send e-mail messages across computer networks. SMTP uses TCP port 25.

SNMP (Simple Network Management Protocol) A network protocol used to obtain and modify the configuration of various network devices. It typically uses UDP ports 161 and 162.

snort A common network-based IDS used to analyze network packets and identify network traffic attacks.

sockd The SOCKS daemon used by the dante package.

socket A connection between hosts that identifies the IP address and port number used on each host for the communication.

SOCKS A widely-used application-independent proxy server standard that translates internal TCP and UDP requests to an external network.

socksify command Used to create a SOCKS connection on a client computer.

Source NAT An implementation of NAT designed for routers that have a static public IP address on the Internet.

SQL injection A network attack that inserts malicious information into SQL queries that are performed on a database server.

squid A common HTTP proxy server package found on most Linux systems.

squidGuard A SUSE Linux package that contains additional tools for the squid proxy server including URL filtering.

SSH (Secure Shell) A remote access protocol that may be used to connect to or copy files between remote hosts using TCP and UDP port 22. SSH protects communication using asymmetric cryptography and is a secure replacement for both Telnet and the r-Tools.

ssh command Used to obtain a remote shell interface using SSH.

SSL (Secure Sockets Layer) An asymmetric cryptography technology used by many Internet services.

standard proxy server A proxy server that provides Internet access to clients on an internal network.

state match A packet filter rule that specifies that stateful or dynamic packet filtering should be used.

stateful packet filter See dynamic packet filter.

static packet filter A packet filter that restricts network traffic based on rules that do not change.

Sticky bit A special permission that is set on directories that prevents users from removing files they do not own.

stunnel command Provides SSL support for applications that do not natively support SSL.

su (switch user) command Used to change the current user account.

SuSEconfig command Used to update various configuration files on SUSE Linux systems from information contained in template files.

symmetric encryption An encryption method that uses a single key to both encrypt and decrypt data.

Syslog-ng The next generation system log daemon used to record system events in log files on modern Linux systems.

syslogd The traditional system log daemon used on older Linux systems.

sysstat package Contains system monitoring utilities such as **vmstat** and **sar**.

tag A configuration parameter in the /etc/squid/squid.conf file.

target The part of a packet filtering rule that specifies the action that is taken when traffic matches the conditions specified in the rule.

TCP wrapper A service component that checks for restrictions listed in /etc/hosts.deny and /etc/hosts.allow before allowing access to certain network services.

tcpdchk command Detects and displays problems relating to the configuration of /etc/inetd.conf.

tcpdmatch command Tests the TCP wrapper restrictions specified in the /etc/inetd.conf file.

tcpdump command A common packet sniffing utility on most Linux systems.

Telnet A remote access protocol that was traditionally used to connect to remote Linux and UNIX computers. Telnet does not encrypt the username and password during authentication.

TFTP (Trivial File Transfer Protocol) A version of the FTP protocol that uses UDP instead of TCP.

The Coroners Toolkit (TCT) A software package that may be used to examine a system after a security breach and collect information related to the nature of the attack.

The Sleuth Kit (TSK) A software package based on TCT that may be used to examine a system after a security breach and collect information related to the nature of the attack.

TLS (Transport Layer Security) An implementation of SSL that is used to secure Internet traffic.

transconnect A package that may be used with the squid proxy server to tunnel HTTPS traffic.

transparent proxy server See intercepting proxy server.

Triple DES (3DES) A version of DES that uses keys that are up to three times the length of the original DES keys.

Tripwire A common network-based IDS that provides similar functionality to AIDE.

tunneling The process of sending data formatted using a specific protocol to a remote computer by encapsulating the data within a different protocol.

unconfined command Lists active programs on the system that are not controlled by AppArmor.

URL filtering A process used by many proxy servers that restricts access based on the URL in the source packet.

url_regex A tag in the /etc/squid/squid.conf file that may be used to perform URL filtering.

user-defined chain A set of packet filter rules that are parsed when a certain rule from another chain is evaluated.

vim (vi improved) command Used to start the interactive vi text editor available on nearly all UNIX and Linux systems.

Virtual Private Network (VPN) A technology that encrypts communications between two different networks or between a host and a remote network.

Virtual Private Network (VPN) A virtual connection between two or more hosts on a public network used to tunnel traffic. VPNs provide authentication and encryption for tunneled traffic between the hosts to provide data security.

vmstat (virtual machine statistics) command Displays process, memory and paging statistics.

w command Displays users who are currently logged into the system and what processes they are running.

Web Proxy Auto-Discovery Protocol (WPAD) A configuration that uses DNS records or DHCP options to automatically configure proxy server settings on client computers.

whitelist A list of resources that proxy clients are allowed to access.

who command Displays users who are currently logged into the system.

Wi-Fi Protected Access (WPA) A technology used to secure the information transmitted across wireless networks. The current version is called WPA2 and provides the most security for wireless networks today.

Wired Equivalent Privacy (WEP) A legacy technology used to secure wireless LAN traffic. WEP keys may be cracked by several freely-available utilities today.

worm (write once read many) When referring to media, it describes the ability to save information a single time only.

wpad.dat A file that stores the configuration script downloaded by WPAD clients.

WWW (World Wide Web) The publicly available collection of Web servers on the Internet.

xinetd The Extended Internet Services Daemon. It is used to start other network services on current Linux systems.

YaST Online Update (YOU) A YaST module that may be used to obtain patches for SLES from the SUSE Web servers.

Yet Another Setup Tool (YaST) The graphical system configuration utility in SUSE Linux.

ypcat command Used to view configuration information on remote NIS servers.

Index